AUSTRALIAN LIBRARY SUPERVISION AND MANAGEMENT

SECOND EDITION

Topics in Australasian Library and Information Studies

Series editors: Professor Ross Harvey and Dr Stuart Ferguson

This series provides detailed, formally refereed works on a wide range of topics and issues relevant to professionals and para-professionals in the library and information industry and to students of library and information studies. All titles are written from an Australasian perspective, drawing on professional experience and research in Australia, New Zealand and the wider Pacific region. Proposals for publications should be addressed to the series editors (RossHarvey@csu.edu.au; sferguson@csu.edu.au).

AUSTRALIAN LIBRARY SUPERVISION AND MANAGEMENT

Second edition

Roy Sanders

Topics in Australasian Library and Information Studies, Number 21

Centre for Information Studies
Charles Sturt University
Wagga Wagga New South Wales

ISBN 1 876938 30 7
ISSN: 1030-5009

National Library of Australia cataloguing-in-publication data

---

Sanders, R. (Roy), 1950- .
    Australian library supervision and management.

    2nd ed.
    Bibliography.
    Includes index.
    ISBN 1 876938 30 7.

    1. Library personnel management - Australia. 2. Library administration - Australia. I. Charles Sturt University--Riverina. Centre for Information Studies. II. Title. (Series : Topics in Australasian library and information studies ; no. 21).

023.0994

This edition published in 2004

Editorial direction: S. Ferguson and G. Eyre
Cover design: M. Taylor, Reprographics Unit, Charles Sturt University
Copy editor: P Whitten
Printer: Active Print, Wagga Wagga

Centre for Information Studies
Locked Bag 660
Wagga Wagga NSW 2678
Fax: +612 6933 2733
Email: cis@csu.edu.au
http://www.csu.edu.au/cis

Acknowledgments

The author wishes to extend his personal thanks to the many students and colleagues who have contributed, knowingly or otherwise, to the development and content of this work. Specific thanks must also go to those colleagues and students who have given the kind of feedback which has encouraged the development and refinement of this book.

Contents

Preface

Each of the topics discussed in this text is worthy of a monograph in its own right. Indeed, there are books written on each. The reader is invited to follow up specific areas of interest and need to develop knowledge of, and skills in, a variety of areas. However, there is also a need for an introduction to library supervision and management, as it continues to develop as a vital field for librarians to study and for experienced librarians and educators to practice and to teach.

As in the previous edition, this work addresses skills useable during the first few years of professional practice, emphasising supervisory and people-centred skills. The 1990s saw further development of team management structures and practices, and of the application of self-management theory to library operations. All of these require considerable management-staff communication and cooperation to succeed. It seems that the skills required to implement such systems and structures continue to be in demand: planning, decision-making, communicating, negotiating, and so forth are among a host of management activities which are practised and applied at all levels of the library.

Since I wrote the initial version of this work during 1992–1995, I have continued to teach library management to undergraduates and graduates, and to talk to colleagues and practitioners about the ways in which librarians and associated information workers are going about the tasks of supervision and management. From those and the innumerable print and electronic sources of information, it seems to me that library supervision and management is still about the management of change, but that a new imperative, the quality movement, is influencing the way we plan, organise, lead, and monitor our services. This influence is seen in the addition of one new topic to this edition, that of Total Quality Management.

In a paper presented at the '2000 LAMA National Institute' held by the Library Administration and Management Association of the American Library Association, Dr Julie Todaro (2001) presented a set of guidelines for effective library management in the 21st century. They included an emphasis on teamwork; assessment of the organisational culture; creation of a flexible management style; clear leadership; strategic planning, evaluation and accountability; and clear and skilled communication. Those are all featured in this work to a variety of levels and extents.

The largest sections of Patricia Layzell Ward's recent survey of the library and information management literature (Ward 2002) are those about managing performance and quality; managing change; and managing human resources, all focus areas for this work in its former and latest editions. Ward also makes the following thoughtful comments which provide support for the need for, and content, of this new edition:

> Leadership remains a concern both in the fields of general management and within the sector. This seems to be exacerbated by the retirement of a generation that entered the workforce in the 1960s – a generation that worked through rapid expansion in comfortable economic conditions and then experienced a decline in funding. They gained considerable experience of management, and it may not have been easy for those entering in the 1970s and 1980s to develop management skills since their chances of promotion may have been less than those of the earlier intake. Now the challenge is to bring new recruits into the profession, particularly in the public sector where salaries and prospects are less than in the private sector. To this is added the level of public scrutiny of the quality of the services (Ward 2002, p. 156).

Otherwise, this edition sees a general updating in some chapters, the total re-writing of others, but maintains its central aim of providing both a theoretical and an instructional guide for the beginning and less experienced supervisor. Examples and practices described are taken, mostly, from the library and information services literature. Included are a number of appendices which present samples of documents which support and assist with the processes involved in the human side of library supervision and management. These are mostly taken from, or are based on, current practice in libraries. I will welcome any feedback on their usefulness.

Much of the best managing in libraries goes unreported in the general literature. Many library managers, and supervisors, do acquire reputations for excellence, and I turned to a number of them for practitioners' views. In the first edition I called their pieces 'A View from the Practitioner's Desk', but in this one I have included them as quoted sources. I hope we all can benefit from the practice of such hands-on, experienced and successful practitioners of both librarianship and management. I am grateful to these hardworking professionals for the time they put into providing another dimension to this book, and trust that you, whether student or practising professional yourself, will use their views in learning the theory, skills and practices of library supervision and management.

Introduction to library supervision and management

Chapter 1
Overview of library management theory

History is fables agreed upon. (Voltaire)

What is the use of theory?

To some readers it may seem incongruous for a text which aims to provide a practical background to the tasks and skills of supervision and management to begin with an outline of the theory. Theory is easily dismissed by practitioners if they believe it will mean the rejection of practical concerns. However, as this book will show, every management or supervisory skill, technique and course of action is based upon the diverse theories, philosophy and values which have been previously developed, and which continue to be examined critically.

The particular use, or value, of theory depends on at least two factors: the validity of the theory itself, and what the theory is used for. We all use theories, even the manager or supervisor who loudly proclaims that practical experience is of greater value than any 'airy-fairy' theories developed by academics in their comfortable ivory towers. For example, you would not (I hope!) attempt to walk or drive across a busy street with your eyes closed. Why not? Because you *know* what is likely to occur. And how did you gain this *knowledge*, this common sense, which allows you to be quite sure that problems will occur if you follow that course of action? You can gain it in a combination of three ways: by having been told, or shown, that it is dangerous to do so; by imagining what would happen; or by practical experience of what happens if you are blindfolded in other less risky situations. This gives you a basis for understanding and predicting what would happen if you were to walk or drive across a busy street with your eyes closed. But this understanding, or common sense, is not based on the actual experience of crossing a busy street with your eyes closed. It is not based on practical experience, but rather is based on a simple type of theory – that is, on a rational proposition as to what would happen. Such propositions are what we tend to use to guide us through our lives. We could not survive without them – or extreme good fortune.

The theories developed by academics are not so different. They may be more complicated; they may be more carefully tested for accuracy using the tools provided by the scientific approach to understanding. But they are essentially the same as the propositions and theories we use to guide our daily lives. The remainder of this chapter provides an overview of some major theories of management but without going into detail about the work of each writer involved in the theory. You are, therefore, not going to gain a profound understanding of management theory by reading the rest of this chapter. Rather, by learning the basic assumptions of each theory or writer and the more noteworthy propositions and theories they put forward, you should understand that there are a number of ways in which you can consider the supervision and management of libraries as organisations, and that no single theory or approach is the perfect one. Each provides some understanding of management; some will correspond with views you hold already based on your own experience.

What you need to do when studying any subject, and not least the management of libraries, is be open-minded and consider critically the material presented to you. When reading this text – and indeed when reading any professional material – always try to relate the theoretical explanation to the realities of your organisation and your job. In this way theory ceases to be just that, and instead becomes an extension and verification of your own experience.

Early management

Management is a process that has its roots in the development of organised society. Stueart and Moran point out that 'as early as 3000 BC the Sumerians kept records on clay tablets; many of those records applied to the management practices of the priests of Ur' and that the Catholic Church can be advanced as 'the most efficient formal organization in the history of western civilization' (Stueart and Moran 1998, pp. 4–5). Although management theory has a strong historical background, it was the industrial revolution that foreshadowed the emergence of a more organised approach to management. In their discussion on the birth of management ideas, Bartol and others comment:

> Much of the impetus for developing management theories and principles came from the industrial revolution and factory growth in the early 1800s. With factories came a widespread need to coordinate large numbers of people in producing goods (Bartol et al. 2001, p. 33).

The industrial revolution, unlike earlier periods, brought workers together in the new urban conglomerates to provide factory fodder for the new relatively large-scale factories. However, it was not only in the industrial sector that management theory was being shaped. Government's role in society altered and grew substantially through the nineteenth century. The political and economic doctrines of utilitarianism were also changed beyond recognition by one of its disciples, J. S. Mill – so much, in fact, that by the 1890s the trappings of the welfare state with its burgeoning bureaucracy were being firmly established.

A century of management

The past 100 years have seen the development and growth of management of increasing complexity as each successive age has added its own needs, styles and social pressures to the management picture to meet the challenge of a highly industrialised and a highly urbanised society. You should consider briefly the major theories to emerge, and for convenience they are presented here in the three main periods suggested by Evans (1976), but be aware that there is considerable overlap between the periods.

Scientific period (1880—1927)

This period is summarised by many writers as the outcome of the age of the machine. The machine was considered 'all powerful' and not only dominated management thought, but also permeated all thought. It was, until the First World War and its aftermath shattered complacency, an era of unbridled optimism that the machine was capable of solving the world's ills. The effect of the war and the alienation of the workforce from the mechanistic view of society had their roots in this period, but they did not play a major role in altering management thought until the advent of Elton Mayo.

The scientific period was dominated by the writings of F. W. Taylor, who presented the following basic goals of scientific management:

> To gather all traditional knowledge and classify, tabulate and reduce it to rules, laws and formulas so as to help workers in their daily work.

> To develop a science for each element of man's work to replace the rule of thumb method.

> To scientifically select and then train, teach and develop the workers.

> To co-operate with workers to ensure that work is done according to developed scientific principles.

> To effect an almost equal division of work and responsibility between workers and managers. That is, managers are to be given work for which they are best fitted, as are employees (Taylor 1947, p. 147).

Taylor's principles expound the basic tenet that increased efficiency could be achieved if scientific observation and measurement were used in managing workers. For example, the job of shovelling coal was scrutinised to determine the optimum load that could be handled with each shovelful. Then the correct size of shovel to handle that load was determined. The workers were given a range of sizes of shovel, helped to decide which one to use, and placed on an incentive payment scheme to motivate them to reach the optimum load. For Taylor (and others of this school of thought) monetary motivation was sufficient. However, as the human relations school soon declared, economic reward is not the sole motivator of people at work.

Taylor's ideas were not universally accepted at the time, and continue to be the subject of considerable debate regarding their validity and limitations. For example, much of Taylor's 'scientific' theory is based on work-improvement tests supposedly carried out at Bethlehem Steel around 1900. However, Wrege and Perroni (1974) showed that the tests, and the report on them, were an improbable string of lies, and that no-one ever attempted to replicate Taylor's tests to check the validity of his results.

Other influential figures of this period include Frank and Lillian Gilbreth who are credited with being the founders of the time and motion study, and who are also credited with stating that the aim of scientific management is to induce men to act as nearly like machines as possible. (See, for example, Gilbreth and Gilbreth 1967.)

Classical management theory

Henri Fayol, who provided what we would recognise as the first definition of management, and who outlined principles which correspond in many ways to the more modern management by objectives approach, wrote during this period but his work did not appear in English translation until 1949, some twenty years after his death. Fayol was an early proponent of the view that management consisted of basic principles and that its successful practice was not necessarily an innate instinct but a skill, like anything else, that could be taught. (See Fayol 1949.)

Many of the texts on management theory refer to the classical management functions and theories. The generally agreed use of the term 'classical management theories' refers to those which first appeared with Fayol in the mid 1920s, and encompasses Fayol's five elements which have become known as the classic functions of management – planning, organising, commanding, coordinating and controlling.

An example of how classical theory differs from scientific management is that in the latter there was no place for a single supervisor who could 'manage' a wide range of jobs and specialised work, whereas the classical concept is that of the 'general manager' who has organisational skills and a broad knowledge of the work being performed. Scientific management would have a worker or foreman in charge of each specialisation and each worker could have several 'supervisors'. By contrast, classical theory promotes the principle of 'unity of command' in which any worker is responsible to only one supervisor.

Human relations era (1927–1950)

Human relations theorists developed their humanist approach to management as a direct, and often compassionate, response to the perceived evils of scientific management. Thus began the wide-scale recognition that people at work have personal, social and emotional needs which they bring with them to the workplace, and that they are not motivated purely by monetary reward.

Elton Mayo is considered the leading researcher and thinker of this period, and his name is inextricably linked with what have become known as the Hawthorne experiments. Mayo (1880–1949) was an Australian who worked at Harvard University and who, between 1927 and 1932, conducted a series of experiments at the Hawthorne Works of the Western Electric Company in Chicago. Space does not permit an account of the experiments, but they make fascinating reading. The results can be summarised as follows:

> Several principles have been demonstrated in their studies: (1) Workers are more motivated by social rewards and sanctions than by economic incentives. (2) The group influences workers' actions. (3) The researchers, after hypothesizing that motivation and supervision, as well as basic social relations on the job were responsible for increased productivity, found that indeed, when the work group felt itself to be in opposition to management, productivity stayed close to the minimum accepted level. For the first time it was recognized that those social factors were important to organizational output. In general, the human behavior movement maintains that if the organization makes employees happy, it will gain their full cooperation and effort, and reach optimum efficiency (Stueart and Moran 1998, p. 17).

Mayo recognised that the needs of the worker were not solely economic and were bound closely to the desires of the group and to the worker's place in the group.

> The individual worker, whether capable of it or not, does not work to develop a blackboard logic which shall guide his method of life and work. What he wants is more nearly described as, first, a method of living in social relationship with other people, and second, as part of this an economic function for and value to the group (Mayo 1960, p. 173).

Management under Mayo's influence, then, was no longer restricted to a scientific measurement of performance and monetary reward for productivity, but also had to recognise the individual's role in the group and work environment. Management began to emphasise the role of the organisation in meeting workers' needs, and to recognise the need for a more participatory and consultative style of workplace interaction.

It is easy, in reading accounts of the Hawthorne experiments, to applaud the studies and results in an uncritical manner. There are, however, some criticisms and a quick look at a few of them helps to place some of our current management skills and techniques into the historical context from which they have developed.

One criticism is that Elton Mayo's studies portray the worker as non-rational, and management as rational on a variety of grounds. For example, workers restriction of output is portrayed as non-rational because it conflicts with the organisation's productivity goals. What Mayo does not highlight is that the goals of the organisation are not necessarily those of the workers; that workers' goals often do conflict with those of management. Thus, to apply, as he does, the management's criteria for rational behaviour to workers' goals is both irrational and biased.

Further, given that the Great Depression of the 1930s began while the studies were in progress, worker restriction on output could be seen as a perfectly rational means of preventing lay-offs as long as possible. After all, what rational person would work harder to make themselves unemployed, especially in the desperate economic conditions of the early 1930s? The studies thus neglected the influence of the environment upon the factory, particularly the depressed economic conditions.

Another criticism is that the group of workers studied was not representative of the workers in the rest of the factory and therefore it is not valid to generalise from the research findings. A particularly interesting criticism also maintains that close study shows that:

1   only one of his many experiments provided clear support for the idea that social factors were of major significance in explaining productivity differences between groups; and
2   contrary to popular understanding of them and the impression given by the authors of the studies, monetary incentives and the piece-rate system had the most lasting effects in raising productivity (Carey 1967, pp. 406–407).

Although in retrospect the Hawthorne studies have been shown to exhibit a number of flaws they did reawaken concern for the human factor in the study of management, and sparked research and debate that has improved our knowledge and understanding.

Modern management

Is there any such thing as modern management? There has been, since 1950, an explosion in management thought and writing, and if the debate between two major strands – scientific and human relations – has continued, it has done so at an increasingly sophisticated level, and as part of a range of strands of management thought. Management by objectives, organisational behaviour, operations management, and contingency theory are but some examples of the paths taken to help managers to plan, organise, lead and evaluate their organisations and the people who make up those organisations.

Diversity, rather than uniformity, is the major characteristic of the modern era. This diversity has led to a bewildering number of attempts to explain the success or otherwise of organisations with a growing realisation that no one theory fits every situation or will necessarily stand up for long in a rapidly evolving society. Thus quick fixes, ready answers and pop psychology may contain some useful elements but the desire to provide simplistic solutions to the highly complex business of managing economic and human resources has seen the rise and fall of countless fads over the last few decades. As Hilmer and Donaldson (1996) note, in the highly competitive and challenging business environment of today, the pressure to be 'doing something', picking up on the latest trend, is intense (p. 8). Yet common sense (and history) shows that what may work for one organisation may be inappropriate elsewhere and what was successful five years ago may not necessarily be the best approach today.

The modern period therefore, sees attempts to synthesise the (at least superficially) conflicting views of Taylor and Mayo and the various interpretations of their theories as the basis upon which to develop more refined approaches that are useful today. Both theorists have a valuable role to play in current management philosophy. They were both concerned with people, organisations and the motivation of people within those organisations. They diverged somewhat in ascertaining and claiming what motivated people. For Taylor it was largely economic needs, whereas for Mayo it was group needs and a sense of belonging.

Scientific management theory has been further refined by applying computers to management problems, and is perhaps seen at its ultimate in attempts to produce management information systems and decision support systems. On the other 'side', the social revolution in the 1960s and 1970s strongly advanced a humanist view of society, and influenced management theory. What emerges is an interplay of philosophies that gives management a greater choice of paths, but also causes confusion about the right way to manage.

Indeed, there is acknowledgement today that no one path will satisfy every situation at every point in time. The growth of contingency theory from the 1970s on takes a situational approach where managers have to accept that no one solution suits every problem encountered. In taking this approach, managers need to exercise high levels of reasoning and critical thinking, based upon developing and exploiting sophisticated management information systems. In addition, the importance of management education in providing a solid underpinning for the professional exercise of traditional management functions has become increasingly necessary to help ensure that managers today can know

> ...how to decide in the face of uncertainty, how to distill the signal from the noise, [and] how to impose order and direction on a messy situation to achieve a worthwhile goal (Hilmer and Donaldson 1996, p. 192).

Library management (pre-1939)

Prior to the Second World War there were individuals within the library profession who employed the prevailing management theory. However, libraries have traditionally been behind other fields in developing management theory. That is due, in part, to the smaller size of the library as an organisation but also reflects the fact that examining library schools and associations were slow developing a library management curriculum. Stueart and Moran (1998, p. 403) stress that there were individuals within the library profession who were at least aware of the need for librarians to have and to use management skills. The authors quote the example of Arthur E. Bostwick who, in his 1891 address to the New Zealand Library Association, advocated adopting business efficiency methods in the operation of a library.

Fremont Rider (1966), in an excellent article on cost accounting in libraries, showed that there were librarians who had the theoretical knowledge to apply scientific management theory in the 1930s.

Until this period, libraries had been run with what we now perceive as a traditional and conservative approach. However, as early as the 1930s, a number of developments in the management of library services can be seen, especially with scientific techniques such as cost analysis, and how to achieve efficiencies in technical services like cataloguing.

Studying the ideas and methods of Taylor and the Gilbreths allowed 'forward-thinking' managers of the time to see that there was a range of techniques applicable to the library situation.

For an example of the influence on librarianship of the human relations school of thought, read Danton (1934). Danton was concerned with the role of personnel administration in the library organisation.

Library management after the Second World War

If library literature does not abound with management theory in the period before 1939, the scene alters significantly in the aftermath of the Second World War. The returning soldier wanted, and was given, access to education and business opportunities; and increased spending in the education field was reflected in the growth of academic libraries in particular. Librarians faced with rapid growth of stock, services, and demand for both had to come to terms with managing growing and dynamic organisations with the associated need for management skills to meet this unprecedented development. Library education and training programs began to include management theory and practice in their curricula.

In 1947 Ralph Shaw, one of the first librarian writers to espouse scientific management theory, wrote an important article for the future of library management in which he explained his concern with the integration of the parts into a functional organisation. Following and learning from Shaw (1947), Dougherty and Heinritz (1966) published the first full treatise on the application of scientific management to the library situation.

From the point of view of the library profession, the human relations theories had a considerable influence from the mid-1950s, and in most libraries human relations management has come to mean democratic management, participative supervisory and management styles, and increasing communication with, and involvement by, staff in the decision-making process.

Since the mid-1960s there has been an obvious upsurge in the publication of material dealing with library management as a science, as a necessary discipline for the modern librarian. There is no one theory of library management, just as there is no one right way to manage any organisation. What we have found are diverse contributions and the influence of many schools of thought and theories – for example operations research, the mathematical school, human relations, social systems and behavioural approaches. Librarians are constantly borrowing from – and often improving upon – the theories, ideas, skills and techniques of public administration and business management. We use the parts that are relevant to our needs as managers of people and resources, and we alter those parts as necessary to suit our particular environment, to ensure that our libraries are as effective and as efficient as possible.

Predictably, the evolution of library management was not without its critics. Ralph Edwards ['The Management of Libraries and the Professional Functions of Librarians,' *Library Quarterly*, 45, 1975] has argued that librarians are becoming too involved in tasks such as planning, budgeting and supervising at the cost of professional functions such as materials selection, information control, and client relations. While accepting that some aspects of management, such as goal formulation and strategic planning, require the judgement of librarians, Edwards believes that broad managerial responsibilities, such as those embodied in human resource management, should be discharged by other than professional librarians. An opposite point of view was expressed by McClure ['Library Managers: Can They Manage? Can They Lead?' *Library Journal*, 105, 20, 1980], who sees no contradiction between the professional and managerial tasks of librarians. He argues that 'library managers must become managers first and librarians second' in order to solve societal information problems (Bouthillier 1993, p. 36).

While views such as those expressed by Edwards above may be held by many librarians today, the reality is that no librarian can avoid the development and exercise of management skills if they are to become successful in their career.

Other useful brief outlines of the development of library management can be found in Stueart and Moran (1998), and Evans (1976). An entertaining article by John Lubans is also worth a look for its reflection on where modern library management has come from, its exploration of the reasons why some management fads have failed, and its suggestion that readers develop their own ideas about management of the library workplace (Lubans 2000).

Chapter 2
Organisational climate and culture and managing change

> There is nothing more difficult to carry out, nor more doubtful of success, nor more dangerous to handle, than to initiate a new order of things. (Machiavelli, *The prince*)

> The art of life lies in a constant readjustment to our surroundings. (Kakuzo Okahura)

> If we want things to stay as they are, things will have to change. (di Lampedusa)

Organisational climate and culture

Definitions and understandings of 'organisational culture' are not unlike the more generally known use of the word culture when applied to a society or to a sub-group of society (for example, teenage culture). It is a pattern of behaviours which we learn, and which we share and pass on to others in our same group, and which generally rule the way we act and interact with others.

Samuels (1982, p. 423) defines organisational climate as: 'A set of attributes which can be perceived about a particular organization and/or its subsystems, and that may be induced from the way that organization or its subsystems deal with their members and environments.' This was clearly a precursor to the now more universally used term 'organisational culture' and it is that term which is used in this chapter. The topics organisational culture and managing change are linked because change may not be implemented successfully without an understanding of the culture of the organisation.

Linda O'Brien provides a comprehensive and authoritative definition of organisational culture, based on E. H. Schein's (1990) *Organizational culture*

> Culture can now be defined as a pattern of basic assumptions, invented, discovered or developed by a given group as it learns to cope with its problems of external adaptation and internal integration, that has worked well enough to be considered valid and therefore is to be taught to new members as the correct way to perceive, think and feel in relation to those problems (O'Brien 1990, p. 630; formatting changed).

However, today, it is generally seen as a system of shared values, assumptions, beliefs and norms that serve to create a working environment that defines the manner in which 'things are done around here' (Bartol and Martin 1998, p. 91). Bartol and Martin go on to emphasise the importance of this culture in shaping individual worker's behaviour and its subsequent impact upon organisational effectiveness. Given the significance of building and maintaining a positive culture, it is important for library managers and supervisors to recognise that they are managing and supervising within a unique and specific culture, that they have a clear understanding of it and are willing to work towards changing it as necessary to ensure longer term success for the organisation.

The organisational culture of any organisation should primarily encourage staff to participate in the planning process, facilitate open communication and be supportive of staff and their development. Other factors which are pertinent to the understanding of a library's organisational culture include management style, the structure of the library, the external environment in which the library operates, interdepartmental relationships and the degree of specialisation.

A high degree of specialisation, for example, can lead to a narrow, blinkered approach to work, to the job, to the library and to the profession as a whole. Alison Crook (1987, p. 13) suggests that job rotations, exchanges, temporary transfers and working parties are means of counteracting some of the negative effects of specialisation. Chapter 12, on team development, has something to say about this too.

Who says the culture of an organisation is important? The following quotes illustrate the changing understanding of organisational culture over the last thirty years.

 Why spend all that money and time on the selection of people when the people you've got are breaking down from under-use. Get to know your people. What they do well, what they enjoy doing, what their weaknesses and strengths are, and what they want and need to get from their job...You can create a climate in which most of your people will motivate themselves to help the company reach its objectives (Townsend 1971, p. 130).

...organisational climate and leadership style, in particular those encouraging participation, will help encourage attitudes, relationships, motivation and morale conducive not only to training and development processes but also organisational change and innovation (Saw 1989, p. 18).

The themes that appear to characterise the organisational cultures of the future, reflecting new global and industry requirements, include flexibility, agility, creativity, innovativeness, quality and quantity foci, responsiveness, high performance and a limited form of commitment from both employers and employees (Nankervis, Compton and Baird 2002, p. 59).

Further to that, every library can – in fact should – create a climate or culture in which people are motivated to extend themselves, to perform at their optimum level most of the time, and to be in a position to welcome and deal with change. For all of the above to take place, the working environment must be conducive to change.

Alan Samuels' article 'Organizational climate and library change' (1982), is worth reading to complement what Crook (1987) and Saw (1989) say about creating or modifying a climate which allows innovation and change. By now you should be getting a sense of how to achieve an organisational culture that will help prevent resistance to change. One message is that participation will enhance acceptance of change and help to provide an environment that encourages innovation and creativity. A creative staff will adapt to change and use innovation to achieve agreed goals.

Participation is one key

Traditionally, libraries have been run by authoritarian managers, with decisions made at the top and communicated down with the expectation that workers will follow directions. But change cannot occur by dictate alone: it is not realistic for top management to decree change and then expect the lower levels to make it work. That would certainly create a climate characterised by uneasiness, resentment and other adverse spillover effects. Successful implementation of new ideas and services requires participation by those who will be affected by such change; and a participative approach takes a great deal more effort than an authoritarian one.

> If there is not a participative culture in a library, managers must recognize this and take the time to see that such a culture develops. This is another time-consuming matter, and it is one that can be frustrating. I've heard from new managers more than once, 'I keep having staff meetings and trying to get people to participate, but nobody says anything.' For whatever reason, these people don't have the skills to participate. As managers, we need to realize that teaching them those skills is part of the staff development process (Burgin and Hansel 1991, p. 78).

Staff should also be encouraged to see themselves as agents of change, and implementing change at an individual level. Managers and supervisors need to use groups, teamwork and delegation to empower their staff and to encourage a shared sense of purpose. A collaborative approach to decision-making will result in ownership through participation, and a reduction in the resistance to change. Participation through training programs, seminars, open discussion meetings, brainstorming, newsletters, working parties and work teams will help to identify problems and provide possible solutions. Part of this will involve seeking questions from staff, and answering those questions openly and immediately.

Participation gives great opportunities for the positive aspects of change to be highlighted. Extensive staff participation, and the resultant increase in information available, can alleviate fears and improve staff relations, which in turn should lead to less resistance to, and more acceptance of, change.

> Even with the best of intentions, skills and cooperation, new supervisors sometimes fail in a culture. The primary reason is tied to their people skills. They are not able to function as a member of the culture because they overlook people. They tend to be insensitive to others, have difficulty in working with authority, and fail to focus on their image and communication skills (Sannwald 2000, p. 12)

Communication is the other key

Acceptance of change is more likely, then, when individual people in the organisation perceive future possibilities as being beneficial to them – when they see them as exciting rather than as threatening. Effective communication during the process of planning for change will help to shape individual perceptions and positive attitudes. That communication should focus on paving the way for change by building a climate of acceptance of the need for change. By assisting staff to relate to the change and its benefits, and by involving them in creating and influencing change, a positive rather than a negative attitude towards change can be created among staff.

Communication with staff at all levels during planning for change is vital. Supervisors can be key facilitators of change because their positions form a bridge between management and staff. If supervisors are 'in tune' with staff attitudes and morale they can help to build staff understanding of the benefits of prospective changes and can ensure that management learns of any operational problems identified by staff.

Revealing a realistic picture of long- and short-range changes and updating staff regularly on the progress towards changing goals forewarn everyone of the nature and extent of the effects of change on them. Any decisions which are made, especially those made without a great deal of staff input (and there are some in this category), should be communicated throughout the organisation by a variety of methods – for example, regular bulletins or newsletters, meetings, memos (be careful of the wording), and training and development programs. These should be an in-built part of the change process, and should be continually occurring.

Managing change requires managers at all levels to provide staff with information, seek discussion and suggestions, and allow for any necessary training and education. As noted previously, management should address questions of how the change affects individuals in terms of their work, their flexibility, their potential for growth and advancement, and their personal levels of morale and motivation.

Communication needs to address both successes and problems. Timely information about, and responses to, both positive and problem areas are essential to help staff to adapt to new situations. All possible communication channels must be open and monitored, feedback must be gathered, welcomed and encouraged, staff must be assured that they are being listened to.

Managing change

It is unfortunate that in some management texts the only contribution on managing change is to list reasons why some people resist change. Resistance to change, like support for change, is made up of attitudes and behaviours which may be rooted in a variety of causes and reasons. Of course we have a need to understand those reasons, but in reading about this topic you should attempt to gain some understanding of how supervisors and managers can cope with change; of how resistance to change can be managed and controlled; and of how change can be harnessed to the benefit of the organisation and its goals.

Why study change?

There is constant change in library and information organisations, and it is a necessary part of the life of a dynamic organisation. For example, consider the changes that have been taking place in industrial relations in our world. When you also consider that the introduction and continual updating of technological tools is another force for change, that maintaining the status quo is a recipe for stagnation, and that resistance to change is both natural and to be expected, it is clear that managing change is a vital aspect of human resources management.

Managing change means taking control of, and influencing, the direction and outcomes of change. A well-managed and carefully coordinated combination of approaches is often needed for the effective implementation of change in the workplace. For example, a simple approach to the introduction of new technology in the library may involve gathering information regarding problems and concerns from members of the library staff, organising the information and communicating the results to the staff involved. Specific action to correct any identified problems would be based on those results and discussions. The strength of such an approach lies in involving all staff in a careful analysis of the change process.

Resistance to change

 The most effective technique for overcoming resistance to change is by encouraging participation in the decision-making, problem-solving and planning processes (Bryson 1999, p. 257).

Resistance to change occurs at individual, group and organisational levels. Since the early days of technological innovation in the nineteenth century, organisational change has been accompanied by the resistance of some to any alteration in the ways in which they work or changes to the conditions under which they work. Resistance to change is still often seen as defensive, irrational and even destructive behaviour.

> Viewing resistance to change as a form of sickness or irrationality is simplistic. The inescapable reality of organizational change is that it is never of equal benefit to all parties affected; at least in the short run, some parties usually realize a net loss in some form when change occurs. Thus, most forms of resistance to change are highly rational and have the understandable purpose of self-interest. This fact must be recognized when identifying factors that facilitate or constrain change and innovation (Johnson 1991, p. 92).

Indeed, while the rioting, machine-destroying Luddites of the early 1800s were seen as a destabilising threat to management, to many of their fellow workers they were heroes. Not much has changed in human behavioural terms.

Why do staff still feel threatened by change? Supervisors and managers, in planned and coordinated ways, will need to help staff to understand the benefits of change to them as individuals and to the library as an organisation whose goals they share. If we can recognise and understand where resistance to change comes from, or where it is likely to occur, then we are well on the way to identifying solutions to the problem of resistance to change, and hence can more effectively manage change. Empowering staff at all levels to be part of the change process from the beginning is a vital step in the success of organisational change (Martin 1998).

One of the most common reasons for resistance to change is that people fear a loss of security, and a threat to their status, their expertise or their place in the organisation. This can be because people feel threatened by change when they have no control over it. If they do not have enough information about the change, and have had little opportunity to influence its planning and implementation, then they are likely to resist its introduction. Surprise and lack of knowledge are common causes of resistance to change – people can be expected to be upset by decisions or requests suddenly sprung upon them without groundwork or preparation. Sometimes the threat is real – this is the most reasonable reason for resisting change. Sometimes people do lose their status, influence or comfort zone because of the change.

As well as being perceived as a threat to comfortable routines, change can also be seen to have potential effects on the individual. When first hearing about planned change, many of us will think immediately about how it will make more work for less of us; or how it will change the way we do things or interact with others. We may see it as having the potential to help or hinder our prospects for being valued members of the enterprise.

Other reasons for resistance to change that you need to consider include:

- loss of face – changes in work practices may be perceived as implying that past practices were wrong

- concerns about competence – people may resist change if they are concerned about their ability to perform new functions and duties
- flow-on effects – people may worry about the impacts of change on other plans or projects
- concern about work levels – implementing change requires more energy and focus, and more time, than routine 'known' work
- resentment – staff who have had a grievance with the organisation may resist and resent being told they now have to do something new (based on Johnson 1991, p. 93, citing Kanter 1985).

Research has shown that the kinds of 'personal' threats listed above are the most disabling. Overcoming resistance to change must be based on a knowledge of what those threats might be.

Overcoming resistance

Most management texts will explain that the best way to deal with resistance to change is to prevent it rather than to remove it once it has developed. Resistance can be controlled and redirected by adopting, or continuing, a participative philosophy of management in the design, planning and implementation of planned change. That is, participation in planning will enhance the chances of acceptance of change and provide an environment that encourages innovation and creativity. A creative staff will more readily adapt to change and use change to meet appropriate goals.

Peggy Johnson (1991, pp. 95–101) provides the following set of strategies for overcoming resistance to change, enabling change to be handled effectively.

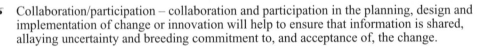

- Collaboration/participation – collaboration and participation in the planning, design and implementation of change or innovation will help to ensure that information is shared, allaying uncertainty and breeding commitment to, and acceptance of, the change.

- Communication – this means communicating information when planning for change. It means listening to negative and positive responses to planned change, and the acceptance of questions and suggestions for and against innovation.

- Leadership – this means the commitment of all levels of management to the change, and the creation of an organisational climate that encourages change and innovation by focusing on future, mission-based, visions.

- Purpose – acceptable change will be accompanied by a clear statement of what it will, or intends to, achieve, and by a statement of why the change will solve real problems.

- Incentives – change which clearly provides those higher-level motivators such as ownership and autonomy, job variety, increased job satisfaction and other social and psychological fulfilments will have a greater chance of acceptance. Change that provides job enrichment opportunities and the learning of new, valid and portable skills will be less likely to attract resistance.

- Consequences – when staff are made aware of how change will affect their work, their relationships (both formal and social) and the culture of the library, they can more readily prepare for and adapt to it.

- Time – allowing adequate time for staff and management to explore alternatives, consider input from all parties and make decisions based upon a full consideration of possible consequences will give staff the opportunity to become used to the idea and nature of the changes being planned.

- Incremental implementation – gradual introduction is important with major change in particular. Not only does it give more time for information to be communicated and for acceptance to occur, it can ensure also that opportunities are available to modify the goals of the innovation. Full consideration of problems and step-by-step evaluation of decisions made can assist in increasing staff acceptance and preventing resistance at various stages.

- Design – applicable mainly to the development and implementation of technological changes, the design process should be flexible and dynamic. This should allow for staff input, consideration of a range of options and alternatives, ensure that those who will be using the new system will not have a fait accompli thrust upon them, and thus make acceptance of the change a more likely result.

- Training – if staff are made aware from the beginning of planning that training in any new skills, methods and practices will be provided, and if that training is developed locally with this specific innovation in mind, then acceptance will again be made easier.

Writers suggest the development of an appropriate organisational culture, or climate, is crucial to the management of change. By building an environment in which staff feel included, involved, and empowered to use initiative, the library and the individual can be masters of change, instead of the victims. The formula for change includes the following basic features:

- plan the change
- create the right climate
- anticipate resistance
- sell the benefits
- listen
- follow-up.

Much of what follows in this book is prepared, written and presented with libraries and change in mind. Many of the theories and practical skills presented are practical tools for implementing change, and can be synthesised as in Figure 2.1 further below.

Eric Wainwright (1988) outlined a number of guidelines to encourage the acceptance of change which can be summarised as follows.

Change is more acceptable when it is understood; when it does not threaten security; when input is received from those affected by it; when it is not the result of a dictated order; when it follows previously successful changes; when it is implemented at a time when the organisation is not affected by other major change; when it has been planned; when the people affected are new and have no time and interest vested in maintaining the status quo; when those affected benefit from the change; and when the organisation itself is forward looking and anxious to improve (Wainwright, 1988).

Practical tools for implementing change	
• *Training*	♦ in leadership and management development ♦ in team building, as mentors and coaches ♦ to allow multi-skilling and the development of career paths which encourage continuous learning
• *Motivational tools*	♦ induction programs ♦ information sharing ♦ delegation ♦ decentralising decision-making ♦ goal setting ♦ finding out what staff attitudes are ♦ reward and incentive schemes
• *Developing responsibility and accountability*	♦ performance appraisal ♦ job analysis and design ♦ problem-solving ♦ team-building

Figure 2.1: *Practical tools for implementing change*

Conclusion

Change is inevitable and constant – nothing stays the same. Providing opportunities for individuals to have influence over, and to participate in, the change process will reduce any resistance to change. Providing continuing involvement after the initial change will produce significant increases in motivation, satisfaction and performance. Effective interpersonal and organisational communication are both crucial to the successful implementation of change. As libraries and information agencies deal with a wide range of technological and attitudinal upheaval, participation and communication are the keys that enable changes to be planned and developed, and once developed, to make them work. Both will help staff to prepare for and cope with change and will help – although not necessarily ensure – staff develop the flexibility to welcome change in a positive manner.

Chapter 3
Total quality management

Introduction

This chapter aims to introduce you to the concepts of quality and total quality management (TQM), and allow you to gain a broad understanding of how and why TQM has been, and is being, applied to libraries. The purpose of this is to consider a modern philosophy of management which underpins much of contemporary library management theory and practice.

TQM is a management philosophy, based on the work of pioneers in industrial management such as W. Edwards Deming, Joseph Juran, Armand Fiegenbaum, and Kaoru Ishikawa. These people helped transform Japan's industrial sector in the 1950s by applying statistical methods to the management of production processes, by making client satisfaction the focus of all operations, and by empowering employees through teamwork and shared decision-making (Morgan and Murgatroyd 1994, p. 200). In the 1980s, when the United States began to see a reduction in its own world market share in relation to Japan, American business rediscovered Deming. Quality management experts, Joseph Juran and Philip Crosby, also contributed to the development of TQM theories, models, and tools. TQM is now practiced in business as well as in government, the military, education, and in non-profit organisations including libraries (Jurow and Barnard 1993, cited in Masters 1996).

Since then, the theory and methodology of TQM has been adopted (and adapted) by many different types of organisations worldwide, including libraries and the organisations of which libraries are a structural part. The central philosophy of TQM is that good quality should be designed into services and processes at the start, to prevent problems from ever arising. Constant monitoring of services and processes is important, to reject substandard products or services, but they cannot raise the quality of products or services produced. Therefore, quality management practitioners have devised a series of tools and methods for managers and employees to strengthen organisational systems, prevent problems, and improve quality.

There are numerous useful introductions to TQM, and I encourage you to read at least one of the introductions listed in the references. The 'Total quality management' chapter in Carson, Carson and Phillips (1995) is especially useful, together with an Australian introduction, *Quality concepts* (1993) by Vallence and Wallace.

Quality in management defined

As the following definitions indicate, quality can be defined in a number of ways, depending on the specific context.

Quality is fitness for purpose. (Found in nearly every text on quality management)

Quality is 'the totality of features and characteristics of a product or service that bear on its ability to meet stated or implied needs...meeting requirements, conforming to specification, fitness for purpose' (Ellis and Norton 1996, p. 134).

'Fundamentally, *quality* is concerned with meeting the wants and needs of customers' (Brophy and Coulling 1996, p. 6;. italics added).

Quality management: 'Although there are many different ways of defining quality, it has been generally recognized in the literature of quality management that those definitions which emphasize a link between the customer, the customer's purpose and the product or service being received are the most helpful. Quality management then becomes a way of delivering products and services which, over time, are closer and closer to the customer's needs' (Brophy and Coulling 1996, p. 19).

Total quality management '...a process of continuous improvement which always puts the customer first' (Ellis and Norton 1996, p. 1).

'*Total Quality Management* involves monitoring and assessing organisations and their products and services to identify opportunities for improvement, then taking action to make and maintain these improvements' (Armstrong, 1994, p. 108, italics added).

Out of all of that, we can discern an emphasis on quality as a process *of continuous improvement that is customer-focused.*

However, there is even more to it.

> It has frequently been observed of organizations, especially of those in the service sector, that staff are their most valuable resource. Staff are also certainly the greatest single cost for libraries. A university, for example, may spend something of the order of 70% of its total library budget on staffing. In addition, as we enter the so-called Information Age, staff have become the repository of a second, frequently uncosted and undervalued resource, namely information and skills. From the perspective of any management system, it makes sense to ensure that this scarce and valuable resource is used to maximum effect. Total quality management places great stress on this issue, since it is recognised that the success of the whole organisation, particularly its ability to meet the needs of its customers, is dependent on everyone taking responsibility for quality and having the skills to deliver the needed 'products' to their internal and external customers (Brophy and Coulling 1996, p. 85).

Therefore, it can be safely argued that customer focus, continuous improvement and employee empowerment are the major principles of TQM in modern organisations.

> Patron focus specifies that library organizations must be responsive to the user. Process improvement is built on the notion that consumers of a library organization can best be served by reducing system deficiencies through a structured procedure using project teams. Finally, employee empowerment involves efforts to utilize the talents of all staff members in the library (Carson, *et al.* 1995, p. 171).

The outcome of quality in management is not an end, but rather a continual striving for excellence. It requires us to deny the common belief that 'if it ain't broke, don't fix it'. One of the keys to quality management is not to leave things alone if they seem to be working. If you find nothing wrong, then you must look harder until you do, and then make improvements. It should not be confused with 're-engineering' (or, business process engineering) which is at the other end of the change scale in that re-engineering is a one-time concerted effort to make major improvements in processes, rather than the TQM approach of making marginal improvements in existing procedures (Rue and Byars 1999, p. 372)

Deming's fourteen points Explained better pg41 Module 1

Masters (1996) notes that one of the 'founders' of TQM, W. Edwards Deming, outlined fourteen steps that managers in any type of organisation can take to implement a total quality management program. The steps are based on Deming's work with Japanese managers and others.

1. Create constancy of purpose for improvement of product and service. Constancy of purpose requires innovation, investment in research and education, continuous improvement of product and service, maintenance of equipment, furniture and fixtures, and new aids to production.

2. Adopt the new philosophy. Management must undergo a transformation and begin to believe in quality products and services.

3. Cease dependence on mass inspection. Inspect products and services only enough to be able to identify ways to improve the process.

4. End the practice of awarding business on price tag alone. The lowest priced goods are not always the highest quality; choose a supplier based on its record of improvement and then make a long-term commitment to it.

5. Improve constantly and forever the system of product and service. Improvement is not a one-time effort; management is responsible for leading the organisation into the practice of continual improvement in quality and productivity.

6. Institute training and retraining. Workers need to know how to do their jobs correctly even if they need to learn new skills.

7. Institute leadership. Leadership is the job of management. Managers have the responsibility to discover the barriers that prevent staff from taking pride in what they do. The staff will know what those barriers are.

8. Drive out fear. People often fear reprisal if they "make waves" at work. Managers need to create an environment where workers can express concerns with confidence.

9. Break down barriers between staff areas. Managers should promote teamwork by helping staff in different areas/departments work together. Fostering interrelationships among departments encourages higher quality decision-making.

10. Eliminate slogans, exhortations, and targets for the workforce. Using slogans alone, without an investigation into the processes of the workplace, can be offensive to workers because they imply that a better job could be done. Managers need to learn real ways of motivating people in their organisations.

11. Eliminate numerical quotas. Quotas impede quality more than any other working condition; they leave no room for improvement. Workers need the flexibility to give customers the level of service they need.

12. Remove barriers to pride of workmanship. Give workers respect and feedback about how they are doing their jobs.

13. Institute a vigorous program of education and retraining. With continuous improvement, job descriptions will change. As a result, employees need to be educated and retrained so they will be successful at new job responsibilities.

14. Take action to accomplish the transformation. Management must work as a team to carry out the previous 13 steps (Masters 1996; formatting changed).

While Deming's points were primarily developed through observations in manufacturing industries, others have looked closely at their application in service organisations such as libraries and information centres. Berry, Parasuraman and Zeithaml (1994, cited in Stueart and Moran 1998) outline the results of a ten year study into the application of TQM in a range of service industries. They found that the following principles formed the core of a successful TQM program:

- Listening to customers is the driver for action.

- Reliable, consistent service delivery is essential.

- Most customers do not have extravagant expectations, they just want their basic requirements handled well.

- Designing a quality service delivery system that allows staff to provide reliable, high-level service is a major management responsibility.

- Quick, effective response to customer complaints is essential in turning around dissatisfied clients.

- Providing unexpected, value added 'surprises' to customers builds loyalty and commitment.

- All clients expect to be treated fairly and consistently.

- Supportive co-workers within well functioning teams promotes the development of quality conscious staff.

- Staff are encouraged to highlight areas of concern and identify problems. They should act as early-warning devices if things seem to be going wrong.

- Managers have to set standards, develop systems and empower staff in order to achieve the quality levels the organisation desires.

All of these principles are applicable to the library environment and a number of major libraries have built on these and Deming's points in order to implement TQM programs in their organisations.

Masters (1996) for example, provides the following illustration of the use of TQM at Harvard:

> Harvard College Library created a task force which rewrote the library's vision statement, and considered changes that would have to be made in order to develop a new organisation culture – one that "highlights the changing nature of staff roles and responsibilities" in an era of pervasive change" (Clack 1993). With the help of consultants, Harvard learned about TQM, and found that its principles of service excellence, teamwork, ongoing training and skill building, process/systems focus, continuous improvement, and cooperation across boundaries could help them make the changes they needed (Masters 1996).

Masters (1996) also describes a TQM project conducted at the Oregon State University Library.

> Two small teams, the Shelving Team from the stack maintenance unit, and the Documents Team from the government publications unit worked with outside facilitators. Each team surveyed users and staff and found that some issues, perceived as critical by staff, were not perceived as critical by customers and therefore needed

rethinking in terms of TQM. The Shelving Team, which wanted to address the problem of longlasting shelving backlogs, found that the shelvers, who worked alone on the floors, felt isolated and unmotivated to make progress. Using this information, the team devised a plan for shelvers to work in small groups and have an assigned floor. The result was an increased "esprit de corps", tidier shelves, and less backlog (Butcher 1993, cited in Masters 1996).

Sirkin (1993, cited in Masters 1996) suggests that TQM operates at a wide range of levels, from the operational level (for example, assisting customers by developing simpler methods for the loan and return of materials) through to the strategic level (for example, updating the mission statement).

Clearly, quality management is not just another fad, or trendy theory, and most modern organisations can bear witness that the focus on quality is here to stay. The major characteristics which libraries embrace through TQM are customer driven quality, continuous improvement, data collection, benchmarking, employee participation and empowerment, and the need for senior management to provide the lead.

Customer-driven quality

TQM has a customer-first orientation. Customer satisfaction is seen as the library's highest priority, taking the focus away from internal activities and constraints. The library's mission statement (discussed in Chapters 5 and 6) should be an indicator that it will only be successful if customers are satisfied. The TQM library is sensitive to customer requirements and responds rapidly to them. In the TQM context, 'being sensitive to customer requirements' goes beyond the reduction of mistakes and inadequate service, or of merely meeting basic requirements or reducing customer complaints. The concept of requirements is expanded to take in not only service attributes that meet basic requirements, but also those that enhance and differentiate them for competitive advantage.

Each part of the library is involved in total quality services, operating as a customer to some functions and as a supplier to others. For example, cataloguing is a supplier to reference and information services, and has to treat internal customers with the same sensitivity and responsiveness as it would external customers.

Many libraries today provide a public face to their mission statement in the form of a Customer Service Charter, and as the following, from the State Library of Western Australia (2002) shows, its relationship to TQM is very clear. 'The State Library's Customer Service Charter demonstrates our commitment to planning for continuous improvement of the services offered to the Western Australia community'.

Continuous improvement

Continuous improvement of all operations and activities is at the heart of TQM. Once it is recognised that customer satisfaction can only be obtained by providing a high-quality service, continuous improvement of the quality of the service is seen as the main way to maintain a high level of customer satisfaction. As well as recognising the link between service quality and customer satisfaction, TQM also recognises that service quality is the result of process quality. As a result, there is a focus on continuous improvement of the library's processes. This will lead to an improvement in product quality, and to an increase in customer satisfaction. Improvement cycles are encouraged for all the library's activities especially the development of new and current services and the way customer relations are managed.

TQM and the concept of continuous improvement focuses on the idea of incremental change. It is all about making modest changes to improve delivery rather than trying to always develop major, structural improvements. This conglomeration of small improvements, quick and simple to devise and implement, adds up over time to higher levels of quality service, minimal disruption to staff and users and increasing awareness of the possibilities that a continual concern for quality can bring.

Eliminating waste is also a major component of the continuous improvement approach. There is a strong emphasis on prevention rather than detection, and an emphasis on quality at the design stage. The customer-driven approach helps to prevent errors and achieve defect-free production. When problems do occur within the product development process, they are generally discovered and resolved before they can get to the next internal customer.

Data collection

The issue of properly evaluating all aspects of work within a library is an area that has received increased attention in recent times. The establishment of a regular international conference dealing specifically with performance measurement and libraries is indication of the importance now being attached to this area. As Lakos, the coordinator of the 2nd Northumbria International Conference on Performance Measurement and Libraries has noted,

> The creation and draw of this conference is just one indication of the greater role that performance measures are playing in libraries today than they have in the past. Measures are being applied in a wide variety of settings and in a number of locations (1998, p. 1)

An overview of the Conference can be found at <http://www.library.ucla.edu/libraries/yrl/reference/aalakos/Present/North97/norsum.html.

In addition, the development of online tools such as LibQUAL+, devised by the American Research Libraries group, are indications of the seriousness with which the measurement and evaluation of service delivery is being taken within the library environment. Cook and Heath (2001) describe one such research project undertaken in a university library using the LibQUAL+ instrument to measure the dimensions of library service quality. Their findings concluded that , in addition to some standard dimensions of service quality, three other variables, possibly unique to the library environment, also played a major part. These were:

> …ubiquity and ease of access to collections, the library as place, subsuming dual concepts of utilitarian space and of the library as a symbol of the intellect and, finally, the overwhelming drive on the part of users to be self-reliant and confident in navigating the information world (Cook and Heath 2001, p. 582).

Assessing the level of service quality relies on the collection of relevant data, but as noted above, in a library this can require the use of sophisticated instruments or techniques and be difficult to obtain. For instance, recording the time for book requests to arrive, for customer requests to be fulfilled or complaints to be resolved, will only shed light on part of the process. Identifying what customers expect from the library and whether they obtain that service is more difficult to assess. With a product, such as a toy, assessment criteria may often be self-evident (for example, is it safe, educational, value for money, appropriate to the target age group?). For a service the issues are far less obvious. A customer may receive friendly service but leave without the information they came to find. Similarly, a customer may find the information they seek but spend excessive time and have difficulty locating it.

Brophy and Coulling (1996) suggest benchmarking as a method to determine data collection criteria for libraries. Benchmarking – the process of identifying, monitoring and evaluating innovative service delivery techniques and adapting them so they can be implemented in a particular environment – is an important component of the TQM approach. The University of Wollongong Library which won the 2000 Australian Business Excellence Award participated in multiple benchmarking activities which they consider to be one of the TQM processes they implemented that contributed to their remarkable success (University of Wollongong 2001, p. 7).

Benchmarking

The development and use of performance indicators is linked, directly or indirectly, to customer requirements and satisfaction, and to management and employee remuneration. Numerous indicators of performance can be found discussed in the literature of library evaluation. Benchmarking is one of these measures which has been closely linked to TQM and the need to continuously improve to meet customer expectations and needs.

> Benchmarking is the process of examining any process your organization performs, finding out who else needs to undertake that same process (whether in your industry or not), then finding out who performs it best, and then using their performance as a benchmark against which to compare your own performance, and with which to generate new expectations and standards about what constitutes first class performance, and to generate new ideas about how to improve your performance (Koenig 1998, p. 33).

For example, it may be the librarian's information seeking expertise which gives the library a strong competitive advantage within their own organisation, with outside competitors such as management consultants, and even with non-library organisations which maintain similar processes or functions (Evans 1999). Benchmarking requires that you find out not only where other libraries provide a better service, but consider going to unrelated services (for example, parliamentary researchers) and discovering how well they do it, what can be learned from them, and what can be used towards improving your own service.

Employee participation

A successful TQM environment requires a committed and well-trained workforce that participates fully in quality improvement activities. Participation should be reinforced by reward and recognition systems which emphasise the achievement of quality objectives. On-going education and training of all employees supports the desire to achieve quality. Employees should be encouraged to take more responsibility, to communicate more effectively, to act creatively, and to always be aware of the potential for innovation. As will be discussed in Chapter 12, the development and maintenance of a team culture in a participative environment relies on individual staff members being empowered to develop and build on the input of those around them, to share opinions, and to listen to and learn from others.

Leadership from senior management

Although it is well-recognised that the successful implementation of TQM depends on empowered staff, it is equally true that TQM has to be introduced and led by senior management. Successful TQM requires that top management is committed to and personally involved in creating and deploying clear quality values and goals consistent with the library's objectives. Management also needs to be involved in supporting the creation of systems, methods and performance measures for achieving those goals. These systems and methods should not only guide all quality activities but should also encourage participation by all employees.

Bringing the two together

The introduction of TQM requires, then, an open, cooperative culture. Front line staff will often have critical contributions to make to the development of quality initiatives (Austen 1996). Staff, supervisors and managers all need to feel that they are responsible for customer satisfaction. They are not going to feel this if they are excluded from the development of visions, strategies, and plans. It is important they all participate in these activities.

An excellent article which demonstrates how this can occur in the changing culture of quality improvement is provided by Helen Ristuccia (1998) from Liverpool City Library, in Sydney, New South Wales. It is a good example of leadership through the empowerment of staff.

Management commitment to TQM should also result in a recognition of the need to inform and train staff. Several initiatives in this area are described in 'Library staff development and training for assessment of services' (Kight and Snyder, 2002).

Quality rewarded

In November 1996, at the annual Australian Quality Awards ceremony, the libraries of the University of Wollongong and the University of Melbourne received Achievement in Business Excellence Awards. The Australian Quality Awards were introduced in 1988 and have contributed significantly to the growing awareness within the community of the importance of quality to Australia's international competitiveness. The Awards provide a framework for defining sustainable organisational excellence.

McGregor (1997) documents the University of Wollongong's achievement. The value of TQM is highlighted in that article, and in the following excerpt from *InCite*.

> For the University of Wollongong Library, the presentation culminated a two-year commitment to the quality journey and almost a decade of planned change within the library. The process has transformed the library from a rigidly hierarchical, reactive organisation into one which is flexible, team-based and client-focused.
>
> Participation in the awards program provided the library with a structured means of critical introspection. It reaffirmed the library's goal of creating a culture which values both team and individual achievement. More pragmatically it has prepared the library for meeting the challenges brought about by changes in University funding. Unlike many other sections of the University, the library has a clear mission statement, can identify its core activities and has data regarding its performance and costs.

The library now has a framework around which to continue developing it services in a manner which is strategic and closely aligned with the needs of its clients. This framework will facilitate the library's ability to meet whatever challenges the future brings.

For the University of Melbourne's library, the award recognises considerable gains in the areas of staff, community relations, planning and products and services, although the library recognises that quality is a journey and they still have some distance to go.

Organisations must lead from the front by effecting their own continuous learning. This requires an approach which encourages audit and review and retains enough flexibility to move resources to new programs and drive change to achieve greater customer satisfaction.

Libraries need a vision which can be owned by the organisation and its customers. The massive increase in information both in print and electronic form requires that libraries change their roles to meet the opportunities and challenges ahead. It is in this context that many libraries have used quality principles as a tool for moving forward.

When the library began [its] quality journey it was seen by some to be 'lagging behind' — although many of the library's services and its collections were extremely good, the library was criticised for its lack of a service focus. It was clear that substantial quality improvement programs needed to be established as a tool for achieving organisational change and development.

A framework for sustained improvement is in place. Libraries have a future, this future will continue to change rapidly and libraries must be able to embrace the opportunities this future will provide (Quality rewarded 1996, p. 7).

Conclusion

Quality management requires exemplary customer focus, and continuous improvement – change of all kinds, to the benefit of the library's clients. Active involvement by all levels of staff and management is essential to the successful achievement of the library's TQM service goals. And the optimum culture for TQM to flourish in is one that empowers staff, and encourages a shared sense of purpose.

Chapter 4
Roles of the supervisor and manager

Dilbert principle: The most ineffective workers are systematically moved to the place where they can do the least damage: management. (Scott Adams)

Introduction

One of the aims of this text is to provide an introduction to the managerial environment of libraries. By considering a number of theories, skills and techniques you can gain a basic understanding of how and why we manage, or are managed, in our working situation.

But why study management?…this is a library! Well, managers and supervisors are people whose jobs involve achieving things through others. This is done by managers allocating resources, making decisions and overseeing the activities of others to achieve the organisation's objectives (Bryson 1999, p. 6). Therefore, if your job involves supervising other people, there is a management aspect to your job. Anyone who makes decisions about other people, equipment, materials, finance or other resources has some element of management in their job. Supervisory and management tasks and practices are required at all levels of the library, to varying degrees, and any organisation can be seen as having three main levels of management.

Levels of management

Strategic or top management

The strategic or top level of management is responsible for the total organisation and will deal with the funding body (for example, City Council, University Council) in the realms of policy making, strategic planning and so on. They are concerned with the long-term threats and opportunities faced by the organisation and deal very much with future directions, rather than the short-term management of specific tasks. Examples of this level are chief librarians of public libraries, university librarians and librarians-in-charge of a variety of other types of library.

Middle management

Middle management manages the operations level, and mediates between the operations level and the clients of the organisation. It must also mediate with the top level of management. Mid-level managers are concerned with developing practices and procedures, organising resources to achieve long and short term goals and setting in place an appropriate climate within which effective and efficient teams can grow. Middle managers are both supervisors and managers, and examples include heads of departments such as technical services and reader services.

Operations management

Often described as the technical level, operations managers and supervisors are directly in charge of the goods and services produced by an organisation. On a day-to-day basis they will be concerned with planning and delivery of services, ensuring that staff and client needs are met. They will also have a major impact on levels of staff enthusiasm and motivation. In a public library, for example, operations managers could include a lending services librarian, or someone in charge of the reference services.

This indicates that the librarian in, for example, a small library in a large commercial organisation will have little or no opportunity to practise a general managerial function. Some education and training in supervisory techniques, communication, planning skills, and so forth will be necessary though. Furthermore, an appreciation of the structures, processes and values of management will be vital in helping the librarian to fit more readily into the total organisation of which the library is a part. An understanding of some management theory and techniques will help newly qualified professionals to survive more readily in a managerial environment with some degree of understanding of its modes of thought and operation.

Managerial roles

Mintzberg (1980, cited in Bartol *et al.* 2001, p. 10) outlines three broad categories of managerial roles.

Interpersonal roles, primarily concerned with interpersonal relationships for example:

- the figurehead role, for example when the manager attends the funeral of a subordinate
- the leadership role, which involves directing and coordinating people
- the liaison role, which involves the manager in contacts outside the vertical chain of command to bring information into the unit and gain favour from the external environment.

Information roles, primarily concerned with the transfer of information, for example:

- the monitoring role, where the environment is constantly scanned to receive and collect information
- the disseminator role, which involves the passing along of special or privileged information that subordinates would not normally have access to
- the spokesperson role, where the manager speaks for the unit and represents it at various meetings.

Decision roles, primarily concerned with decision-making for example:

- the entrepreneurial role, where the manager works to bring about changes that will improve the effectiveness or efficiency of the unit, or perhaps even alter its goals
- the disturbance handler role, which involves the taking of corrective action in response to pressures and changes that are beyond personal control
- the resource allocator role, where the manager decides who will get what in the unit
- the negotiator role, where the manager discusses and bargains with other units or managers, or externally, to obtain advantages for the unit.

All of these roles are closely interrelated, but each manager or supervisor puts a different emphasis on them – often unconsciously – which gives each a distinctive 'style'. The relative emphasis also depends a great deal upon the level in the management hierarchy and on the specific nature of the job involved. For example, chief librarians of large universities spend much time in the figurehead and liaison roles, whereas a head of lending services would rarely fulfil the figurehead role.

The type of organisation can also be relevant here. For example, librarians in business companies may be more involved in the entrepreneurial role than would librarians in government departments. Conversely, the latter often spend more time in the negotiator role because of the frequent contact with the public that some government departments experience.

Supervision

Supervising, then, is the often complex process of getting things done through people; of ensuring that workers perform their jobs efficiently and effectively so that the library's objectives are achieved. Supervision requires considerable understanding of people, especially how they interact and relate within organisations. Supervisors must have an understanding of what motivates people to work and to achieve, and what supervisory styles will work best for which people in which situations. In order to do so, to get to know the individuals and their needs, and to help fulfil those needs in conjunction with the needs of the library, supervisors must communicate and have a clear understanding of the importance of communication in the library.

Supervision styles

The supervisor is one key to the employees' attitudes to their work and their jobs, and plays a major role in the quality of work performance and in productivity. As a result supervisors can influence the job satisfaction and morale of the staff they supervise. The following are examples of supervisory styles.

- Predominantly production-centred – this style of supervisor feels responsible for getting the work completed; employees are made aware that they are to do only what the supervisor tells them.

- Predominantly employee-centred – this style of supervisor recognises that employees do the work and that they should have a major input into determining how it is done. This supervisor's role is to coordinate and maintain a harmonious environment.

- The 'good sort' – this sort of supervisor wants to be part of the group he or she is managing. However, this can create problems when the supervisor is required to discipline, realign or deal with a subordinate 'mate'.

- The distant boss – this style of supervisor maintains both a formal and informal distance between him or herself and the staff. Staff may consider such a supervisor to be uninterested in their work and their welfare.

The examples above represent some extremes, and use the word 'predominantly' advisedly, because no one person is always the same.

Qualities of a successful supervisor

The following list of qualities of a good supervisor is provided to give a frame of reference for what follows in this book in terms of key skills required for successful supervision. See how many you have already, and make plans to develop those in which you are weak.

- A supervisor should have ambition: the desire to manage and grow. You should always be willing to learn, to develop new skills, to broaden the job. You cannot be afraid to take a chance, but instead should possess confidence that you will succeed.

- A supervisor should be a self-starter. You should think and act on your own initiative, and not wait to be told by others to do something. To do this, you also need self-confidence and the courage to take risks and develop.

- A supervisor should be able to think. This is perhaps the hardest skill for most supervisors to practise constantly. Most of us find it easy to do and to act, but have more difficulty in thinking clearly about a problem. The mind wanders, noises and other problems can distract, and we prefer to take some immediate action – no matter how precipitate – rather than to take time to think about how to solve the problem.

- A supervisor should be able to communicate clearly. The best idea in the world is worthless unless it is communicated well. Supervisors spend most of their time communicating, therefore they need to do it well. This does not mean great speaking and writing skills. Instead, it is simply that a supervisor needs to get ideas across to staff clearly so they can understand what they are expected to do.

- A supervisor should be a salesperson. Any idea that you have and communicate to others still needs to be sold. Selling an idea, convincing others of its worth, is one of a supervisor's main tasks. Selling a plan of action to others is a vital part of communication and motivation by supervisors.

- A supervisor should have well-developed ethics. Truthfulness, honesty, integrity are vital ingredients if you wish to inspire your staff's trust and confidence in you.

- A supervisor should be able to organise. This is an obvious, but important, attribute because supervisors are constantly called on to organise their own work, and the work of their staff, in order to achieve service and productivity goals.

- A supervisor should have the ability to work with and through other people. This involves the supervisor in the key skill areas of leading, delegating, motivating and directing in order to ensure that section and library goals are achieved. A supervisor should like people, enjoy working with others, and have a sense of loyalty and empathy for colleagues.

- A supervisor should be willing to tackle and make tough decisions. Anyone can make the simple and easy decisions, but a good supervisor must have or develop the character to consider hard problems and make tough or unpopular decisions.

- A supervisor should be dynamic and have the ability to inspire others. The personal characteristics (many of those mentioned already), the behaviour, and the style of the good supervisor will portray leadership qualities that are regarded as worthy of allegiance and respect.

- A supervisor should have the ability to evaluate others and recognise individual strengths and weaknesses. This is critical in the staffing function, which involves ensuring the right person is in the right job, possessing the appropriate skills and displaying the right attitudes. This ability will also be vital in the staff development function.

Bearing these qualities in mind, have you ever thought that different things are important to different supervisors? For example, is it true that supervisory style depends on the type of work being done? Is it true that the style of supervision adopted in any situation is contingent upon that particular situation? Think about your own situation now, or in previous positions. How did your style, or the style of your supervisor, change to fit different circumstances of work, environment, or people?

Traditionally, it has been considered that supervisors require skills in four main areas:

- conceptual skills – the ability to obtain, interpret, and apply the information necessary to make sound decisions
- human relations skills – the ability to work with, and through, people
- administrative skills – the ability to plan, organise, and coordinate the activities of a work group
- technical skills – the ability to perform the actual jobs within the supervisor's area of responsibility.

In recent years many observers have added political skills – the savvy to ascertain the hidden rules of the organisational game and to recognise the roles that various people play in getting things done outside formal organisational channels. (See Hilgert and Leonard 1995, Rue and Byars 1999.)

The results of a recent (unidentified) survey of staff in an Australian government agency (cited in Pymm 2000, p. 9) provide an interesting insight into the common, and divergent, views of what managers expect from their staff, and what staff would like from their managers. Thus managers' expectations of staff were to:

- deliver agreed outputs to agreed deadlines
- reach agreed quality standards
- accept personal responsibility for the outputs and deadlines
- try and improve systems and processes
- be a loyal, effective and contributing team member
- assist other team members as required
- participate in meetings and discussions
- support management decisions once consultation and discussion were completed
- bring concerns initially to their immediate supervisor
- implement OH&S policies and practices
- share responsibility for personal development and training.

Staff expectations of their managers were to:

- provide guidance and leadership to the team
- show respect for individuals and the team
- provide a safe, healthy and 'respecting' work environment
- allow opportunities for input into the decision making process for issues that affect them
- develop creative and innovative solutions to problems
- negotiate deadlines and priorities
- organise adequate resources to undertake the task
- delegate responsibility

- provide adequate training and career development opportunities
- effectively represent the area to peer groups, higher level management and external bodies
- act as an information conduit between senior management and the work group
- undertake fair and proper recruitment and promotion practices
- have the ability and willingness to make the 'hard' decisions.

While there are common threads in many of the issues expressed by both groups, being aware of the occasionally divergent views represented in the survey can help managers better understand the motivation behind actions and assist them in helping teams achieve their goals. It also helps outline the skills and strategies necessary to ensure that team supervisors in particular can create successful, motivated teams providing quality service.

Key skills in supervisors

Later in this work the discussion turns to some of the broader supervisory skills. Basic skills such as communication, problem-solving and decision-making are needed by all workers in all organisations. If the goals of the current movement towards gaining key competencies at the completion of secondary education are achieved, teachers of management and supervision will have a sound basis upon which to build.

However, that is for the future. Before you can begin to consider the skills of the supervisor and manager, you need to spend some time looking at the general process and functions of management. Traditionally, these involve the major tasks of planning, organising, leading and controlling. Within each of these functions, managers utilise their technical, human or strategic skills to a greater or lesser degree in order to achieve organisational goals. Part 1, which follows, considers a simple strategic approach to the management of libraries. Setting objectives, planning for their achievement, organising the work in such a way that objectives are achieved, leading people, and evaluating progress towards goals provides a framework within which the skills and techniques of supervision and management can be considered.

Part 1

The general functions of management

Chapter 5
Objectives and policy development

Alice: Would you tell me please, which way I ought to go from here?
Cheshire cat: That depends a good deal on where you want to get to!
(Lewis Carroll, *Alice's adventures in wonderland*)

As indicated earlier, there are numerous approaches to studying and considering the processes and functions of management. Whatever approach is applied, managers and supervisors function as part of a process in which a cooperative group directs action towards common goals or objectives. The primary step in any activity, in any organisation, must therefore be a consideration of the objectives of that activity, and/or the aims of that organisation. Setting and monitoring objectives, both short- and long-term, must be a fundamental function of management at all levels; and that is where this study of the functions of library management begins.

The present situation

Defining the present situation is the first step. We can all say vaguely what it is, but ask yourself these questions.

- What proportion of your library's potential 'public' are members, or regular users?
- What reasons might the others give for not being members or regular users?
- What proportion of your 'public' knows how to join the library?
- What proportion has never used the library?
- Why do people mainly visit the library?
- What hours do people prefer the library to be open?
- What proportion of users prefers not to use the catalogue?
- What are the characteristics of this group?
- What proportion of your public use the library as a resting place?
- How frequently do users use the library?

Try now to see if you know the answers to some, or all, or any, of these questions. Relate them to the library in which you work, or at least a library you know well.

The answers to some of these questions can give an indication about what proportion of the library's time, resources and budget needs to be spent on which areas of service. Objectives can be set from that kind of information and analysis. The answers to other questions will raise further questions. If you discover that only 20 per cent of members use the library regularly, you need to ask whether, for example, more would use it more regularly if it were better located; if service points were available in a wider range of locations; or if it were open for longer hours.

The important point about answering such questions is not to guess. We cannot define our present situation and discover useful planning information, nor can we set objectives based on that information, unless it is factual and valid. We cannot, for example, take the answers to the questions from the survey undertaken by another library. We need to ask those questions within our own environment, in our own library's 'catchment area'. Only our own 'public' can give the answers.

Once you have defined the present situation you can set your objectives.

Objectives

The meaning of the word 'objective' is self-explanatory, but in the management context a number of synonymous terms are used, generally to denote longer- or shorter-term aims, and those distinctions will become clear as you read this chapter.

To formulate objectives, you need to answer questions like 'where do we want to be?' or 'what is the mission (aim, purpose) of this library?' Answers might be 'to provide a free public library service to the citizens of this city (or town, or region)'; or 'to maximise effective access to recorded information by the university's academic and student community with resources acquired for that purpose.'

You must, of course, define what you mean by terms like 'free public library service', 'effective access' and 'resources', to make your mission statement as clear and specific as possible. For example, you may decide that 'free public library service' encompasses the provision of educational, information, recreational and community-oriented materials for every resident in the city (or town, or region).

That, then, would be the library's mission. To move towards the fulfilment of that mission, the library will need to set broad, or long-term, goals and objectives that will identify the strategic direction of the organisation. In turn, the library's various sections, departments and teams will need to set shorter-term goals which aim to fulfil long-term goals. The day-to-day activities and tasks performed throughout the whole library must all be linked to the short-term goals, long-term goals and ultimately, to the overall mission.

The hierarchy of objectives identified in Figure 5.1 helps to put this in perspective. It is a model only, and not a prescription for setting objectives, but it helps to explain the interdependence of goals and activities.

Try the exercise yourself, using your own organisation and the types of activities in which you are engaged. If you don't find it easy, it is probably because it is difficult to set realistic objectives unless you have a clear understanding of the situation in which you find yourself, and that requires some ongoing and detailed research. Chapter 6 also looks at the need to define the present situation as part of the planning process.

Setting goals and objectives requires the cooperation and involvement of everyone in the library. Long-range goals and missions are the responsibility of the Chief Librarian and his or her political 'masters', but should contain input from, and the support of, library staff at all levels. Setting shorter-term objectives will also be a product of all library staff. After all, what the circulation desk staff in a large library know about client needs is often different from what the senior management levels perceive as their needs. As indicated in Chapter 2, all management functions and activities depend upon good communication and participation.

Mission			
Long-range goal		**Long-range goal**	
Short-range objective	**Short-range objective**	**Short-range objective**	**Short-range objective**
Task **Task**	**Task** **Task**	**Task** **Task**	**Task** **Task**

Example:

Mission: to provide a free public library service to the residents of X city.

Long-range goal: to provide library users with access to materials to enable them to meet their information need by providing a current, efficient reference and information service.

Short-range objective: to purchase the most up-to-date reference works on the dramatic arts.

Tasks: ensure budget has funds available; read review journals and selection aids, talk to experts in the subject area and decide on works to be purchase, undertake acquisitions procedures.

Figure 5.1: *Hierarchical model of objectives*

There are a number of features that turn a vague declaration of intent into a workable objective. It must:

- be measurable
- be specific
- identify expected results
- be within the individual's or group's power
- be realistic and attainable
- contain clear time limits
- be part of a hierarchy.

This can be condensed into an easily remembered mnemonic, SMART (specific, measurable, actions and tasks, realistic, timing). Use these or similar headings across the top of a page and evaluate your objectives, work related or personal, against the headings to help focus on the effort required, and likelihood of success in reaching the goals. See how the following examples measure up to these criteria. Consider first the following goals of a public library:

- *Long-range goal*: To provide library users with access to a range of information materials which enable them to pursue a sustained program of lifelong learning.

- *Short-range objective*: To provide Internet access for public use in all branch libraries by the end of the financial year.

These could be seen as managerial objectives, but their setting and designing should have input from a range of staff.

The *National Library Act* (1960) sets out the functions of the National Library of Australia, and these can be seen as the mission, or long-term objectives of that organisation, as set out in Section 6 of the Act:

The functions of the Library are, on behalf of the Commonwealth:

a. to maintain and develop a national collection of library material, including a comprehensive collection of library material relating to Australia and the Australian people;

b. to make library material in the national collection available to such persons and institutions, and in such manner and subject to such conditions, as the Council determines with a view to the most advantageous use of that collection in the national interest;

c. to make available such other services in relation to library matters and library material (including bibliographical services) as the Council thinks fit, and, in particular, services for the purpose of:
    (i)   the library of the Parliament;
    (ii)   the authorities of the Commonwealth; and
    (iii) the Territories; and
    (iv)   the Agencies (within the meaning of the *Public Service Act 1999*); and

d. to co-operate in library matters (including the advancement of library science) with authorities or persons, whether in Australia or elsewhere, concerned with library matters.

These broad objectives, enshrined though they are in legislation, merely provide the basis for more detailed long-term strategies, short-term goals, right down to policy statements and specific plans. Their compilation, dissemination and achievement are the particular responsibility of senior management.

A useful comparison can be seen at another level where objectives, or targets, may be set in your library in order to assist with the assessment of each employee's performance. Specific objectives will be agreed upon between supervisors and their staff. The objectives have to be accomplished over a set time, and their achievement is the direct responsibility of the individual, with support from supervisor and other staff; but the targets will still be part of the hierarchy of objectives for the library.

Measuring objectives can be achieved by a variety of means, provided that the means form part of the objective (see Table 5.1).

Type	Frequency
Percentages	Per cent satisfied reference queries Per cent 'hits' on Kinetica
Frequency of activity	Mail to be opened and sorted twice a day Stocktaking to be undertaken every six months
Averages	X items to be catalogues per day/week Y interlibrary loan requests to be processed per day
Time limits	All urgent interlibrary loans to be processed within 24 hours All complaints to be investigated within 24 hours All phone calls to be answered within four rings
Absolute prohibition	No staff use of email or Internet for personal purposes No mobile phones to be used in library precincts
	(Adapted from George *et al*. 1987, p. 266)

Table 5.1: Terms for targets

Benefits of setting objectives

Setting objectives has many benefits for the individual staff member, the supervisor, the library, and the clients. The library's mission statement should be an indicator that it will only be successful if customers are satisfied. Quality management demands that libraries are responsive to their clients, and objectives ensure that the library and its staff focus on specific tasks and services which will fulfil client needs.

Clear objectives also provide motivational triggers to supervisors and to staff, and when staff are aware of the results they are expected to achieve, they are empowered to control their own work performance. And if everyone in the library is striving toward objectives which they have helped to produce, the library's culture becomes one of striving to achieve, rather than one of being satisfied with merely getting the day's work done.

Most importantly, however, most writers on organisational behaviour, and on motivation and morale in particular, argue that when clear objectives are set and agreed upon people perform better, especially if they receive regular and constructive feedback on their performance. This in turn leads to higher individual morale, because staff then have more purpose and direction and will derive greater satisfaction from their work. Research findings to support this are considered in more detail in Part 3, 'Human resources management'.

In order to articulate this and to introduce the next section, consider the following short quotation in which the authors distinguish between objectives and policy: 'Objectives emphasize aims and are stated as expectations; policies emphasize rules and are stated as instructions' (Stueart and Moran 1998, p. 69).

Policy development

A policy is a guideline or rule for action, setting the boundaries within which an individual or group can act. As someone once said facetiously 'A policy is what you accidentally find you have after taking a number of ad hoc decisions on related matters'. Decisions taken on the basis of a stated policy will be consistent no matter who makes the decision. Knowledge of the library's policy makes staff feel confident to make decisions or to take creative action. Policies provide a basis for planning. Policies help to provide better and consistent service to clients. Policies help to prevent patron complaints, especially those complaints which play off one staff member against another. If they are clearly formulated and communicated to all who need to know, policies can foster staff morale and public relations.

Try to find a written statement of policy for an activity or function of your library. If you cannot find a written policy statement, then try to discover what the policy is, and write your own. The following areas are among those on which most libraries will have a policy:

- interlibrary loans
- loan of books
- loan of serials
- the imposition of penalties for overdue items
- staff study time
- acquisition of recommended texts
- job rotation
- equal employment opportunity.

Now answer the following questions.

- Does the policy encourage uniform handling of similar cases by different staff members (for example, does it allow for, or eliminate, preferential treatment, and/or discrimination)?

- Does the policy act as a guide for handling problems as they occur? Is it firm or flexible (for example does the overdue policy allow room for reasonable excuses such as hospitalisation, kidnapping, or the man [this is true!] who objected to paying a fine on his overdue book because he had followed the instructions in the car service manual he had borrowed, the car blew up and had to be sold for scrap!)?

- Does the policy provide a predetermined answer to normal problems without the need to refer to a higher level in the decision-making hierarchy?

- Does it serve, and is it used, as a method of communicating with both staff and clients?

- Is the policy open to interpretations which may be contrary to library objectives?

Answering these questions should provide some understanding of the functions and requirements of a sound policy. A policy must not degenerate into a rule rather than a guide. Staff members should not be 'policied' into a corner so that all possible areas for decision-making are removed. There must be room for decision-making within all policies, just as, for example, there should be no job description that is so specific that there is no room for individual decision-making. Be aware, too, that there are many types and levels of policy.

Policy formulation

Whether a policy is formulated by the library's funding body (with input from senior management), or senior management (with input from supervisory level staff), or by any other combination of levels in the hierarchy, there are certain requirements for a sound and effective policy.

- Any policy must reflect, and advance, the objectives of the library. In stating the policy, then, it must be clear why it is a policy.

- The policy should be stated as concisely as possible without ambiguity or confusion.

- The policy should include limits to, and delegation of, authority. This should also include a note of who is to be referred to for problem decisions not covered by the policy.

- The policy may need to refer to other overlapping or related policies.

- The statement of policy should not outline procedures or routines to be followed. Too much detail will change the policy from a guide into a firm rule, and prevent that latitude in decision-making that was mentioned earlier.

Examples of a policy statement

Figure 5.2 provides an example of an interlibrary loans policy statement which helps to meet two of the library's aims: to make a positive contribution to the university's learning-teaching program; and to act as a clearing-house and coordinating distribution point for resource materials.

Figure 5.3 depicts a circulation policy for a public library. The statement clearly relates to the library's goal of making information and recreational materials accessible to its users.

Consider how these policy statements match up to the five requirements outlined above. Rules and procedures that will more fully specify how interlibrary loan and circulation will be organised and operated can be developed based on the policy statement. Much of that detail will be delineated in work or procedures manuals to which the interlibrary loan and circulation staff can refer when necessary.

Interlibrary loans policy (Academic library)

1   Items not held in this library may be acquired from another library through interlibrary loan (ILL).

2   The loan period, and conditions of use, will normally be set by the lending library.

3   Individual users of the service are required to meet the cost of photocopied materials. No other charge will be levied on the user.

4   Undergraduate students may use the ILL service only with the written approval of their lecturer.

Figure 5.2: Example of an interlibrary loans policy statement

---

Circulation policy (Public library)

1   All registered borrowers of City Library are entitled to borrow from any of its twelve branches. Each user is allowed to borrow ten items per visit, with a maximum of 40 loans at any one time. Exceptions to this include 'holiday borrowers' who may borrow only four items per visit with a maximum of eight loans allowed.

2   The normal loan period is four weeks, the exception being housebound users who have an eight-week loan period.

3   Items may be renewed once, by telephone or in person, provided that the item is not overdue and that it has not been reserved by another user.

4   Failure to return library materials by the date due will result in fines being imposed. If overdue materials are not returned within four weeks, borrowing rights may be suspended.

Figure 5.3: Example of a circulation policy statement

Policy manuals

Many libraries collate all their policy statements into a policy manual. Not everyone agrees that this is a useful idea.

Opinion 1:

Don't bother. If they're general, they're useless. If they're specific, they're how-to manuals – expensive to prepare and revise.

The only people who read policy manuals are goldbricks and martinets. The goldbricks memorize them so they can say: (1) 'That's not in this department', or (2) 'It's against company policy.' The martinets use policy manuals to confine, frustrate, punish, and eventually drive out of the organisation every imaginative, creative, adventuresome woman or man.

If you have *to have a policy manual, publish the* Ten Commandments (Townsend 1971, p. 135).

Opinion 2:

...an up-to-date policy manual allows everyone to know what is and what is not policy. It is surprising how few libraries even have policy manuals. Very few manuals in use are really current (Evans 1976, p. 95).

Opinion 3:

To be effective, policies must be communicated and not filed away in the written policy manual, never to be seen again (Scanlan and Keys 1983, p. 71).

Opinion 4:

A policy manual is an important record and is invaluable as a decision-making guide and as a way of communicating within the organization. It is also a basic tool for indoctrinating new staff members and assuring some degree of uniformity in approaches or responses to issues (Stueart and Moran 1998, p. 70).

From these four opinions we can see that policy manuals:

- are an efficient *written record* of policies
- can be referred to when situations arise requiring action
- make policy analysis and change more easily achieved
- are a useful training and induction tool

but

- can be used to the wrong ends
- can be ignored.

Communicating policies is one key to their usefulness. In addition, it is important to note that they must not be considered to be set in concrete. Policy formulation is an ongoing process as changes occur within the library, or as staff place a different interpretation or emphasis on particular policies. For example, if other libraries introduce a charge for interlibrary loans you might need to change your own policy regarding charges for interlibrary loans.

In order to communicate policies outside of the institution, particularly those that impact upon dealings with external clients, it is useful to post the full set of policy documents on the Web. Thus most collection development policies for major libraries and archives are accessible through their web sites and standards for client service are also often available.

Developing policies such as these is not done in a vacuum but should, for instance, involve staff, users and other institutions to ensure that there is a level of cooperation across the board that limits any overlap or contradiction. This is particularly important in the area of collection development where scarce resources need to be used in the most appropriate manner and not wasted in duplicating effort. Thus neighbouring libraries may work together to share resources, focus on specialities and avoid collecting the same material. The concept of a Distributed National Collection (DNC) where libraries cooperate in order to provide the broadest coverage possible without duplication of effort is an important policy that directly affects collection building activity. Effective implementation of the DNC concept is contingent upon policies being well publicised and readily available to other institutions.

Finally, note that external policies over which an institution may have little control, also drive an organisation's work practices. There are a number of state and federal government policies that impose restrictions, regulations and direction on the day-to-day work of the library. Areas such as occupational health and safety, basic wage provisions, privacy, freedom of information, copyright and discrimination are all covered by high level government policies that have to be implemented by the organisation whether it likes them or not. Making these well known and understood by all staff is another responsibility of the management team.

Chapter 6
Planning

We must ask where we are and whither we are tending. (Abraham Lincoln)

Introduction

Planning is not an easy activity, and it can be very time consuming. It is also a function which many librarians find themselves resisting – for any number of reasons. It is easy, for example, to be constantly caught up in the immediacy of daily routines and crises and forget about the need to plan ahead. It is much easier, for example, to decide what materials to purchase from this year's book vote than it is to plan and prepare for next year's!

The importance of planning must not be underestimated, because the alternative is random and uncoordinated activity. Planning provides direction for the activities within the organisation (as do objectives), provides a shape for the future, and prevents the managerial and supervisory roles from becoming ones of pure reaction to crisis and the incessant solving of immediate dilemmas.

Definitions

- *Planning* is the conscious predetermination of courses of action and basing decisions on purpose, facts and considered estimates.

- *Strategic planning* is long-term in approach and incorporates the library's mission statement in determining the library's future direction and the strategies and resources required to make progress towards achieving the mission.

- *Operational planning* focuses on the short-term programs and activities necessary to make progress towards the longer term objectives detailed in the strategic plan.

Planning

Planning is making things happen which would not otherwise. It is, essentially, attempting to control the future – without planning, events would be left to chance.

Planning is everybody's responsibility – while it is a primary function of supervisors and managers, who plan on behalf of others as well as for their own specific functions, it is practically impossible to delegate authority so specifically that no area of choice remains. It is within this area of choice, for all librarians, that their area of planning lies.

Planning is really a process of logical decision-making – if carefully carried out it will enable you to achieve results more quickly, more efficiently and more economically. Note that while planning always involves decision-making, the converse is not always true.

Time spent on planning is never wasted. In fact the higher the level of supervision or management you are in, the more time you will spend in planning.

Advantages of planning

Most writers on management list a number of advantages of planning, and claim that the effort is well worthwhile in assisting organisations to achieve their objectives, to survive and to grow. The following are some specific advantages of planning.

- Coping with change – planning can help minimise the potentially negative impact of change and maximise the benefits by drawing attention to threats at an early stage and by identifying opportunities.

- Coordination of activities – planning helps to achieve a coordinated effort by all sections of the library by focusing attention on goals. Without this, sections could tend to formulate their own goals in isolation which can lead to conflicting goals within the library.

- Purpose and direction is provided to the organisation through the planning process. This is particularly important as organisations increase in size and complexity. Maintaining unity of purpose and commitment across a wide range of activities and geographically and functionally diverse work environments is only possible through an organisation-wide acceptance of the planning process.

- Efficiency of operation – one of the major steps in the planning process is to consider the costs and benefits of the various options being considered for future action. This process helps to identify the most efficient means of achieving the library's objectives.

- Effective control – the planning process includes identifying procedures and standards for evaluating progress towards achieving objectives. Performance standards provide guidelines which enable us to exercise effective control over the library's operations. (Chapter 8 addresses issues relating to control and evaluation at greater depth.)

- Staff development – involving all staff in planning, and especially in strategic planning, allows the development of a range of skills. For example, planning requires skills in the areas of research, communication and decision-making. Being part of the various levels of planning requires staff to address the same issues that their supervisors and managers are addressing.

The planning process

There are almost as many models of the planning process as there are writers on the subject. The models may include as few as four major steps or phases, or at the other extreme, as many as eighteen phases. All the approaches have much in common despite differences in the numbers and order of the steps. My own brief synthesis of the various planning models appears below.

Planning steps

1 Define and quantify the goal

This must be as specific as possible, and should be measurable, enabling you to audit progress towards the goal. There can be political and other environmental influences on the setting of objectives. This step is vital, however, and links most closely with step 7 because performance indicators need to be considered now, so that progress can be monitored later.

2 Identify the relevant policies

Are there any standards, staff regulations, library policies already in effect –for example, union rules; government regulations, laws or by-laws; council, university, company, or board policies – which must be taken into consideration before planning can proceed further, or which will affect later steps or implementation? Constraints in areas such as freedom of information, equal employment opportunity, occupational health and safety, disabled access, privacy, and copyright must be considered at this stage.

3 Identify the planning premises

A number of questions need to be answered in relation to the planning premises. What is the present situation of the planning area? How far from stated goals is it at present? What is the situation regarding staffing, materials, resources, equipment and so forth of the section, or the library as a whole? What conditions exist now which could affect the planning and the plan's resultant operation?

4 List alternative courses of action

Do not be confined by looking only at the obvious courses of action: look at all possible alternatives. Enlist the help and cooperation of others here, especially those staff who are experienced in the planning area involved. If there is one step which is most important in the planning process, it is this one – the consideration of *all* possible alternatives.

5 Evaluate each alternative

List and weigh up the pros and cons, the costs and benefits, of each alternative. There are many ways of doing this, depending on the type and level of the planning. For example, some of the decision-making methods discussed in Chapter 11 will be applicable in this step. Teamwork (discussed in Chapter 12) will be of great benefit in this phase in particular.

6 Select the best alternative, decide upon a course of action, and implement it

Make sure, as part of this step, that plans have been communicated to all staff and that staff have been motivated towards achieving the objectives. Seek the advice of staff on the best way of fulfilling the plans. Ensure that the library's internal structure is adequate to cope with the plans, and that resources will be available when needed. Set a timetable for the action to be taken.

7 Follow up

Check that you really are achieving the results you planned for. Be prepared to modify the goals and methods if necessary.

But do librarians ever plan like this? It is to be hoped that they do, because planning is an essential component of the management of change, and change is constant in the library environment today.

A colleague once admitted that she was a disorganised cataloguer who, because of lack of time to plan, allowed items to build up until finally she had no choice but to offer an on-demand cataloguing service for staff and users alike. Her productivity was high, but without forward planning, and without a plan for setting priorities in advance, it was impossible to ensure that the number of items leaving the department kept pace with the number being received. Hence the cataloguing department, and her work area, constantly looked like an uncoordinated mess, and an outsider would assume that the cataloguers were not working to capacity. Staff morale and self-esteem were low as a result.

Some of the reasons why planning is not always done have already been noted. However it is useful to consider these a little further in order to be able to guard against this problem arising in your organisation. Generally, the main issues summarised by Pymm (2000, p. 47) are:

- a manager's inability to set goals which may be due to a lack of confidence, lack of knowledge about the organisation and its aims or a lack of understanding and training in the planning process
- a lack of confidence can lead to a fear of failure which is far more apparent when a clear plan exists against which progress can be measured
- resistance to change can be an issue where managers or staff are happy with the current situation and see no reason to plan for change
- the time taken in the planning process can be significant and for busy managers, this is an issue that can be a major determinant in the depth and level of planning undertaken
- building in controls and measures to assess progress of any plan can be difficult if not carefully thought through beforehand. Not having these controls limits the usefulness of any planning activity
- concern that in such a rapidly changing environment any medium- or long-term plan is likely to become rapidly outdated.

While all of these issues have a degree of validity, it is up to managers to work through these perceived difficulties in order to ensure the best possible environment is created that fosters a successful planning process.

For confirmation that librarians do plan, look no further than the American Library Association's *A planning process for public libraries* (Palmour *et al.* 1980) as an ideal example of the theory of planning put into practice on a large scale in libraries. Krueger (1985) describes the planning process and highlights the formulation of strategies for reaching goals, their evaluation (particularly in relation to resources), and the selection of the optimum alternative.

Most of the above applies to planning at all levels of the library, and the advice and methods can be used by all staff. The next section considers the 'managerial' level planning – planning at the macro level.

Strategic planning

Strategic planning is the process of setting major organisational objectives and developing comprehensive plans to achieve them. It involves decisions related to the major directions of the organisation in terms of its structure, strategies, policies and the contributions of its resources (Nankervis *et al.* 2002, p. 58). As suggested earlier, strategic planning is long-term in approach, and incorporates the library's mission statement in determining the library's future direction and the strategies and resources required to make progress towards achieving the mission. Strategic planning sounds like something new that libraries have only started doing in the past few years. But the definition covers what many libraries have been doing for years. What is important is the recognition that is now given to this type of planning, and the effort being given to it by libraries today.

Strategic planning is a key component in the management of change. Rather than simply reacting to change as it occurs and affects library goals, operations and services, library managers are seeking to be proactive by creating a vision, mission, and strategic plans. That in turn gives them the opportunity to continue looking forward, and to constantly monitor the plan and its effectiveness in taking the library towards its mission.

The process of strategic planning is covered in most management texts. Most libraries, being part of larger institutions, will be guided or driven by the parent body's strategic planning processes. But often the library will be able to customise and develop beyond the basic principles. One of the most striking examples of this is the Auckland City Libraries (New Zealand) strategic framework for 2000-2020.

Their process and results linked with the corporate planning and objectives of their parent body, the Auckland City Council, and can be found at the following site:

Auckland City: <http://www.aucklandcity.govt.nz/council/documents/focus/strategic.asp> (viewed 27 April, 2003).

The structure of their final framework is of most interest. It contains not just a mission statement and goals, but rather the following main areas of concern:

> Our Guiding Principles
> - Our Assignment – Vision – He Wawata
> - Our Organisation – Mission – He Whakatakanga
> - Our Commitment – Bicultural Partnership
>
> Our Values – Nga Uaratanga
> - First Class Service – Painga
> - Partnerships – Nga Hononga Mahi
> - Outstanding value – Maiatanga
> - Integrity and respect – Mana
> - Support for each other – Tautoko
> - Professional service – Ngaio Matatika
>
> Our Strategy – He Kaupapa Neke Atu
> - Customer focus – Nga Ratonga
> - Technology – Hangarau
> - Physical environment – Turangawaewae
> - Resources – Nga Rauemi
> - Partnerships – Nga hononga mahi
> - Leadership – Arahina
> - Finance & Business Systems – Te Tahua
> - Staff – Nga kai mahi (Auckland City Libraries 2000)

Of course, what this does not reveal is the time, energy and cooperative effort that is needed to carry out the process. The following section gives a more detailed indication of that.

Strategic planning steps

According to Hobrick (1991), the detailed formal strategic planning effort may require all of the following steps.

- Establish the ground rules:
  - top management must be committed to, and understand the process, to ensure participation at all levels
  - a task force or team should coordinate the process
  - all participants should understand the whole process before beginning
  - there must be realistic expectations that the plan will be implemented
  - time to plan must be available
  - reading materials and paperwork should be kept to a minimum
  - communicate progress to all levels of staff.

- Develop the library's mission statement:
  - defines the purpose of the library
  - recognises and fits within the parent body's mission and objectives.

- Conduct an environmental analysis:
  - consider opportunities and threats, internal and external, that do and will affect the library.

The steps will include:

- Resource analysis:
  - assess the strengths and weaknesses of the library
  - include input from management, staff and users.

- Identify strategic issues:
  - 'visualise' the library's future
  - develop statements of intent regarding the library's future, based on its mission.

- Define future strategies:
  - state where the library is going rather than how it will get there
  - describe new approaches, new services, or new directions in, for example collection development, management style and so forth

- Decide on programs:
  - define the organisational activities required to carry out strategies; how the library gets to where it wants to go
  - grassroots involvement is vital here
  - consider budget and other resources now.

- Implement, and plan to evaluate:
  - requires management resolve and staff commitment
  - consider effects on staff and users
  - constant (at least annual) review and evaluation (based on Hobrick 1991, pp. 48–52).

Two of the major steps noted by Hobrick – environmental and resource analysis – deserve further attention. No organisation exists in isolation and a good understanding of both the external world in which they operate, as well as the internal environment that shapes their work culture, is essential for successful long-term planning. The processing of analysing these environments is known as a SWOT analysis.

The SWOT analysis (strengths, weaknesses, opportunities, threats) is a common methodology used to identify those factors, both internal to the organisation and external to it, that it is anticipated will influence the success or otherwise of the plans being developed.

Thus within an organisation it is essential to identify the strengths and weaknesses that may help or hinder the achievement of corporate goals. Strengths are those internal resources held and fostered by the organisation that enable it to provide a high quality service. Usually strengths take time to become established (for example, well-trained staff, a comprehensive collection in a particular field) and it is essential that in any forward planning these are not overlooked or overridden when developing new strategies – once lost it can be difficult and costly to regain them. Weaknesses are apparent in all organisations and are usually more volatile than strengths. Often they will suddenly appear (for example the loss of a key staff member) but also, it may be easier to overcome them once identified. Again, being aware of weaknesses and ensuring they are taken into consideration during the planning process is essential for success.

The external environment offers opportunities and threats. Most organisations have little influence over the external environment – no library can impact say, the exchange rate of the Australian dollar yet it has a major influence on collecting activity. It is therefore important for forward planners to try and identify trends in order to be able to take advantage of opportunities and to foresee difficulties in order to guard against their impact. Scanning the external environment in order to make these assessments is a major task for those involved in strategic planning.

It must also be borne in mind that goals and objectives considered and set towards the library's mission must be both current and visionary. Setting goals and objectives helps to provide a starting point and base for individual and team planning. Action and contingency plans will in turn be based on the goals set, and will include consideration of resources required, time frame, allocation of staff, the means of achieving the goals, and the means of monitoring progress towards goals.

If you have a vision of how your library service should be, then you need a strategic plan to carry you towards that vision. Strategic planning is a dynamic and ongoing process which gives libraries the opportunity to decide their future themselves, within certain boundaries and as part of a wider environment. As such it can be a powerful tool in the management of change. If strategic planning and thinking become part of a library's culture, it can help to build a commitment to the library's mission. This assists managers in their function of guiding cooperative effort. Involving staff in the strategic planning process will in turn help all staff to prepare for the future with their morale and esteem intact.

For an excellent resource on the process of strategic planning, and a range of case studies, read *Charting the future: strategic planning in the Australasian library and information industry* (Bridgland and Hayes 1996). Mark Grosvenor (1998) and Helen Ristuccia (1994) provide realistic introductions to the strategic planning process, and many libraries have presented their strategic planning process and results on the Internet.

Conclusion

All successful supervisors and managers will have the desire and ability to plan. Effective service cannot be achieved without planning. Effective planning will be based upon:

- having the authority to plan – you must have that authority yourself and give that authority to others where necessary
- ensuring everyone understands the value of planning
- knowing how to plan – in particular, considering all possible alternative courses of action, and clear and cooperative assessment of alternatives.

Planning has relevance at every level of the library, just as everyone must be involved in setting and achieving goals. In fact, if you do not have plans, the likelihood of achieving your goals is not very high. Planning undertaken carefully and consciously will enable you to achieve the best possible results.

Chapter 7
Organising human resources

Organizing is what you do before you do something, so that when you do it, it is not all mixed up. (A.A. Milne)

Introduction

Newcomers to a library or information organisation generally discover that one of their first needs is to gain an understanding of the organisational structure. This means finding out about the various parts of the organisation such as departments, sections, branches, divisions and how they relate to one another.

This chapter, which provides a basic understanding of organising human resources, is included for a number of reasons. To be able to supervise and manage within an organisation, you must first understand the characteristics of the organisation itself. To define one's own role in an organisation, it is necessary to understand where you and your job are placed in relation to other jobs.

To become, or develop as, a supervisor, you need to know how the various relationships with which you will be dealing are structured, and how they are affected by any changes you may wish to initiate. In a situation of amalgamation or reorganisation of libraries, for example, the study of the organisation takes on an even more important role in the working lives of staff, supervisors and managers. The larger the library, the more complex and important is the function of organising.

Traditional forms of organisational structure

It is surprising how many definitions of organising or organisation appear in management texts with very little emphasis on the needs and concerns of individual people. For example, Ivancevich and others (1997, p. 19) define 'organisation' as a *structure*, 'the formal pattern of activities and interrelationships among the various subunits of the organisation.' Other business management texts emphasise the creation of *structures* to maximise efficiency and effectiveness. We can also call it:

- a management function, and one which becomes more important as an organisation grows in size and complexity
- the process a manager follows in arranging the work to be done so it can be performed most effectively by the people involved
- a group of people working toward some common objective
- a set of activities, consciously coordinated.

Organisation, then, can be seen as a management function involving activities, people, a structure and a process. This text takes a people-oriented point of view.

The formal structure can be understood as:

- the pattern of formal relationships and duties as revealed in the organisational chart and in job and position descriptions
- the ways in which the various activities and tasks are assigned to, or by, different individuals, teams, sections and departments in the library
- the ways in which these activities and tasks are coordinated
- the power and hierarchical relationships of the library
- the planned and formalised policies, procedures and controls that guide the activities and relationships of staff.

The structure of an organisation consists of much more than can be seen in the formal organisational chart with which most of you will be familiar.

The process of achieving a balanced organisation becomes more complex the larger the library. In larger systems the number of activities being pursued is greater and the number of people involved is greater. At the other end of the scale, in one person organisations (for example, a sole charge research, special, school or public library) there is no need to develop an elaborate structure – one person must do all of the activities and perform all of the functions. Even a small organisation, however, is generally still part of the structure of a larger organisation, and as such must have a clearly defined relationship to that organisation.

Relationships of authority, responsibility, delegation and power are especially important in considering the relationships in an organisation. Many decisions in this area are based on the abilities of individuals already in place, or even on the forecasted abilities of those who might fill the positions involved.

In your own organisation, how do you know to whom each person is responsible, and for what each is responsible? Are those responsibilities clearly defined, and how? What authority is given, from whom and to whom, for spending funds, purchasing materials, planning new services, changing policies at various levels, undertaking public relations exercises, or speaking on behalf of parts of the system or of the system as a whole?

These are serious questions. You cannot make decisions about people and their relationships in the organisation without a clear understanding of the structure and policies of your own organisation. In the functional structure in particular, fully defined policies can actually inhibit good staff relations.

Alternative structures

There are criticisms of the traditional, mechanistic or functional form of organisational structure. The most telling, from the point of view of organisation in libraries, is that they tend to be most suited to organisations which involve the performance of routine tasks and which are part of a very stable and secure environment. Neither of those two criteria applies to the modern library organisation.

There are alternative approaches, and one you should consider (not necessarily accept) as especially appropriate for the dynamic, modern library is the organic organisational structure. As one management text notes, an organic structure has the following features:

1   work is defined in terms of general tasks, rather than specific focused jobs;
2   tasks are adjusted as required through interaction with others as the job evolves and do not adhere rigidly to set instructions;
3   the authority, communication and control structure is not simply hierarchical, but a network;
4   decisions are made by the individuals who have the knowledge, not based upon their position in the hierarchy;
5   communication is across all work levels – subordinates, superiors and colleagues;
6   communication comprises advice and information, not straight instruction;
7   the emphasis is on commitment to organisational goals and possession of the relevant knowledge and expertise rather than simple loyalty or obedience to instruction (Bartol *et al.* 2001, p. 317).

This can be seen as organising around people, creating structures that use and develop staff already within the system. While an entire library system may not be organised along such lines, sections and departments within the organisation may find it an appropriate means of organising. For example, participative and decentralised structures are highly desirable in the context of team building and development.

The importance of the organic form of organisation to communication, team development, motivation, morale and organisational climate is highlighted by the following quotation in which the author considers the difference between mechanistic and organic systems.

> Mechanistic systems tend to be rigid. People who work in them tend to work in isolated units with no overall knowledge of the final product or how it is achieved. There is a precise definition of roles and rights and obligations and methods, and everything is turned into a very precisely described functional role. There is a very rigid hierarchic structure of control and a tight bureaucracy. Any interaction in the system tends to be vertical and the factors governing work behaviour are instructions issued by superiors. There is a demand for loyalty to the concern and obedience to superiors as a condition of working (Smith 1982, p. 60).

The modern organic organisation is almost the exact opposite, in that staff understand – through participation and open communication – their roles and tasks in the context of all aspects of the organisation. Commitment to library-wide objectives is encouraged rather than required, and the structure of control is less bureaucratic, especially in those libraries where team structures prevail. Communication is more often in the form of information and advice rather than instructions about the decisions to be implemented.

One important element that is influenced by organisational design is the 'span of management' – the number of staff who report directly to a particular manager. Too few staff reporting to an individual may mean the manager is not being used to their full effectiveness and may tend to be too closely involved with their subordinate's work. Too many staff and managers risk losing control and becoming overloaded, with the subsequent risk of a breakdown in relations between manager and staff.

Under mechanistic systems, with fairly rigid means of instruction and control, the span of management can be larger and still be successful. Under a more organic structure, smaller spans work better, facilitating closer communication between staff and management. Bartol and Martin (1998, p. 266) note other factors influencing the span of management:

- the level of interaction necessary between subordinates and managers – simple, repetitive work requires less supervision than more complex tasks
- experienced well-trained staff work effectively with less direct supervision

- if the frequency and seriousness of mistakes or problems occurring is low, there is less need for close supervision
- where subordinates work in close physical proximity to each other, managers can coordinate higher numbers of staff
- where the manager's main duty is staff supervision, they can be responsible for larger numbers
- where the work itself is highly motivational, staff need less direct supervision and thus managers can supervise more people.

From this it can be seen that the span of management influences the number of levels in the organisation's hierarchy. A tall structure, with many levels, indicates a fairly narrow span of management while flatter structures, with fewer levels, suggest wider spans of control. No one structure or span of control is appropriate for all organisations. Each is different and at different times in its evolution will benefit from variations in its structure. Importantly, restructuring by changing levels and hierarchies needs to be carefully considered and its implementation thoroughly planned in order to minimise the inevitable disruption it will cause. Integral to any such changes is its impact upon human resources and how this can be properly managed.

Human resources planning

Planning for the future human resources needs of an organisation is a management, rather than supervisory, function. Human resources planning is a process which aims to ensure the efficient and effective use of people. It is concerned *first* with ensuring that enough staff are available to do the work (and that there is no overstaffing), and *second* with improving the efficient use of staff.

To plan carefully for the library's human resources needs, it is necessary to have at hand – and to study – data on job requirements, data on the library workforce and data on the skills and abilities of current staff. Armed with such data, the library manager may plan for current and future staff needs with some confidence. But where does the information come from?

- Data on job requirements will be obtained through strategic planning, and through the processes of job analysis, job description, performance appraisal and training needs analysis.

- Information about the library workforce in Australia that has been generated through 'manpower' studies and conferences.

- Undertaking job analyses, the consideration of person specifications produced for new and existing positions, and consideration of training needs analyses will help to isolate the skills and abilities of existing staff. (These issues are discussed in Chapters 15 and 17.)

The process of workforce planning can be seen to cover four main steps:

1 Supply analysis

This is a data gathering and analysis of recruitment and resignation trends, aimed at developing a profile of the current staff establishment as it would exist if all recruitment, training, and staff development programs are suspended.

2   Demand analysis

The purpose of demand analysis is to forecast the competencies that will be required by your future workforce for your library to be successful. It involves predicting how the nature of the work will change.

3   Gap analysis

This step compares the supply and demand data collected during Steps 1 and 2. The result is the determination of skill surpluses and deficiencies.

4   Solution analysis

This step requires the development of strategies for closing the gaps identified in Step 3. Specifically, it is the identification of ways to *build* skills that are in short supply and *reduce* those that are overly-abundant in relation to your organisation's projected needs. This can involve specific recruitment drives, staff development, and new measures to ensure the retention of staff.

For the purposes of this text it is sufficient that you be aware of what human resources planning is, without delving into the techniques of the process of forecasting human resources supply and demand. Most organisations will use consultant specialists to undertake the human resources planning process for them. It is important, however, to be aware that while the task of human resources planning as a long-term strategy is a function of senior management, input from supervisory level staff will be vital to its success.

Conclusion

Organising has long been a function of management. The organisation of people, the tension between the need to divide the labour tasks and the need to coordinate them, is something we can study, but only experience in an individual situation can teach you how to handle that situation. What this chapter has aimed to do, is to give you some indication about the ways in which organising human resources affect the role and functions of the manager and supervisor.

Chapter 8
Evaluation

Achievement is a journey, not a destination. (Source unknown)

Introduction

The aim of this chapter is to briefly introduce the idea and characteristics of the 'control' function of management, including a further look at the evaluation of library services. As with the other chapters in Part 1, we are concerned with the theory and principles involved rather than practical, how-to-do-it skills. The control function rounds out the cycle of management functions. A process model is useful here as it provides a framework for understanding the functions carried out to achieve library goals, including the control function.

Definition

Control is the managerial function of measuring actual performance, and comparing that with the performance level that was planned. It is concerned with setting targets, ensuring staff are aware of those targets, locating deviations from planned steps, and then taking corrective action. Control requires management to:

- establish standards – what should be achieved, when, within which parameters?
- measure performance against the established standards
- correct deviations.

Control is the basis of organisational learning, because without it the library will not be aware of its strengths and weaknesses. Control is the basis of organisational learning, because without it the library will not be aware of its strengths and weaknesses. There is a close relationship between planning, objectives, accountability and control. As indicated in Chapter 6, identifying procedures for evaluating progress towards the achievement of objectives is one of the steps built into all models of the planning process. Chapter 6 also indicated that effective control is one of the many advantages of careful planning.

Controlling, or evaluation, must relate to objectives, and should always concentrate on improving performance. If the objectives are specific and measurable, then you will be able to ascertain whether or not they are being achieved. What is needed, then, is evidence that what was supposed to happen, does happen.

Libraries and control

Libraries, by their very nature, are service organisations, and as a consequence their objectives are necessarily service-oriented. With this in mind, we can see the process of library activity as:

- seeing a *need* (or needs)
- setting *objectives* to fulfil those needs
- obtaining the means to achieve those objectives (for example, buying books and other materials, employing staff, purchasing appropriate equipment, providing a building) – these are *inputs*
- providing the needed services through efficient use and management of the inputs – the services are the *outputs* of the library.

If the cycle of library activity is not entirely clear, then try to think of a need which you know the library can fulfil for its 'community' – this is the *need.* Then consider what the library aims to do to fulfil that need – these are the *objectives.* How, and with what people, facilities and materials, does the library try to meet those objectives – these are the *inputs.* As a result of this activity, what does the library provide for that community? – these are the *outputs.*

Library activity revolves around needs, objectives, inputs and outputs. Objectives and inputs are largely internal factors which are the result of systematic organisation and activity *within* the library. The objectives and inputs influence how effective the library is because the *efficient* management and organisation of staff and other resources will help to make library operations run more smoothly. The real test of library *effectiveness,* however, is the relationship between outputs and needs.

In other words, the test of library effectiveness is the answer to the question 'do the services provided meet the needs expressed?' If the library's primary objective is service to its user community, then the measure of library effectiveness is the satisfaction of needs, no matter how efficiently that objective is achieved. The measurement of that satisfaction is crucial in determining library effectiveness from the users' points of view.

Setting objectives and planning require choices from among alternatives: alternative ways of undertaking an activity; alternative resources; alternative possible results. Such choices are the basis of policies, activities, programs and, importantly, ways of measuring their effectiveness. The alternatives chosen are selected because certain results are expected. That expectation provides the basis for evaluation, but to carry out that evaluation, one must monitor not the actions themselves, but rather the impact of those actions on the environment, on the community, and on the users. Measures of achievement, or effectiveness, should relate to output.

Library performance evaluation, then, is really a way of answering a series of questions about how well a library or information service is fulfilling its obligation – that is, questions about its performance.

- How well is the library meeting its strategic objectives?

- What is the optimal allocation of library resources (stock, staff, equipment)?

- How can the library achieve its optimal use of resources and services?

- What is the most appropriate balance between the costs and quality of service provision?
- How well is the library satisfying user needs and user demands?
- Is the library/information service operating economically, efficiently and effectively?

Performance evaluation is also undertaken for the following reasons:

- to collect information to help with decision-making and marketing
- to evaluate overall service quality
- to identify the extent to which problems can be solved
- to identify differing or contradictory needs of different groups of customers
- to provide feedback to, and to evaluate, suppliers
- to involve customers in the development of services
- to provide a basis for continuous improvement (Crawford 2000).

Input measurement

Levels of input in areas of library service such as the provision of facilities, organisation, and the provision of staff have become a common means for librarians and their funding bodies to compare their services with others. Annual statistical reports on library use usually contain figures relating to the number of books and other items purchased, staff size, extra building space provided and circulation of materials. The statistics are often used to demonstrate to the funding body that a larger financial injection is required to develop and improve services. However, they are not a measure of service, and cannot truly be justified in this manner.

Often such measures of input (including limited measures of use such as circulation statistics) are compared with the levels of input recommended in a published standard. Examples include the guidelines and standards for Queensland public libraries (Library Board of Queensland 1997), and more recently, the United Kingdom's new standards for public library service (Department for Culture, Media and Sport 2001).

However, standards are not a measure of effectiveness because they emphasise inputs and *quantity* measures which will help provide the service, rather than emphasising the outputs and *quality* of the service. For example, we cannot assume that we are providing a better quality of service just because we have managed to buy 20 per cent more items, employed 20 per cent more staff and opened a new branch or given the users more space in which to browse and study.

The following excerpt from the British public library standards gives you an idea of some *quality* measures.

> **OBJECTIVE: Library authorities must ensure user satisfaction with the services provided (PLS 12 to 15)**
>
> **PLS 12**
> Percentage of library users reporting success in obtaining a specific book:
> - adults
> - children
>
> *To be based on the National PLUS standards (Public Library User Surveys).*

The target for the three year planning cycle commencing in April 2001 will be 65% for both adults and children. Authorities may also inform this measure with information about the number of searches for books leading to reservations, and satisfaction with the outcome.

PLS 13
Percentage of library users reporting success in gaining information as a result of a search or enquiry.

To be based on the National PLUS standards (Public Library User Surveys).

The target for the three year planning cycle commencing in April 2001 will be 75% for both adults and children. In addition, the Library Association and the Audit Commission will be invited to advise on the development of a formal "unobtrusive testing" or "mystery shopping" process which will provide for a measured professional assessment of the quality of the enquiry service. This is expected to develop into an indicator in its own right.

PLS 14
Percentage of library users rating the knowledge of staff as "good" or "very good".

To be based on the National PLUS standards (Public Library User Surveys).

The target for the three year planning cycle commencing in April 2001 will be 95% for both adults and children.

PLS 15
Users rating the helpfulness of staff as "good"or "very good".
- adults
- children

To be based on the National PLUS standards (Public Library User Surveys).

The target for the three year planning cycle commencing in April 2001 will be 95% for both adults and children (Department for Culture, Media and Sport 2001, pp. 13–14; formatting changed).

Standards are useful as a basis for planning, provided that:

- they are not regarded as the maximum desired objective
- they are not allowed to stifle flexibility and initiative
- they are only regarded as a basis from which to work.

One of the major problems with developing standards for comparison is that it is difficult to allow for variations in local conditions and hence to ensure that similar situations are being compared. Adhering to input-based standards rather than output targets makes the assumption that there is little variation in libraries' communities. But this is patently not so. While the same problems may occur in most library communities, the extent will vary, the needs of each community will be different, client groups and their aspirations will vary, and the solutions and resources available to support those solutions will be different.

Output measurement

For many years, standards and input measurements were widely accepted as measures of library effectiveness because there were no alternative evaluation measures. Now there are other means of evaluation. For example, output measurement has been 'discovered' as a common private sector practice, and, with adaptations, is becoming more commonly used by libraries to determine whether an appropriately high level of service is being achieved.

The most readily obtained figures about output in a library service are the volumes of loans and users. The figures provide only a partial indication of the library's effectiveness, but many libraries still rely on such purely quantitative measures to evaluate the library's service. Even when compared with data from other libraries, and even when measured against published minimum standards, the figures tell only part of the story.

The number of books borrowed, or the number of people who enter the library, bear no *direct* relationship to the *quality* of the service. They do represent some measure of satisfied need in that it is clear that the community is using the service because it is serving needs they have expressed. What those figures do not tell us is how many needs the community has which are not being met by the library but which the library could and should meet. Some of those needs may be met by other information agencies, and some may not have been recognised by, or expressed to, the library.

A great deal of work has been done in the past to help librarians in the evaluation of their services through the development and application of output or performance measures. These attempt to measure the 'product' of the library. The American Library Association, following the success of their planning manual for public libraries (Palmour *et al.* 1980), produced a set of output measures for public libraries (Zweizig and Roger 1982; Van House *et al.* 1987; Childers and Van House 1993). Some examples include:

- circulation per capita
- library visits per capita (number of visits divided by the population served)
- reference transactions per capita (or at least those in which staff are involved)
- reference fill rate (proportion of reference transactions completed)
- title fill rate (titles desired by library users that are available in the library at the time of the request)
- subject and author fill rate (the proportion of subject and author requests filled from the library's own resources)
- registration as a percentage of population.

The Australian Library and Information Association worked in this area for some years, with *Towards a quality service: goals, objectives and standards for public libraries in Australia* (Australian Library and Information Association 1990) taking into account both standards and output measures. Combining quantitative and qualitative measures to assess both public and academic library performance is well described in Peter Hernon's *Assessing service quality: satisfying the expectations of library customers* (Hernon and Altman, 1998).

Any library, not just public libraries, can use these kinds of measures to evaluate aspects of their service. Academic libraries need to demonstrate their effectiveness to their funding body and to outside bodies, such as the Commonwealth Department of Education and Training and Youth Affairs (DETYA), which also require universities to have mechanisms to monitor performance. Nancy Van House's *Measuring academic library performance* (Van House 1990) is a most useful tool, with easy-to-use survey and questionnaire instruments, technically sound, built on previous work and concentrating on quantitative measures. Examples of these output measures include:

- materials availability and use – for example, circulation, in-library use, materials availability, and request delays
- facilities and library use – for example, number of user visits, remote use, use of seating and equipment, and use of service points
- information services – for example, number of reference transactions, evaluation of manual, online and Internet reference searches
- user satisfaction – for example, user success rates, and evaluation of information transactions and service.

In implementing measures of library outputs, it is important to remember that they must relate to user needs; and that means that libraries must develop their performance measures in conjunction with their strategic planning process. Planning and control, as noted earlier, are inseparable. As the library environment changes, new competitive forces emerge and user expectations increase

> libraries must begin listening and acting on the voice of customers, staff, work processes, and the organisation for the purpose of learning new directions and partnering with customers (Phipps 2001, p. 635).

Conclusion

Recognising the relationship between user needs and library outputs as the key to evaluation of library effectiveness will enable librarians to begin to discover whether they are meeting their objectives of service to their community – and if not, how far there is to go to achieve those objectives. It will enable librarians:

- to provide for reassessment and readjustment of library activities to fulfil library goals more effectively
- to provide a record of achievement which justifies continued financial and political support from the library's funding authority.

Measurement and control can make the difference between attempting to provide an excellent service and ensuring that the output service is excellent and meets the needs of the users. 'The quest for accountability should not, however, blind us to what must be the real value of performance measurement. That is, to identify excellence in library service from the client's point of view' (Garlick 1992, p. 52).

Last word goes to Jennifer Cram, from her inspiring address to a New South Wales Country Public Libraries Association conference.

> The bottom line is that librarians have to be able to demonstrate the value that libraries add to the goals set for senior officials. Whatever the rhetoric about services and benefits the truth in publicly funded organisations, is that the CEO has mandated goals which are usually short-term and financial. The goals have measures, which, of course, become the goals of the person(s) who report to the CEO, and this is replicated all the way down the line. So, unless you can demonstrate that your operation contributes to the CEO being seen to be a good financial manager, you have little hope of survival, of ensuring that those who allocate resources will continue to support allocation of funds to the library. Therefore, short-term performance reporting requires demonstrating value in terms of return on expense, on the budget for the year, in order to demonstrate that your operation benefits the personal agendas of decision-makers (Cram 1998).

Part 2

Supervisory skills

Chapter 9
Communication

The art of communication is the language of leadership. (James Humes)

Introduction

The success of every enterprise depends upon communication, since in any undertaking involving two or more people it is essential for the coordination of activities. In a survey of the management education and training needs of librarians, nearly all respondents, from senior managers through to entry-level professionals, ranked communication skills as those most needed in their library (Sanders 1993).

Communication takes place in all parts of the organisation, between staff at all levels, between staff and users, and between staff and other clients such as suppliers, parent body administrators and representatives of the funding body. Every other topic in this book is affected by communication to varying degrees. Unfortunately, in some libraries, as in many organisations, poor or non-existent communication is one of the main barriers to progress and effective service.

> Effective communication is not just a matter of luck or something we are born with. We are born with the sensory equipment and the brain structures which enable us to send and receive messages and to code and decode them, but how we do this is a learned skill.
>
> **Most people do not communicate well**.
>
> If you do not communicate as well as you would like to, all is not lost; you can change. If some of the ways you have learned to communicate in the past prove to be ineffective or destructive you can unlearn them and relearn new ways. It takes time and effort and the willingness to persevere (Kotzman 1989, pp. 38–39, formatting added).

Definition

Communication is the exchange of words, letters, symbols or messages in such a way that an individual or group receives information and understanding from other individuals or groups.

Communication models

As communication is simply the process of sending and receiving messages, models representing the process generally incorporate the following features:

- A *source* (or, sender) – this may be an individual (speaking, writing, gesturing) or a group (speaking or writing, for example) or even a communication organisation (like a newspaper, radio station or a television station). The sender encodes a message, that is, translates what they want to convey (thoughts, feelings, ideas, instructions, and so on) into symbols for transmission.

- A *message*.

- The *channel* – this is the means of conveying the message (for example paper, voice/air waves, telephone lines, email).

- The *receiver* – this is who decodes the message and assigns meaning to it.

- *Feedback* – after receiving the message, the receiver provides a response to the original message. This in turn may require a further response, and so the cycle continues.

- *Noise* – this is anything that interferes with, or disrupts, the accurate transmission and/or reception of messages. Also called barriers to effective communication, noise can, and does, occur at any point in the communication process.

White and Bednar (1986) argue that although such a model appears relatively uncomplicated, there are some issues we should keep in mind. First, messages merely *represent* feelings, perceptions and thoughts. We are not able to communicate an actual belief or feeling, so instead we are reduced to sending messages about them. Second, communication involves both the sending and receiving of messages – it is not a one-way process. Third, communication is a process which is continuous, both reciprocal and dynamic. For example, you cannot be with another person and not communicate – think about it! The communication process does not necessarily begin, end, or proceed as and when we want it to.

This is a fairly straightforward model and further consideration has given rise to a number of other models that describe parts or all of the communication process from a different perspective or through taking a different emphasis. Rather than go into these in detail here, a readily accessible overview of these models is available at the following site created by the University of Wisconsin's School of Library and Information Studies: <http://www.slis.wisc.edu/academic/syllabi/450/communication/sld001.htm>.

Problems in communication occur largely because we do not place enough importance on understanding these issues. We should study our own communication style, pattern, network and needs if we are to be effective in our work and, more especially, if we are to become effective supervisors.

Types of communication

Some writers divide communication types into three general categories: written, oral and non-verbal. However, rather than follow that categorisation, I have considered it in two types: verbal and non-verbal. Verbal communication is message exchange using written or spoken symbols. Non-verbal communication, on the other hand, is conveyed by behaviour such as eye contact, body movements, facial expressions, gestures, posture and other body positioning – even style of dress and use of personal space.

Verbal communication

Verbal communication has been studied and written about more than any other type of communication. Books and articles on management, supervision, organisational behaviour, interpersonal relations and many other topics abound with writings on verbal communication. A detailed study of some of that literature will bring rewards and further insight into the subject.

On first appearances verbal communication seems to be a very clear, simple and easily defined and explained topic. However, further reading about it quickly exhibits the complexities with which we are faced as supervisors. Verbal communication relies on, and involves, both the written and the spoken message. It relies on words to provide information and is part of a communication system based on symbols that stand for the objects and ideas to which we refer.

One of the keys to successful verbal communication is deciding when to speak your message, and when to provide it in writing. Both types are important, but there are certain situations which require one type rather than the other, or one type followed by the other.

Written communication

Written communication is rife in any organisation, through letters, memos, reports, and email messages. Written communication provides a clear record of the message which can be kept by all parties for future reference. (As someone once said, a memo serves not to inform the reader, but rather to protect the writer!) Written communication does ensure that everyone receives the same message, and it does give the opportunity to write, rewrite and edit before sending the message.

Policies, procedures and instructions should always be presented in written format, although they will generally be introduced and monitored through oral messages as well. The oral follow-up is often necessary to ensure that the message is clearly understood, that the words convey the same message to all parties involved, and to allow for immediate feedback. This helps to overcome problems created through a variety of interpretations of policies, ambiguous instructions, and the like.

Oral communication

Oral communication can be between individuals or within group settings. Most supervisors will spend more of their communication time and effort in oral communication. The major advantage of this mode is that it allows for feedback and immediate clarification of any confusing points. The message can be more readily decoded for meaning. People are more readily motivated by oral messages, especially if they are transmitted in an appropriate manner – the written word cannot take the place of an enthusiastic and friendly voice. If the communication is face-to-face (as opposed to telephone, for example), then content and information, conveyed verbally, can be supported by the non-verbal component to aid in interpretation.

Non-verbal communication

Non-verbal communication reinforces the verbal or information content of the message and performs a number of functions in our society. These include:

- communicating interpersonal attitudes and feelings – for example, many gestures, stances, eye movements, and postures will communicate what we are feeling or what attitude we want to convey, with or without any accompanying speech
- supporting verbal communication – this is achieved by complementing the meaning of what is spoken; signalling attentiveness; obtaining feedback from the person or group with whom you are communicating
- replacing speech – this can take place, for example, in a noisy environment; or in sports, where umpires cannot be close enough to all the players and the spectators to make themselves heard.

What we communicate will nearly always be affected by the manner accompanying our communication. If a colleague asks you for assistance when designing a training program and you answer 'Yes!' in an enthusiastic manner, your colleague can pretty safely interpret your response as a willingness to help. However, if your response of 'Yes' is accompanied by evasive eye movements and a tired tone of voice, your colleague might be safe in assuming that you really mean 'No'. When a contradiction arises between the verbal and non-verbal messages, we usually accept the non-verbal. This generally happens without us being aware that it is taking place.

Compared to verbal communication, non-verbal communication is very limited. Usually, non-verbal messages are used to communicate feelings, likes, attitudes towards a subject, or preferences – they typically reinforce or contradict feelings that are communicated verbally. There are a number of forms of non-verbal communication.

Key concepts in communication (O'Sullivan *et al.* 1994) outlines the major sources of non-verbal communication as:

- eye contact (that is, the amount of looking at the other person)
- mouth (especially smiling or grimacing in relation to eye contact)
- posture (for example, sitting forwards or backwards)
- gesture (for example, the use of arm movements when talking)
- orientation (of the body to the addressee)
- body distance (as when we stand too close or too far away from others)
- smell (including perfumes)
- skin (including pigmentation, blushing and texture)
- hair (including length, texture and style)
- clothes (with particular reference to fashion).

You can even add to this the size and location of an office, or desk space, or type of furnishing, or the types of posters and clippings you place on your noticeboard or walls.

Recognising your own uses of non-verbal communication, and practising positive rather than negative means, will increase your ability to communicate effectively. If, for example, you wish to become more assertive (not necessarily aggressive, just a step or two forward from being a sponge or a doormat) in your face-to-face communication, then make sure you get the other person's attention before beginning. You can help with this by looking directly at them, speaking firmly and not too fast. Hold a solid posture with your head up and feet firmly planted. The opposite, with head drooping, shoulders slouched, eyes looking elsewhere, whispering, will ensure that you are not taken seriously. Figure 9.1 provides further information on body language and communication.

Defensiveness	Cooperation	Confidence
Arms crossed on chest	Body in sprinter's position	Hand-to-face gestures
Legs crosses	Open hands	Sideways glance
Fist gestures	Sitting on edge of chair	Hands behind back
Pointing	Hand-to-face gestures	Back stiffened
Frustration	**Nervousness**	**Insecurity**
Short breaths	Throat clearing	Chewing pen
Tssk sound	Fidgeting	Thumb over thumb
Clenched hands	Perspiration	Nail biting
Hand wringing	*Phew* sound	Hands in pockets
Suspicion	**Openness**	**Evaluation**
Touching of nose	Open hands	Steepled hands
Backing away	Coat unbuttoned	Head tilted
Hands on lapels		Chin stroking
		Peering over glasses

Figure 9.1: Some attitudes communicated through body language

Communication barriers

Communication barriers are those things that create a gap between what the sender intends as meaning, and what the receiver effectively understands or receives. They come about mainly because the sender makes assumptions about how the receiver will understand, and most arise because we communicate automatically, without thinking too closely about our intended meaning (Dwyer 1999, p. 11).

The term barriers does not imply we communicate like machines, rather it tries to convey that 'meaningful interpersonal communication may lose some of its effectiveness when communicators behave or think in certain ways' (DeVito 2001, p. 178).

Figure 9.2 depicts a highly exaggerated example of what can happen when messages are passed in writing, and orally, from one person to another. It is a funny, but somewhat edifying, example of noise and lack of feedback – two barriers to successful communication. A more detailed consideration of those barriers follows.

Openness and cooperation are necessary for effective communication to take place, but the process which sounds so straightforward – sending and receiving messages – is complex and is fraught with potential difficulties. The following list is not exhaustive, but it indicates where and how some of these problems occur through barriers to effective communication.

Language

Clearly, someone speaking to you in a different language will have great difficulty getting their message across. Even an accent, or the use of slang, can make communication very difficult. Likewise, technical language and jargon which is unfamiliar to one party will blur meaning. Semantics (meaning) can have a considerable influence at times. We need to be literate enough to understand that when words have more than one meaning, we may need to 'translate', or make it clear which meaning applies in a particular circumstance. Written communication requires particular care in this area. The examples in Figure 9.3 highlight many of the points just made.

A school superintendent told his assistant superintendent the following:

'Next Thursday at 10:30 a.m. Halley's Comet will appear over this area. This is an event which occurs only once every 75 years. Call the school principals and have them assemble their teachers and classes on their athletic fields and explain this phenomenon to them. If it rains then cancel the day's observation and have the classes meet in the auditorium to see a film about the comet.'

Assistant superintendent to school principals:

'By order of the superintendent of schools, next Thursday at 10:30 Halley's Comet will appear over your athletic field. If it rains then cancel the day's classes and report to the auditorium with your teachers and students where you will be shown films, a phenomenal event which occurs only once every 75 years.'

Principals to teachers:

'By order of the phenomenal superintendent of schools at 10:30 next Thursday Halley's Comet will appear in the auditorium. In case of rain over the athletic field the superintendent will give another order, something which occurs once every 75 years.'

Teachers to students:

'Next Thursday at 10:30 the superintendent of schools will appear in our school auditorium with Halley's Comet, something which occurs every 75 years. If it rains the superintendent will cancel the Comet and order us all out to our phenomenal athletic field.'

Students to parents:

'When it rains next Thursday at 10:30 over the school athletic field the phenomenal 75 year old superintendent of schools will cancel all classes and appear before the whole school in the auditorium accompanied by Bill Halley and the Comets'

(Source: <http:///www.frc.ri.cmu.edu/~mcm/halleys.html>, viewed 28 April 2003).

Figure 9.2: *Example of what can happen when messages pass through too many channels*

Notices intended to communicate simple messages

The following are from actual Church Bulletins - announcements that were misspelled due to typos, or Public Announcements that were just badly put together in the first place.

* Bertha Belch, a missionary from Africa will be speaking tonight at Calvary Memorial Church in Racine. Come tonight and hear Bertha Belch all the way from Africa.
* Our youth basketball team is back in action Wednesday at 8 PM in the recreation hall. Come out and watch us kill Christ the King.
* Ladies, don't forget the rummage sale. It's a chance to get rid of those things not worth keeping around the house. Don't forget your husbands.
* Next Sunday is the family hayride and bonfire at the Fowlers'. Bring your own hot dogs and guns. Friends are welcome! Everyone come for a fun time.
* The sermon this morning: 'Jesus Walks on the Water.' The sermon tonight: 'Searching for Jesus'.
* The peacemaking meeting scheduled for today has been cancelled due to a conflict.
* Next Thursday there will be tryouts for the choir. They need all the help they can get.
* Barbara remains in the hospital and needs blood donors for more transfusions. She is also having trouble sleeping and requests tapes of Pastor Jack's sermons.
* The Rector will preach his farewell message after which the choir will sing 'Break Forth into Joy.'
* Remember in prayer the many who are sick of our community. Smile at someone who is hard to love. Say 'hell' to someone who doesn't care much about you.
* Irving Benson and Jessie Carter were married on October 24 in the church. So ends a friendship that began in their school days.
* A bean supper will be held on Tuesday evening in the church hall. Music will follow.
* At the evening service tonight, the sermon topic will be 'What is Hell?' Come early and listen to our choir practice.
* Eight new choir robes are currently needed, due to the addition of several new members and to the deterioration of some older ones.
* The senior choir invites any member of the congregation who enjoys sinning to join the choir.
* Scouts are saving aluminum cans, bottles, and other items to be recycled. Proceeds will be used to cripple children.
* For those of you who have children and don't know it, we have a nursery downstairs.
* Attend and you will hear an excellent speaker and heave a healthy lunch.
* The church will host an evening of fine dining, superb entertainment, and gracious hostility.
* Potluck supper Sunday at 5:00 P.M. Prayer and medication to follow.
* The ladies of the Church have cast off clothing of every kind. They may be seen in the basement on Friday afternoon.
* Ladies Bible Study will be held Thursday morning at 10. All ladies are invited to lunch in the Fellowship Hall after the B.S. is done.
* Low Self Esteem Support Group will meet Thursday at 7 PM. Please use the back door.
* The Associate Minister unveiled the church's new tithing campaign slogan last Sunday 'I Upped My Pledge – Up Yours.'
* The eighth-graders will be presenting Shakespeare's Hamlet in the Church basement Friday at 7 PM. The Congregation is invited to attend this tragedy.
* Weight Watchers will meet at 7 PM at the First Presbyterian Church. Please use large double door at the side entrance

(Source:<http://www.pastornet.net.au/jmm/ahmr/ahmr1831.htm> Viewed 16 August 2002)

Figure 9.3: *Examples of what can happen when written communication is not clear*

Perceptions

Based on their own unique frame of reference through which they perceive the world, each individual perceives events, activities and messages in their own way. Beyond language and meaning, this barrier affects our responses to non-verbal communication. Chapter 10 includes a more detailed explanation of how perception affects behaviour in general.

Attitudes

Our attitudes involve matters like age and status, and these can block successful message giving and receiving. Different sets of values can be at work here. Attitudinal assumptions about whether someone else will listen or think you have any value can affect communication.

Interference

Interference – often called noise – is anything that interferes with, or disrupts, the accurate transmission or reception of a message. External noise – sounds, like a radio blaring, or someone else shouting nearby, can distort or obliterate the message. Internal noise – for example, pain, fear, or hunger – will prevent concentration and distract from full reception of a message.

Distortion

The Halley's Comet example in Figure 9.2 is a classic example of distortion. It's a bit like 'Chinese whispers', the party game in which participants whisper a message from one to another along the chain, until the final recipient states what they have received and it is compared with the original message. The distortion increases in proportion to the number of people involved. Keeping the number of stages down, using written forms of communication, and sending brief and simple messages will help eliminate, or reduce, distortion.

Prejudice, prejudging, bias and stereotyping

Prejudging a person's ability to understand, or take on, a task can be a significant communication barrier. Statements like, 'I know you don't like working on the circulation desk…' or, 'You probably won't understand this…' are clear barriers to favourable reception. We tend to be more receptive to people we have a high regard for, and less receptive to those for whom we have less respect or regard. This kind of barrier will happen, but we need to be wary of these attitudes degenerating into more extreme prejudice, such as that based on race, ethnicity, or religion. The section on interviewing in Chapter 16 gives further examples of prejudice, and considers in more detail such factors as the 'halo' and 'pitchfork' effects.

Blocking phrases

Some statements or responses close the door on further conversation. Many of them are commonly used without the speaker being aware of their potential for erecting a communication barrier. Phrases that command, threaten, preach, lecture, judge, criticise, ridicule, interrogate or distract have a high potential for blocking communication. Think about how you would feel about talking to someone who uses the following phrases in communicating with you.

- 'Don't use that PC.'
- 'You'll be sorry you did that.'
- 'That's a terrible thing to say.'
- 'You should be more tolerant.'
- 'Why don't you work hard like [a fellow employee] does?'
- 'How long have you had such bad breath?'

What effect would these have on your desire to communicate with that speaker?

Defensiveness

Defensiveness occurs when a participant in the communication process perceives they are under threat from one or more individuals in the process. It arises from a variety of factors, including manner of speech and tone of voice, negative body language, dogmatic or ambiguous behaviour. These in turn evoke a defensive response in which the listener will be forced to spend their communication efforts in defending themselves, in working out how they can 'win', rather than in assembling a constructive response. Studies (for example, Miller *et al.* 1989) have also shown that when people are worried or anxious about approval, they have difficulty in concentrating on what is being said. Arousing defensiveness, then, reduces the effectiveness of communication and makes it difficult for the speaker to convey their message accurately.

Selective reception

In oral communication selective reception is really a listening problem (addressed later in this chapter), but it can happen with written communication as well. We screen out those parts of the message which are not readily understood, and latch onto those parts which are. We hear, or read, those things with which we are most familiar, and concentrate less, if at all, on the unfamiliar, unless the message is presented in an exciting, ear- or eye-catching, manner.

Physical abilities

Be aware of people's potential communication difficulties. For example, with those who are hard of hearing, have visual impairment, or literacy problems, tailor your method and form of communication to suit the other party.

The role of language

Most of the above are psychological barriers that are due to the nature of language and the emotional character and mental limitations of human beings. Language is a poor substitute for the realities it attempts to represent. Although it enables us to send messages to one another as well as making the analysis and comparison of experiences possible, language in operation often tends to conceal and obscure meaning.

However, according to DeVito (2001, pp. 178–192) there are specific obstacles in language that merit special attention, including that language symbolises reality but is not reality itself; that language expresses both facts and inferences; that language is static, while people are dynamic; that language can create the appearance of discrimination; that language is used for lying, gossiping and the use of stereotypes (the assimilation of material to familiar frames of reference).

Communication barriers: how to avoid them

- Be positive. If you are experiencing a communication block, don't withdraw into negativism and discouraging behaviour.

- Be specific and personal about what you say rather than using vague generalisations.

- Be empathetic and try to see situations as other people see them. Try to understand and be sensitive to the other person's feelings, and let them know that you understand.

- Avoid making judgmental comments.

- Try to avoid personal biases. Even if you do not like, for example, the way a person dresses or the sound of their voice, don't let this prevent you from listening to, hearing and understanding the message.

- Decide that you want to communicate, not compete to win.

- Avoid sending mixed messages (where the verbal and non-verbal content contradict each other).

- Be aware that negative emotions – for example, anger and resentment – are communication barriers.

- Use silences to give the other party time to consider, think and respond. If you feel uncomfortable during a pause, focus on the other person and how they may be feeling. If it is important that they be leading the conversation, allow them the time and space to do so.

- Use repetition to make sure the message sent has been received accurately. For example, 'So you will be back from the workshop after lunch; that means you'll be able to do your desk duty at 3 o'clock.'

What you should learn from this is that barriers do exist and that you can prevent them or inhibit their effects if you take care with your communication. You must always bear your audience in mind (whether one person or a group) including their background and what you know about them that could influence their reception. All of the above barriers help to prevent us from communicating accurately and effectively. They also contribute to poor listening.

Listening

> Nature gave us two ears, but only one tongue.

> Use your two ears and one mouth in that proportion [listen more than you talk]. (Two gems from the desk diary)

Listening as part of the communication process is no longer overlooked, because it is vital if messages are to be interpreted correctly. To develop an effective work environment, it is essential to listen carefully and intelligently to work colleagues. This section is concerned with listening skills that will help you to gain a clearer understanding of the situation, and that in turn will assist you in taking responsibility and will help you when seeking the cooperation of others.

How do we become adept at poor listening? Research and observation has shown that:

- people tend to retain only about 30 per cent of what they hear, and yet fail to take notes to assist their memory
- people tend to latch onto some of the comments (perhaps because they are presented in an attractive manner, or because they already agree with them) rather than keeping an open mind and hearing the point of the message
- people often think they already know what is about to be said
- if people are critical of the speaker, then they will treat the message accordingly
- because people are too busy with their own concerns to be good listeners, they often pretend that they have heard or understood all of the message
- people are often working on their response before the other party has finished conveying their message
- people can think much faster than they speak so poor listeners tend to think around the subject, mentally go off on a tangent, and then miss important parts of the message.

As Alessandra (1998) notes in a discussion on improving listening skills:

> While we hear, we only pretend to listen. Listening doesn't just mean shutting up while someone else speaks – though that's a start...But listening – real listening – takes more work than that. It's more than the physical process of hearing. It also takes intellectual and emotional effort. To get a full appreciation of the other person and what's being said, you need to ask questions, give feedback, remain objective, figure out what's really being said and what's not being said, and observe and interpret body language.

Figure 9.4 gives some of the many reasons why we should all attempt to improve our listening skills, and a few practical suggestions for improving your listening skills.

Good reasons to become a better listener		
To get the best value	To control distractions	To improve discipline
To learn something	To be entertained	To understand a situation
To get information	To be courteous	To be responsible
To prevent accidents	To be a team player	To ask intelligent questions
To improve confidence	To protect freedom	To find out a person's needs
To reach a productivity quota	To use money more wisely	To be valued and trusted
To solve problems	To show you care	To satisfy curiosity
To be safe	To be good lover	To make intelligent decisions
To prevent waste	To make money	To avoid embarrassment
To save time	To stay out of trouble	To build rapport
To enhance relationships	To be a discriminating consumer	To be more efficient
To make comparisons	To be a supportive friend	To make accurate evaluations
To give an appropriate response	To enjoy the sounds of nature	To settle disagreements
To increase concentration	To create a 'win-win' situation	To improve your vocabulary
To be prepared for sudden shifts in a speaker's topic or intention	To be a better family member	To improve your personality
	To maintain a flexible attitude	To analyse the speaker's purpose
	To use the gift of hearing	

Source: Hale 1991 (adapted from Bone, 1988)

Figure 9.4: Why you should become a better listener

Consider the reasons for, and benefits of, effective listening, and make your own list from the above, of the top ten reasons for effective listening in the work context. Which of the above reasons are imperative for the supervisor?

Tips for effective listening

Stop talking: You cannot listen if you are talking. 'The ears don't work until the tongue has expired.' Don't begin speaking yourself until it is clearly appropriate to do so.

Put the talker at ease: For good listening, and therefore good communication, it is important that both parties are at ease. Make it clear that you are available, and attend to any immediate needs which may have a distracting influence if left unattended. Create a permissive environment in which all parties feel free to talk and listen.

Show the other person that you want to listen: Look and act interested. Use appropriate non-verbal behaviour. Effective two-way communication tends to be encouraged when the listener is relaxed and alert, leaning slightly forward and facing the other person, clearly concentrating, and maintaining an appropriate distance from the other person. You can show that you are actively listening by nodding your head, making occasional comment, looking at the person who is talking.

Ignore, remove or avoid distractions: Don't doodle, shuffle papers, tap your pen, or look at your computer screen. Shut a door, move to a quieter environment, ask to have 'phone calls redirected, if necessary.

Empathise with the speaker: Try to help yourself to see their point of view. As mentioned above, try to understand and be sensitive to the other person's feelings, and let them know that you understand.

Be patient: Allow plenty of time, avoid rushing them to a conclusion. Don't interrupt them. Don't walk away before they have finished speaking. If you wish to help a colleague, you need to take the time to respond in such a way that they can make their feelings clear and work towards solving their own problems.

Beware of argument and criticism: These can put the speaker on the defensive, and that can have two results: they may become angry, in which case the wrong meaning and emphasis may go onto words and phrases; or they may clam up, which does not make for useful communication.

Ask questions: This should encourage a speaker, and demonstrates that you are listening. You can develop the communication further by asking leading questions to clarify a point, or open questions to gain information and allow the other person to expand. Decision-makers who do not listen, and who do not ask questions, will have less information for making sound decisions.

Stop talking: I repeat myself in order to emphasise that all of the other tips to effective listening depend on it. You cannot be an effective listener while you are talking.

Figure 9.5: *Tips for effective listening*

Listening is a sophisticated skill – it is hard work, and requires considerable effort and practice. Examine your own listening habits in relation to the tips in Figure 9.5. Do you consciously, or otherwise, follow these tips regularly? Which do you not follow? Why? Can you place yourself in a recent work-related conversation or discussion and recall how you handled it? How could you have improved your listening? Take note of how you listen, and recall the tips above, the next time you are communicating face-to-face. See how your perception of communication, and listening, is changed and sharpened. The results will be worthwhile.

Communication in organisations

Much of the literature and discussion of communication is in terms of personal communication. However, we need to be aware of some aspects of organisations which affect what is called organisational communication.

Organisational communication is the exchange of messages along predefined paths directed by the organisational hierarchy. In the workplace these predefined paths allow communications to circulate so that everyone affected can know what is happening. They aim to encourage unity and coordination so that the organisation operates as a unit instead of as a series of unconnected parts.

One of the main functions of the supervisor or manager is to be certain that their network of communication is effective. By encouraging coordination, communication helps to bring together different decision-making areas, and allows for feedback to be a regular part of the monitoring or control process. Communication in libraries can be seen to flow through the organisation in three ways: downwards, upwards, and horizontally.

In the formal 'system' of communication, *downwards communication* flows from senior to lower levels through a chain of authority and responsibility. This flow of communication is used for giving orders, delegating authority, announcing changes and plans, reinforcing policies and goals, asking for suggestions, and so forth. Almost all communication channels are used.

Upwards communication consists of messages which flow from lower levels to more senior levels. From the supervisor's point of view, this flow is vital if feedback on staff attitudes, performance, expectations and disappointments is to be obtained. Channels of communication can fall into the informal category, although supervisory group meetings, face-to-face interviews (for example, in appraisal programs), reports, and grievance procedures, are all channels for the feedback process.

Horizontal communication is the lateral exchange of information within the library organisation, and is based on a variety of working relationships between individuals, teams and sections. This flow of communication is used for problem-solving, task coordination, information sharing, conflict resolution, and so forth. It uses all possible channels, both formal and informal.

Channels of communication

There are decisions to be made about frequency, style, form, type and origin of messages, and supervisors need to be selective in the way they approach another section of the organisation. Some methods are more suitable than others for getting an immediate resolution of a day-to-day problem; for lengthy details of policy; for advising on career prospects within the organisation; for announcing a social club activity; for requesting an immediate response to an important new issue; for presenting initial plans for a future development; or for necessarily restricted information – to mention just a few.

The choice of channels of communication within an organisation can be divided into formal and informal. Formal channels usually follow the library's lines of authority and responsibility from the top to the bottom which indicate who is supposed to talk to whom, or who is to report to whom, and include:

- email
- memo
- fax message
- newsletter
- noticeboard
- letter
- meeting

- report
- telephone
- survey/questionnaire
- conference/seminar/workshop
- interview

The informal 'system' of communication in organisations is often known as the 'grapevine'. This involves messages which cut across structured communication channels, which do not follow the networks and paths specified by the formal organisation. They indicate who really talks to whom without regard for officially designated positions. Informal communication channels include:

- email
- telephone
- general conversation
- suggestion box
- social gathering
- noticeboard
- newsletter.

Informal channels are neither as predictable nor as neatly structured as formal channels, but they are remarkably efficient at moving information. The term 'grapevine' originated during the American Civil War, where, for concealment purposes, telegraph lines were strung between trees to resemble wild grapevines. Today the term applies to those informal channels of communication that develop as part of a social relationship between colleagues, regardless of hierarchies, work practices or formal communication channels (Bryson 1999, p. 278).

Since it is an impossible task to destroy the grapevine, library supervisors and managers should learn to live with it and use it and similar informal channels to their advantage. There are a number of benefits to be gained from such practice.

It's fast. The grapevine exists largely because it is a much faster method of communication than any of the formal channels.

It's accurate. Various studies indicate that the accuracy of information communicated through the grapevine is 75–90 per cent (Bedeian 1989, p. 499). Any inaccuracies are usually because the message is transmitted in an incomplete manner.

It's efficient. Better than any circulation listing, the grapevine selectively routes information to those who will find it to be of the greatest interest. In contrast, formal channels tend to send information to staff who have no interest in it, resulting in information sitting on a desk somewhere and not being passed on to those who really do need to know.

It fulfils needs. The grapevine satisfies the need for staff members to communicate with each other. A major problem faced by libraries, especially in these days of change, is the rumour – information without a factual basis. Rumours are encouraged where there is a lack of communication. By providing adequate, accurate and timely information, managers can reduce the number and extent of rumours floating around among their staff.

Library supervisors and managers can also tap into the grapevine to obtain the opinions, attitudes and beliefs of staff about proposed changes, incidents, events and services. The grapevine can also be used to spread information quickly. Information can be 'fed' to those staff members who are likely to spread the information. Some organisations also use the grapevine to release favourable information that has yet to be confirmed or that they do not want to keep records of.

So, the grapevine is accurate, fast and very active, and no-one is exempt from it. However, the grapevine is also a vehicle for rumour and gossip, and it is this which has created the image and sense of the grapevine as the medium of unreliable and unconfirmed information. Thus, while it can be very effective in relaying information, it should not be relied upon as the only way to give information to staff.

Most staff would rather obtain important job-related and personal information directly from their supervisor. We should be aware of, and sensitive to, the existence of the grapevine as a way of helping us to deal most effectively with communication in our organisations. Any formal oral communication should be followed up and confirmed, in writing, to prevent the kinds of problems already mentioned.

Supervisor's role in communication

Why does a supervisor communicate?

A supervisor communicates to, for example:

- inform
- solicit information
- appraise
- persuade
- coordinate
- build and support teams
- motivate
- solve problems
- lead
- counsel
- praise
- discipline.

The list of reasons for communicating is endless. Supervisors spend the largest percentage of their time communicating with other people: it is the key element in the success of their role. The supervisor is a vital link in the communication chain between departments, and between senior management and the staff for whom they are responsible. Supervisors are at the forefront of establishing and maintaining open and dynamic communication among the staff. The supervisor's influence can be major in terms of the library's climate, the section's productivity and the morale of staff.

What does a supervisor communicate?

A supervisor communicates the following, for example:

- specific job instructions
- the reasons for undertaking a task
- library policies and procedures
- specific section needs and practices

- feedback on employee performance
- answers to questions
- plans for the future
- decisions of senior management.

How does a supervisor communicate?

A supervisor uses a number of methods of communication, including:

- talking
- emails, memos, letters
- noticeboards, newsletters
- reports
- procedures manuals
- meetings, group discussions
- individual interviews.

Add to this the endless opportunities to influence through gestures, actions (for example, a pat on the back, facial expressions, tone of voice) and you will begin to see that the supervisor is always communicating in one form or another. The need for managers and supervisors to have an understanding of what communication is, what it involves, and of some of the skills involved in successful and effective communication has never been greater than it is today.

Many work problems are created or magnified by poor communication. The library's total culture is made up, in large part, of the interrelationships between formal and informal communication. Constant change affects a library's communications, although flexibility of communication form and style will help alleviate the effects. Supervisors and managers must be prepared to communicate explicit information when and where it is needed, and obtain accurate and timely information through feedback and listening skills. Everyone in the organisation has a stake in ensuring that all staff receive the information required to fulfil the potential of their jobs. When a system is being managed well all staff should be aware of how messages are sent and received, and should be alert for ways to improve the communication systems. Staff at all levels, but especially supervisors, should take the initiative to improve understanding and communication with colleagues to build a more effective organisation.

Conclusion

Mastering the theory, skills and techniques of communication is still not the whole answer to success in the communication role of managers and supervisors. To paraphrase one respondent to the study of management education and training needs (Sanders 1993), qualities needed in addition to communication skills include honesty, integrity, openness, compassion, common sense, courage, optimism, being nice occasionally, and having respect for staff as people.

As Ann Kotzman quotes from Bolton (1979):

> Communication techniques are useful only insofar as they facilitate the expression of essential human qualities. The person who has mastered the skills of communication but lacks genuineness, love and empathy will find his expertise irrelevant or even harmful. Important as they are, the techniques of communication

by themselves are unable to forge satisfactory relationships (Bolton 1979, cited in Kotzman 1989, p. 102).

Kotzman goes on to a detailed discussion of three main qualities that foster good relationships of various kinds, the theory being based on the work of Carl Rogers, which in turn is supported by more than a hundred different studies. Kotzman discusses these qualities under the broad headings of genuineness, acceptance and warmth, and empathy, and concludes:

> When these three qualities are present, relationships of all kinds are enhanced. Children learn better…business relationships work better, people are freer, healthier, happier and become more mature…We all have the capacity for these qualities by virtue of being human. Sometimes they atrophy from disuse or become blocked for various reasons…Learning and using communication skills such as reflective listening and self-assertion can help to enhance your capacity for [these qualities] (Kotzman 1989, pp. 102–104).

If you want to study the issue of communication in greater depth then *The interpersonal communication book* by Joseph DeVito (2001), is an excellent place to start.

Chapter 10
Leading

The wicked leader is he who the people despise. The good leader is he who the people revere. The great leader is he who the people say, We did it ourselves. (Lao-Tzu)

Nobody motivates today's workers. If it doesn't come from within, it doesn't come. (Source unknown)

I'm famous for my motivational skills. Everyone always says they have to work a lot harder when I'm around. (Homer Simpson)

The best morale exists when you never hear the word mentioned. When you hear a lot of talk about it, it's usually lousy. (Dwight D. Eisenhower)

Definition

Leading can be defined as the supervisory and managerial function of providing direction and influencing individuals to achieve goals. To be a successful leader requires leadership, that is, the ability to motivate and influence others through the display and use of certain types of behaviour.

Leadership can be defined further as the ability to guide, influence and motivate the opinions and actions of others toward the accomplishment of organisational goals and objectives. (Hilgert and Leonard 1995, p. 432). There are many different approaches to the study of leadership, and they are presented in terms of the traits that the leader should possess, the power needed, the position in the organisation, or even the style appropriate to a particular situation.

Introduction

We study leading for a number of reasons. If managers and supervisors agree with the definition above, then they will want to become effective leaders, because that will help achieve the library's goals. We also want to be able to identify those staff members who show the potential to become leaders and develop them towards that. Leadership is a major influence on how people perform at work, and we want to know how to become, and develop, successful leaders.

Many positions in a library require, by virtue of their designated roles and descriptions, the incumbent to lead others. These are formal leaders, as a consequence of their formal position within the library. But that does not necessarily mean they will be good leaders. On the other hand, libraries can have leaders who do not hold formal leadership positions. These leaders are 'appointed' by their colleagues, generally because they demonstrate a knowledge of the job and personal qualities that the group respects and wants to follow.

The formal leader can allow leader behaviour in others to be developed in certain situations, provided they are working for the library and its goals and are meeting genuine needs of the work group. Teamwork, in particular, is the home of many such informal leaders.

Theories of leadership

We can learn to become more effective leaders and that is the purpose of studying this topic. There has been an enormous amount of research to discover what makes a good leader, and what characteristics a good leader must possess. I suggest that you go to the management literature to read about that in detail.

There is also, within the literature, an ongoing discussion over the difference between management and leadership. The definition that management involves getting things done through people suggests that the employees in an organisation, in terms of management, are simply a means to an end – a way of achieving organisational tasks (Bratton and Gold 1999; Robbins, Millet, Cacioppe, and Waters-Marsh 1998). The most important tasks in management at a supervisory level are planning, organising, staffing, controlling and problem-solving. On the other hand, the most important leadership activities include defining a vision for the future, aligning employees with that vision, and inspiring and supporting them towards reaching that vision by creating an organisational environment where obstacles are viewed as challenges to be overcome rather than setbacks to be avoided (Kotter 1998).

The essence of what makes good leadership is yet to be precisely defined, lending evidence to the view that the appropriateness of leadership style to a particular situation is more important than the style itself. Despite many attempts to define the ideal leadership style (see for example, Sarros and Butchatsky 1996) and studies pinpointing essential leadership traits (for example, Kirkpatrick and Lock's study quoted in Ivancevich *et al.* 1999), success as a leader does not seem to hinge on a consistent and readily definable set of common personality and behavioural traits.

Leadership is more readily associated with seeking to motivate and inspire staff, and encouraging them to align their work lives and aspirations to those of the library vision. Leaders stretch and enhance others by providing a vision for personal and organisational goals; they get results through expectations rather than directions, and by encouraging employees to reach their potential as humans rather than pushing them to complete job tasks (Batten 1989).

The combination of planning and organising skills, along with those associated with leadership (including the ability to motivate and inspire employees, to encourage independence and the acceptance of responsibility, and to develop trusting interpersonal relationships with others) are the foundation for the most effective leaders.

Leadership style

Leadership style refers to how one behaves as a leader in terms of influencing and relating to others, and the success of different leadership styles will be contingent on specific situational variables (Leigh and Maynard 1997). This includes selecting the appropriate style of leading contingent on the competence, motivation and developmental level of the staff involved (Hersey and Blanchard, in Robbins *et al.* 1998). Those leaders who are able to adapt their leadership style (for example, directing, coaching, supporting, delegating) to suit the challenge at hand will therefore be the most successful across different leadership situations.

Traditional perspectives of leadership tend to focus on autocratic and directive styles of leadership, which are characterised by limited dissemination of information, close supervision and control of workers, little delegation of responsibility, authority based on a strict hierarchy, and the articulation of detailed instructions, even for simple work tasks (Hilgert and Leonard 1995). These characteristics tend to result in little or no trust either of or between employees, and mistakes are usually punished rather than viewed as a necessary aspect of creativity and innovation (which will therefore also suffer under this kind of leadership).

By contrast, modern approaches to leadership propound the virtues of participative leadership, which focuses on open communication, distant supervision, team approaches to decision-making, high levels of work task delegation, and flatter organisational authority structures. These characteristics tend to lead to the development of mutual trust amongst employees and their leaders, and reward systems are often geared towards supporting initiative, creativity and innovation. On the other hand, traditional leadership styles built on structures of command and control can act as barriers to creativity, innovation and risk-taking. Autocratic leadership styles within organisations can also slow work processes because of the expectation that employees will seek permission from someone higher in the organisation before making decisions rather than taking the initiative to get the job done.

That 'softer' styles of organisational leadership have gained more attention in recent times is not so much an indication of their inherent superiority over directive styles of leadership, but more a reflection of trends in organisational change – that is, trends towards teamwork, flatter structures and employee participation.

Leadership: a behavioural approach

Leaders who are aware of what motivates people to work will be in the best possible position to understand and relate to their staff. That gives the best opportunity for satisfactory working relationships, which in turn will ensure that efforts to achieve both organisational and individual goals will be most effective. Conversely, lack of an awareness of motivational factors will be more likely to create a work culture in which initiative is limited, creativity is stifled, and workers do not feel a need to think for themselves. This relates to the intrinsic theories of motivation where it is assumed that the worker is more productive if the task is intrinsically worthwhile and the worker is allowed to undertake it with minimal supervision, resulting in the 'reward' coming from the job satisfaction itself (see the section on motivation later in this chapter).

To be a successful leader requires the ability to motivate and influence others through the display and use of certain types of behaviour. A good leader, within the modern library context, will develop the employees under his or her influence to fulfil their organisational and personal potential, and generate employee commitment, flexibility, innovation and change. Individuals do not become good leaders because of their personality traits, but rather through their ability to harness them as resources for leadership and apply them differently in a range of contexts (Heifetz 1998).

Empirical evidence for the benefits of a team-like, participative approach to leadership within organisations has been generated by applying behavioural science principles to organisational situations. These include five basic principles related to shared participation, mutual trust, open communication, conflict management and responsibility (Reese and Brandt 1993).

In behavioural science, it is asserted that shared participation in problem-solving and decision-making is basic to growth, development and contribution. That is, people can develop a sense of identity with, and control over, their work when they are encouraged to participate in decisions that directly affect them. Leaders who encourage participation rather than direction will aid in the development of staff who can understand and identify with the goals and purpose of their own work, and also those of the organisation as a whole.

A second principle states that mutual trust and respect underpin productive human relationships. In an organisation, this means that people are more likely to develop honest and open relationships when trust is present, and the development of these relationships, in turn, will facilitate employees' abilities to work with others, in a team or otherwise.

Behavioural science further proposes that, when applied to an organisational setting, open communication supports mutual understanding. Leadership in organisations should facilitate the open sharing of information among employees because it can promote trust and respect (also seen in the second principle), which can deepen interpersonal bonds among members of an organisation.

A fourth principle suggests that conflict management by direct problem-solving confrontation promotes personal health. That is, leadership that manages conflict in a thorough and timely manner can help reduce stress amongst employees. This is beneficial not only for the employee, but also for the organisation, as paid stress leave is becoming the major health and safety issue for many. Jordan and Lloyd (2002) note that there is a growing tendency for the courts to hold employers responsible for employee injuries related to stress, providing a financial as well moral impetus to ensure stress levels are minimised in the workplace.

The assertion that handling responsibility for one's own actions stimulates initiative is the basis of the fifth principle of behavioural science that supports a participative leadership style. When adults are not allowed to be self-directing, the result can be built-up resentment and resistance to management (Reece and Brandt 1993); expanded responsibility and authority will counteract this, and give adults the opportunity to grow and develop to their potential.

Whatever theory is followed, it must be agreed that supervisors and managers have a leadership function. They are dealing with, and achieving through, people. That means not doing all the work yourself, but ensuring it is done by delegating the responsibility for it.

Delegation

Definition

Delegation is the supervisory and management function of granting, to other staff, the authority and responsibility to carry out tasks and duties which are usually seen as the responsibility of the supervisor or manager themselves. This does not necessarily mean that the accountability for such duties and tasks is handed over as well.

Authority is the right of a supervisor or manager to decide what is to be done, and who will do it.

Responsibility is an obligation to the organisation, or to someone more senior, to undertake and complete certain work.

Accountability is being held answerable to the organisation, or someone more senior, or to the community, for performing the duties for which one is responsible.

It is important to delegate, otherwise supervisors or managers can end up trying to do everything themselves. However, many people find it difficult to do, because in order to delegate, supervisors and managers must give both authority and the responsibility to the person to whom they are delegating. This can be seen as a loss of control, and it is not uncommon for managers and supervisors to fail to delegate for that reason alone. The job of the manager and the supervisor is to achieve *through others*. Delegation is also essential to ensure that work is carried out at the appropriate organisational level.

Supervisors will become familiar with the distinction between informal and formal delegation. Formal delegation will be an integral component of the organisational structure and policies. For example, purchasing or financial powers, or personnel management functions, are delegated through formal regulations which make allowance to do so.

Informal delegation implies that the supervisor gives another staff member the authority to take certain actions, to use specific resources, or to make certain decisions within defined limits. This will often mean giving staff more, or better, control over their tasks. This does not mean that the supervisor surrenders accountability, but it can help to engender trust and allow a greater measure of ownership of the tasks they are engaged in. Ownership is empowering, and it is true that people who own something tend to look after it.

Barriers to delegation

Some reasons why some supervisors find it difficult, or impossible, to delegate include:

- they feel their staff are not experienced enough for the task or duty
- they feel they haven't the time to do the necessary training
- they don't want to impose on staff who are already too busy
- they can't give responsibility for something for which they themselves are accountable
- they believe no one else is capable of carrying the responsibility
- they cannot bear to lose control and feel that they will not know what is happening
- they fear that someone else will do the job better and show them up
- they feel the task is too important to be entrusted to someone else
- they feel that they will have to be constantly checking on the person and might as well do it themselves
- they feel that people will see it as passing the buck.

These are excuses for not delegating, but they are also the very real feelings of many people who are in a position to delegate. One of the main reasons why people feel like that is a lack of supervision and management training prior to appointment to such a position. It can be too late once someone is in the job, and, unfortunately, the consequences of not delegating can be severe. The supervisor who does not delegate will become overworked and unable to sort out priorities. This will lead to feelings of confusion and dissatisfaction among other staff, and the work of a whole team or unit will suffer as a result.

How to delegate

Delegation is a motivational tool, not a tool of control, and if it is seen in that light, the guidelines that need to be followed become quite clear.

- Delegate to those who have the skills and background that will enable them to succeed at the new responsibility.

- Make it clear why the persons was chosen for a particular responsibility.

- Explain carefully and in some detail what the delegation is and why the task is being delegated. Arrange for any training to be appropriate and timely.

- Ensure the recipient of the delegation is clear on the limits to their new authority and responsibility, and the results expected.

- Make sure other staff are aware of the new delegation.

- Be available for further guidance and advice.

- Pursue and accept feedback on performance, and be prepared to modify the delegated authority if necessary. Make some allowance for the new situation.

- Don't delegate just because it is an unpleasant or monotonous task or responsibility. Some things, such as firing and disciplining, can be done only by the manager or supervisor.

- Be wary of the staff member who wants to shift the responsibility back without giving it a fair trial. The reason may be reflect a failure on your part to consider all of the above points. For example, their training may be inadequate, or you may have been unavailable for support and advice.

Individual behaviour

One feature that separates the human being from other animals is our ability to choose. Behaviour is not necessarily related to any deep-seated instinct, or range of instincts. Man is often free to choose from among alternative ways of behaving in any situation, with the result that there can be a wide variety of behaviour exhibited by the various individuals that make up a profession or an organisation. The individual is the basic component of the library as an organisation, and, in turn, individuals form groups, and groups are a large component of the library.

An understanding of individual behaviour is a prerequisite for the effective leader. It is an important part of the supervisor's and manager's role to deal with people, as individuals and in groups, and an understanding of how and why people behave differently will help them to fulfil their roles.

Consider two library assistants in circulation, or cataloguing, or reserves, who are doing exactly the same job – like charging or discharging materials, sorting or filing. Routine though the job may be, one person manages to get through their work more quickly than the other. Given the situation, one could expect their 'output' to be identical. If it is not, and all other elements being equal, then the underlying reasons need to be identified. The answer will probably lie with the individuals. It is these kinds of differences that make it important to understand why individuals behave as they do in certain situations.

To understand individual behaviour in organisations, it is necessary to consider the personality of the individual. The concepts of perception and motivation are central to the study of personality.

Perception

Perception is the psychological process through which we organise, interpret and assign meaning to what we see, hear, feel, smell and taste. It is subjective in that each of us perceives our lives and our environment from our own unique position – a position based on our physiological and psychological make up and on our own experiences.

As a supervisor or manager, it is essential to remember that different individuals can interpret the same event differently. These different perceptions will influence their behaviour. Chapter 9 briefly discussed this point in conjunction with communication barriers. For example, if you have ever said to someone 'Can't you see that I wanted that done?' you should realise that perception barriers prevented them from doing so. Stereotyping is one kind of perception barrier. For example, the supervisor who believes that all graduates of a particular university course lack practical skills may fail to give them opportunities to work on programs and projects for which they do have the requisite skills.

We may not be able to see, or perceive, things just as others do, but we can try to be aware of, and sensitive to, the causes of perceptual differences. Other perception barriers, apart from stereotyping, include:

- the halo effect – allowing one characteristic of a staff member to influence your perception of their other characteristics
- projection – the expectation that others share characteristics that we have ourselves
- selective perception – whereby individual differences cause us to filter information about a situation and produce a unique interpretation of it
- first impressions – also called the primacy effect, we often keep our first impressions as the only way to perceive a person or event
- recency effect – when the most recent information about an event or person colours the way we perceive it or them. Having the last word in an argument or discussion, for example, is an attempt to influence through the recency effect.

Supervisors and managers need to learn about human behaviour, how it is influenced, and how to be aware of, and sensitive to, those with whom they work. What motivates people to work is another area of behaviour in organisations that is worthy of our study. Once it is realised that motivational forces vary from one individual to another, it is possible to begin to understand why individuals react differently to the same situation.

Motivation

Simply defined, motivation is the drive to reduce the tension created by an unsatisfied need. If we were able to satisfy all of our needs, then we would not be motivated to perform, achieve, act, anything. Similarly, if a supervisor or manager were able to satisfy all a staff member's needs, then they would not be motivated to perform and achieve.

Why are you reading this book? Is it because it is a set text for your studies, and that if you do not study, you will not pass, and that if you fail, you may be excluded from the course? Is this pressure a motivating force? Are you reading it to satisfy your own needs for professional development? Is professional development a motivating factor?

Why do you want to be a supervisor or manager? Is it because success will lead to promotion, or further promotion; and hence to more money, more status or more power? Are these things motivators? Or is it a lack of power, status or money that motivates you (the 'push' as opposed to the 'pull' of a motivating force)?

Handy quotes Aristotle as writing:

> All men seek one goal; success or happiness. The only way to achieve true success is to express yourself completely in service to society. First, have a definite, clear, practical ideal – a goal, an objective. Second, have the necessary means to achieve your ends – wisdom, money, materials and methods. Third, adjust your means to that end (Handy 1976, p. 24).

Both success and happiness seem to be internal motivating forces which the library manager needs to harness towards the goals of the library. Some managers believe that organisational goals should motivate staff, but in doing so they may be misinterpreting one of their functions.

A number of theories have been developed and proposed to explain the complexities of human motivation. A study of some of these will help us, as supervisors and managers to work with staff to achieve the goals of the library and of the individual.

Theories of human motivation

The scope of this book does not allow more than a summary of some of the major theories of motivation. Most texts on organisational behaviour give more detail if you wish to read further. See for example Ivancevich and others (1999), and Robbins and others (1998).

Maslow's hierarchy of needs

Abraham Maslow's (1943) theory is one of the more familiar ones. He developed a hierarchy of needs, where lower needs must be satisfied before higher needs can be met (see Figure 10.1).

```
┌─────────────────────────────┐
│    Self-actualisation needs │
│         Esteem needs        │
│         Social needs        │
│         Safety needs        │
│      Physiological needs    │
└─────────────────────────────┘
```

Figure 10.1: Maslow's pyramid of human needs

Maslow's pyramid of human needs illustrates that the basic need to be satisfied is the physiological or survival one. Only when that need is satisfied will the next highest (safety or security) become important. Self-actualisation is the highest and last need, and can only be reached when all other needs are met.

The implication of this hierarchy of needs can be helpful in understanding what motivates people, and can be used to understand what motivates staff. If a person's physiological needs are not met (for example, if they do not have enough food or water, or shelter) then none of the higher level needs can act as motivators.

Maslow's theory has been criticised as being oversimplistic, but it does provide managers with some basis for understanding the motivation needs of their staff. It also led to the development of further theories on motivation.

Herzberg's two-factor theory

Frederick Herzberg and others (1959) adapted Maslow's theory and focused attention on motivation in the workplace. After extensive studies of management, Herzberg was able to divide people's needs into two significantly different classes of factors (see Figure 10.2):

- *Motivators* which relate to the content of the job (for example, the needs for achievement, recognition, meaningful work, growth, responsibility and advancement). These are all related to motivation on the job.

- *Hygiene* factors are characteristics of the work environment (for example, working conditions, pay, benefits). It is important to realise that these factors in themselves do not serve as motivators. However, if they are present, they prevent the worker from feeling dissatisfied.

Hygiene factors	Motivation factors
Salary	Work itself
Status	Recognition
Working conditions	Achievement
Benefits	Responsibility
Interpersonal relations	Advancement
Job security	Growth
Policies and administration	

Figure 10.2: Herzberg's two-factor theory

Herzberg maintained that if the organisation satisfied hygiene factors, then employees would not be dissatisfied but would be ready to be motivated. However, only the motivating factors would be able to provide motivation. This means that any activities, such as teamwork and job enrichment, which are designed to increase opportunities for growth, achievement, responsibility will provide motivation.

Like Maslow, Herzberg's theory has been the subject of some criticism about the simplistic methodology used to support its findings. However, as long as results are not interpreted too literally, the question and answer survey approach used to assess the strength of satisfiers and dissatisfiers can still be helpful. As Jordan and Lloyd (2002) note:

> ...the answers are illuminating, and do not divide neatly into Herzberg's motivators and hygiene factors, unless the researcher has set out with that particular methodology in mind (p. 53).

Vroom's expectancy theory

Victor Vroom (1964) was among the first to expound the expectancy theory of motivation. His theory is much more complex than the previous two, but can be expressed quite simply. Vroom's theory maintains that the degree of motivation rests on the probability of the desired outcome being achieved; and on the value we place on the reward we will receive in return for the effort we put into achieving the outcome.

In other words, 'What's in it for me?' If the answer to such a question is something we value, and if there is a high probability of success, then we will be motivated to achieve it. The expectancy theory requires an assessment of the relationship between effort and performance (*expectancy*), and an understanding of the connection between performance and outcome (*instrumentality*). Figure 10.3 shows how this is translated to the work situation.

Effort (amount of energy expended)	Performance (output-related behaviour)	Outcome (the goal or reward desired)
A librarian works late to complete a special project on time.	The project is completed on time.	The librarian feels good. The supervisor thanks the librarian for the extra effort, and formally acknowledges the effort at a staff meeting and on the librarian's personnel file.

Expectancy (the probability that a given effort will yield performance)	Instrumentality (the probability that a given performance will achieve an outcome
The librarian expects that the extra work will mean the project will be finished on time.	The librarian believes that finishing on time will lead to positive outcomes such as recognition.

(Based on White and Bednar 1986, p. 251.)

Figure 10.3: *Expectancy theory of motivation*

Other theories of motivation

There are other motivation theories in the literature of organisational behaviour. The more important and useful are:

- *satisfaction theories* – which assume that the employee who is satisfied will work to attain the organisation's objectives
- *incentive theories* – which assume that workers are more productive when they are given encouragement and reward
- *intrinsic theories* – which assume that the worker is more productive if the task is intrinsically worthwhile and the worker is allowed to undertake it with minimal supervision, resulting in the 'reward' coming from the job satisfaction itself
- *path-goal theories* – which assume that the worker is self-activating, and has freedom of goals and methods.

Not everyone is motivated by the same factors, and this to some extent mitigates against the simplicity of theories of motivation. For example, Schein (1980) sees people as belonging to one of four major categories:

- *Rational-economic man*, motivated mainly by the lower, economic needs. These passive staff members can be controlled by others who are self-motivated.

- *Social man*, who finds meaning in social relationships at work because much of the meaning in work itself has disappeared due to essential rationalisation. Management therefore should utilise social relationships within the work group.

- *Self-actualising man*, who is sufficiently motivated and self-controlled to match his or her own goals with those of the organisation without interference from management.

- *Complex man*, who has several motives which hierarchically change from time to time. This assists with the development of a certain flexibility in dealing with management as deemed appropriate in any given situation.

Levinson and others (1978) postulate a fifth category:

- *Psychological man,* who (similar to Maslow's two basic sets of needs in his hierarchy) passes from a physiological to a psychological stage of development. This person develops an ego ideal, and experiences a need to strive towards that ideal. Work is part of it, and motivation will depend on opportunities being provided by management for progress towards this ideal.

The variety of theories presented here indicates that there is no single formula that supervisors and managers can apply to motivate staff members for whom they are responsible. Effective motivation can only be based on a study of the principles derived from research into the subject. A good supervisor or manager needs to take into account the individual characteristics of the worker, as well as the work environment, in order to motivate and encourage staff members to perform, achieve and grow.

Supervisor's role in motivation

As noted earlier, if a supervisor or manager were able to satisfy all a staff member's needs, then they would not be motivated to perform and achieve. Fortunately, there will always be new goals, needs and aspirations. As present needs become satisfied, people keep developing new, and (as you have just seen) higher level and more complex needs. The various theories and ideas which seek to explain human motivation does provide some insight into why people behave the way they do.

Supervisors and managers who are aware of what motivates people to work will be in the best possible position to understand and relate to their staff. That gives the best opportunity for satisfactory working relationships, which in turn will ensure that efforts to achieve both library and individual goals will be most effective.

The theories also suggest that supervisors and managers cannot motivate staff: people motivate themselves – motivation comes from within.

What supervisors can do is to provide their staff with the opportunity to achieve personal goals and satisfy needs by:

- providing clear standards and objectives
- providing adequate job training
- providing opportunities to take responsibility
- being a supportive, interested supervisor
- giving regular, clear and honest feedback on performance
- providing, or keeping staff informed about, opportunities for advancement
- treating staff as worthwhile individuals.

Effective use of motivation depends on the manner in which supervisors apply their knowledge of employee needs and desires, the organisational climate that releases the capacity for work, the quality and appropriateness of training received, and the pride of the employee in the organisation.

Morale

Whereas motivation, from the point of view of the organisation, is best understood as the degree to which staff achieve satisfaction of needs via job-related activities, *morale* is the *extent* to which the same workers are satisfied, or how they feel about things.

If a worker has negative attitudes towards the library as an organisation and feels generally down about things, they could be said to have low morale. High morale is at the opposite end of the extreme. It is accompanied by positive feelings towards the library, plus a feeling of general wellbeing.

High morale, or positive feelings towards the job, is usually accompanied by a high level of job performance. Therefore, it is in the interests of the library to encourage high morale in order to improve productivity. (Measuring productivity is easy for production-line type jobs, but jobs involving less routine activities, and especially those in which there are supervision requirements, are far more difficult to measure.)

However, it is important to realise that there is not always a correlation between productivity and morale. If morale is down, it does not mean that productivity will go down as well.

> Morale reflects a person's attitudes about many things, not all of which affect productivity. It is fair to say, however, that high morale increases an employee's motivation and puts them in a frame of mind to be productive. If good supervision and good working conditions are also present, productivity will usually go up. It is possible though, to have high productivity and low morale but it is doubtful that this condition would last for any length of time. Low morale, reflecting negative attitudes, would sooner or later adversely affect output (George and Massie 1987, p. 311).

As a supervisor or manager, it is important to realise that morale is not something that you can demand from staff. Good morale is something that must be encouraged, and the best way to do this is to employ positive management characteristics such as effective communication, recognition of the individuality of the worker and respect for the individual person. To encourage high morale, it is very useful to be able to recognise the signs of low morale. Some of those signs are:

- high staff turnover
- loss of respect for management
- low productivity
- excessive waste
- high number of conflicts and grievances
- reduced cooperation
- drop in quality of work
- lack of regard for library materials and property
- rise in complaints from clients
- excessive lateness and absenteeism
- loss of interest and enthusiasm among teams.

There are a number of constructive techniques which can be used to help build morale among staff members, whether library-wide or within specific teams.

- Develop effective communications between supervisors and staff – for example, offer praise where it is due, and provide positive criticism if it is needed. Criticism should be given in a private and constructive manner.

- Be willing to speak to staff about their feelings and needs. Be open to ideas and suggestions for improvement from staff for whom you are responsible.

- Be willing and able to delegate responsibility.

- Encourage staff input to all areas of decision-making.

- Be truthful to staff. Tell them what is happening, rather than leaving them to guess.

- Try to introduce variety into job routines.

- Be certain that staff understand the expectations that you, and the library, have of them.

- Treat staff equally – don't play favourites.

Interpersonal relationships

Since supervision and management involve dealing with, and even directing, people, it is appropriate that any study in this area includes some discussion of interpersonal relations. Rather than study the individual as merely a work unit or part of the larger group, it seems reasonable to incorporate a discussion of the individual as a human being.

We all have personal needs and desires that can be satisfied only by interacting with others. Career success, family success and success with friendships all depend on building and maintaining relationships with other people. The importance of interpersonal relationships for our own personal wellbeing cannot be overemphasised. Interpersonal relationships are essential to help both cognitive and social growth. They also help us to form a positive identity and maintain psychological good health.

It is important to develop the basic interpersonal skills in order to form relationships that are essential for a happy and productive life. If we do not develop appropriate social skills, then we can expect to find ourselves alienated and isolated, and be generally at a distinct disadvantage. As children we are usually encouraged to become aware of, and interact within, their peer and social circles. Later on when we are ready to enter the workforce, we can usually adapt to the demands of the work organisation and are able to build and maintain further relationships.

Johnson (1986, p. 2) notes that 'our social and intellectual growth and development are determined by the quality and nature of our relationships with other people.' He goes on to say that our identity is built out of relationships with others. If others view us as worthwhile, we usually tend to view ourselves similarly. So it is through relationships with others that we discover ourselves as a person.

Our psychological health is dependent to a large extent upon our relationships with others. (Obviously, our physical health and wellbeing have some effect as well.) The ability to be able to form and maintain satisfying relationships is often viewed as a sign of good psychological health, whereas people who have psychological problems are often unable to form and maintain relationships and have poor interpersonal skills.

The need for acceptance is important too. Acceptance involves a response from other people to indicate we are worthwhile, whereas non-acceptance suggests we are unimportant and of little real value. This will cause people to take a negative view of themselves.

> Obviously, there are many factors that converge in our lives whose sole function is to drive us crazy. Some of those factors are in ourselves, some are in other people. But the most stressful factors are in the interpersonal process between ourselves and other

people, in the ways we interact with each other, communicate together, interpret each other, and define ourselves in the relationship (Fine 1985, p. 202).

Interpersonal skills

People are able to develop and encourage good relationships by employing a few basic skills. Johnson (1990) divides these skills into four general areas:

- Knowing and trusting one another. To establish a relationship, a high level of trust must exist between the people involved. Such openness relies on self-awareness, and if you are unaware of your own feelings and reactions, then you are unable to communicate them to others.

- Communicating with each other accurately and unambiguously. Unless both people believe the other person likes them, a relationship of any sort will not grow. This is one reason why it is important to send out unambiguous verbal and non-verbal messages.

- Accepting and supporting each other. It is important to respond in ways that are helpful to another person's problems and concerns. Communicating acceptance and support are important relationship skills.

- Resolving conflicts and relationship problems constructively. It is important to learn how to resolve conflicts to bring you and the other person closer and to result in a more developed relationship.

Sara Fine (1985, p. 207) outlines three interpersonal rights which must be part of any successful relationship.

1   The right to know 'what's going on around here anyway.'
2   The right to feel – and to resist, criticize, or challenge any change that affects our lives.
3   The right to have impact – to be heard, heeded and recognized.

The skills required to keep these rights in place are covered to some extent in this book. The discussions of supervisory skills certainly have these rights as a cornerstone when those skills are seen to affect work relationships.

Conclusion

To talk of the complexity of human interaction as though it were simple and clear is to trivialize what we are. When we speak casually of human behavior and motivation, we always risk that we fall into 'the banality of explanation' (Fine 1985, p. 202).

That risk has been ever-present in writing this chapter, but this introduction to leadership, motivation, morale and interpersonal relationships is essential. Supervisors and managers who wish to succeed as leaders must learn that simply to give, or pass on, orders is not to lead. Leading is a complex, active function; it is interpersonal; and it is, most importantly, the function through which the supervisor has most influence on staff, and on the wellbeing of the library. We can learn, through study, and through the practice of a range of skills, to become better and more effective supervisors.

Chapter 11
Decision-making and problem-solving

Nothing is more difficult, and therefore more precious, than to be able to decide. (Napoleon Bonaparte)

In any moment of decision the best thing you can do is the right thing, the next best thing is the wrong thing, and the worst thing you can do is nothing. (Theodore Roosevelt)

It isn't that they can't see the solution. It is that they can't see the problem. (G.K. Chesterton)

No problem is too big it can't be run away from. (Linus)

Introduction

As indicated in Chapter 6, every person at every level of the library is responsible for, and involved in, planning. It is impossible to set working guidelines, design job descriptions and delegate authority so specifically that no area of choice remains. Within that area of choice, and in order to plan, every member of staff is required to solve problems and make decisions.

Decision-making

Definition

A decision is a conscious choice between alternative courses of action and is a characteristic of human behaviour, individually or in groups, in all aspects of life.

We decide whether or not to cross the road; whether to have tea or coffee for breakfast; whether or not to catch up on correspondence; whether to do something today or tomorrow; whether to do or not do something. As such, decision-making is an integral part of all organisational, particularly management and supervision, activities from the most junior to the most senior levels.

In our non-work lives we are continually making choices, both conscious and unconscious, between alternative courses of action. We base those choices on rational judgment, experience, social or personal needs and desires, and on group or peer pressure. While we make decisions as a matter of course, we need to acquire some techniques and skills in organising our decisions into problem-solving statements.

My survey on library management education and training (Sanders 1993) indicated that, after communication and interpersonal skills, the skills of problem-solving and decision-making were those most required of newly qualified graduates. It is equally a requirement of managers and supervisors that they be able to make decisions and solve problems; indeed, it is seen as their job, as a delegated part of the responsibilities of those positions. Decisions need to be made about people, about materials, about equipment, and about resources, on a daily basis. Deciding how, when, what and where to communicate, for example, involves supervisors and managers in constant decision-making.

There are many types of decision – many types of problem. Some decisions can be made with little need to research or think about them. Others may require the decision-maker to, for example, gather information, consult other people, and check on policies. There are also many ways in which to tackle problems and decisions. Some of those are discussed in this chapter. However, whatever the nature of the problem, whatever the style and method we adopt, we can improve our decision-making by using problem-solving processes. This is why decision-making and problem-solving are inextricably linked, and why they are combined in this chapter.

Types of decision

There is a wide variety of ways in which decisions can be classified. Two of the most useful to consider are programmability and rationality.

Programmability

Programmable decisions are those which are routine or which recur frequently, and for which there are definite and systematic procedures established to determine the choice the manager or supervisor should make. It is possible that most of the decisions to be made in a library are of this type, with the relevant procedures being laid down in various policies, procedure manuals and regulations or rules. Typical examples would be ordering and requisitioning library materials, employment conditions, budgetary and accounting procedures, and situations which require only a form letter or memo as a response.

The supervisor's or manager's role in relation to programmable decisions areas is threefold. First, they must be involved in developing and writing policies, rules and procedures to cover such situations which recur, and to be involved in their modification when necessary. Second, they must ensure that the prescribed policies and procedures are operating in the appropriate fashion. Third, they need to decide on which matters should be regarded as exceptions and which should be removed from the standard procedures to be dealt with separately, either by the supervisor or by a more senior manager. As noted in Chapter 5, a policy may even include a statement prescribing the type of problem or situation that needs to be referred elsewhere, and to whom it should be referred.

Unprogrammable decisions, by definition, are less repetitive, less routine, more unusual. In the rarest form there may be no procedures or policies to help the manager or supervisor to deal with them, and a decision has to be made on the basis of the judgment of the individual. Typically, decisions about new policy or new major objectives fall into this category. These arise from the kinds of problems that can have many possible solutions. They will require creative thought, and some kind of decision-making process to solve them.

Rationality and decisions

A rational decision is one where appropriate means are chosen to reach desired outcomes – where appropriate methods and techniques are used to reach desired objectives. From that definition it is possible to envisage a 'rational decision-maker' as being characterised as follows.

- They are always clearly aware when they are in a choice situation – that is, they recognise that there is more than one possible alternative course of action open to them.

- They are certain that if they choose any one of the alternatives open to them, then they can predict what will happen.

- They can make a ranked preference choice between the alternatives. For example, take the case of a man who when asked what he would like to drink, has a choice among beer, scotch whisky and water. He prefers beer to scotch, scotch to water, and hence prefers beer to water as well. He can then be described as having a ranked preference of beer, scotch and water, in that order. When he faced with a choice among these drinks, he will always choose them in the order described.

Similarly, when faced with a management problem, the rational decision-maker will be aware of the need for choice; be aware of, or work at discovering, the alternatives open to them; weigh up the consequences of the choice made; and have a consistent ranked preference among the choices available. Unfortunately, such people do not exist, and thus most of the decisions that we ordinary mortals make are not perfectly rational, despite all efforts to make them so.

Some years ago I attended a library committee meeting of a city council and had to sit through part of another committee meeting first. At the first meeting the councillors made a decision to spend $1 million on upgrading the runway at the local airport. The discussion on that item took about one minute, and the recommendation was endorsed unanimously. The same group of city councillors then spent thirty minutes discussing the size and price of sandwiches to be sold in the airport cafeteria. Why was this?

The following excerpt from Robert Townsend's *Up the organization* provides some insights.

> All decisions should be made as low as possible in the organization. The Charge of the Light Brigade was ordered by an officer who wasn't there looking at the territory.
>
> There are two kinds of decisions: those that are expensive to change and those that are not.
>
> A decision to build the Edsel or Mustang (or locate your new factory in Orlando or Yakima) shouldn't be made hastily; nor without plenty of inputs from operating people and specialists.
>
> But the common or garden variety decision – like when to have the cafeteria open for lunch or what brand of pencil to buy – should be made *fast*. No point in taking three weeks to make a decision that can be made in three seconds – and corrected inexpensively later if wrong. The whole organization may be out of business while you oscillate between baby-blue or buffalo-brown coffee cups (Townsend 1971, p. 42).

Chapter 6 described planning as a process of logical decision-making, and indicated that every librarian has an area of choice within which they must undertake planning. The same applies to decision-making, and the process is very similar.

Decision-making process

A number of factors are involved in making decisions, and an awareness of these will help the individual to improve their decision-making. It is a skill, and practice and experience will obviously help.

- The *process* of decision-making contains a series of steps which, if followed, will ensure that you attempt to impose some rationality where possible. The process is to analyse the problem; develop alternative possible solutions; evaluate each alternative; and decide on the best solution for that situation; and implement it.

- *Problem analysis* involves stating what the situation is, or identifying the problem which needs to be solved; gathering the facts; deciding on objectives of the process; and discovering the constraints on the solution. Getting the facts is critical. Even at the level of day-to-day problems, getting the facts may not be easy. It becomes even more difficult the more complex the problem becomes, particularly decisions that have to be taken in the area of planning. The fewer facts that are gathered or known, the higher will be the risk and uncertainty involved in the solution.

- *Developing alternative solutions* depends upon having all the facts, and depends a great deal upon experience. However, in an environment of change, problems occur that have not been experienced before, and new approaches must be considered. Using the combined talents and ideas of a team or group, through brainstorming and other group techniques, will contribute to a greater range of possible alternatives being developed. Often the best alternatives come from creative or lateral thinking (the generation of novel solutions to problems: the point of lateral thinking is that many problems require a different perspective to solve successfully). To that end, a brief consideration of lateral thinking appears later in this chapter. As with the planning process, if there is one step which is most important in the process, it is this one – the consideration of all possible alternatives.

- *Evaluating alternatives* requires consideration of the pros and cons of each, and consideration of the extent to which each will solve the problem. At the managerial level, sophisticated data and cost-benefit techniques may be called on to assist with the most complex problems.

- *Implementing the decision* requires further use of planning skills in developing a timetable and strategy for putting the decision into action, and the means whereby the decision is communicated to those who need to know. This must take into account human factors. Acceptance of the decision can be the most important factor in the quality of the decision, and will rely on the effective use of communication and interpersonal skills.

Considering the stages in the decision-making process should help you to understand what a decision is and what it involves. The difficulties and problems associated with the process at each stage can be limited or even overcome. You will not be able to use the process in every situation, particularly where a rapid or instant decision is called for. But you will be able to apply it to a variety of other situations, and it will also enable you to reassess the validity of those past decisions that you have had to make in a hurry and which might well recur.

> Positive procrastination is a valuable management technique in this rapidly changing world. (A gem from the desk diary)

The following reflections from Marion Bannister, a former regional librarian at the Riverina Institute of TAFE and lecturer in library science and information management at Charles Sturt University, Wagga Wagga, NSW, highlight the positive benefits to staff of collaborative decision-making.

> When I invite staff to collaborate in decisions which affect services in a profound way I know that the results will be quality decisions. One of the major benefits from collaborative decision-making is that it capitalizes on the expertise and judgment of staff who, on a day-to-day basis, operate the service.
>
> Collegial involvement in decision-making is crucial to the empowering process that assists in the personal and professional development of staff. Staff members know and feel that they are valued as colleagues when they are invited to contribute to the decision-making process. Staff who have provided input and have played a significant part in the decision have a stake in the outcome of their decision and bring a personal commitment to its implementation. Collaborative decision-making provides staff members with a sense of ownership, a pride in their work and a stake in the outcome of special projects. The library manager demonstrates she or he values the staff member's judgment and skills when collaborative decision-making occurs. Staff feel empowered, supported and have an enhanced sense of self-worth when they know their leader respects their professional judgments because she or he takes their advice.
>
> An example of collaborative decision-making that I was involved in occurred recently. Staff had identified the need for more structured training sessions in reference skills. The Reference Librarian, Support Services Coordinator and I had discussed the need for more formal long-term strategies for in-house training. We met to brainstorm ideas. We discovered that the Support Services Coordinator was best at refining the strategies and I was best at encouraging the development of ideas. After what was a very short period we came up with a new and innovative way to address the training problem in both the long and short terms. In this way together we identified the area of greatest needs, how we should address them, and how we could find the time to do this. Most importantly, the three of us were committed to finding the time and implementing the decision.
>
> When I have reservations with the advice from staff, and the consequences are not far reaching, and time is not critical, I often suggest piloting or trialling as a way of testing decisions. After trialling and evaluation by the staff member, then the decision can be examined critically. Such trialling often demonstrates to me or to the staff member that the decision was workable and worth integrating into the system, or that it will need to be modified or discarded.
>
> Ultimately the leader must take responsibility for the decision made in the organization. However, the leader is able to do so with the confidence that the staff are not only committed to the decision but have contributed their expertise and valuable experience to the best possible outcome at that time and that place (Bannister 1995, quoted in Sanders 1995, pp. 167–168).

Problem-solving

Research into problem-solving has shown that:

- problem-solving procedures can be learned, and are not necessarily an inherent skill
- problem-solving can improve with practice
- the better problem-solvers have a tolerance of uncertainty; are creative; are reflective; and are not impulsive

- problem-solving is better in organisations that promote questioning; encourage critical enquiry; value new ideas; encourage independent work; are non-directive; provide all staff with the knowledge required to attack problems occurring in their work.

As with decision-making, there are many approaches to problem-solving.

Note that problem-solving is not the same as decision-making. Decision-making is but one process of problem-solving and is only concerned with deciding between different existing ideas. Problem-solving includes the actual formation of those ideas and can involve varying degrees of problem analysis and solution generation.

The decision-making process outlined above bears a remarkable resemblance to the many versions of the process of problem-solving which appear in the literature. What is useful in the context of this book is to consider some strategies and aids for solving problems and making decisions. These are by no means all-inclusive, as you will find when you read further.

Strategies

The following list of strategies is not a step-by-step process for problem-solving, although the first five items do constitute the beginning stages of the process. The idea is to use whatever strategies are appropriate in the situation.

- read the problem carefully; re-read if necessary
- determine the meaning of key words or special terms
- state the problem in simple words
- list the important information or facts
- consider what additional information or facts is required
- draw a picture or diagram of the problem
- look for patterns
- break the problem into smaller parts
- recall similar problems and how they were solved
- use systematic trial and error (guess and check)
- work backwards from the final result
- be flexible; try different approaches beyond the obvious
- match the solution with the original problem – does it make sense? is it accurate?

The guide in Figure 11.1 may be of use to those who feel their problem-solving processes need some organisation or improvement. Keep a record of the problems and solutions, see if they are effective, and monitor the results.

Exploring the problem-solving process, and the strategies employed in solving problems, should provide some insight into the assumptions made, the evidence required and the logical processes involved.

Problem-solving guide			
Define the problem in simple terms			
List possible solutions			
Weigh up each alternative			
Solution	*Cost*	*Probable effect*	*Comments*
Recommended solution			
Implementation plan			
Evaluate the decision *When first implemented*			
Three months later			

Figure 11.1: *Problem-solving guide*

Decision matrix

Hill and others (1979) describe a decision matrix method that can be used to analyse alternative ways of solving a problem, or making a choice of decisions. It can be used, or at least considered, when confronted with a complex problem, and when faced with making non-routine, unprogrammable decisions.

Reflect back on the comments earlier in this chapter on the decision-making process. The decision matrix method focuses on the *evaluating alternatives* aspect of the process, and involves a number of critical steps:

- identify your alternatives
- establish selection criteria that will help in making an appropriate choice
- assign a number to each feature or criterion according to its relative importance or priority

- identify weighting factors
- identify a consistent scoring system
- evaluate your identified alternatives.

Figure 11.2 is an example of a decision matrix proforma, although there are, of course, numerous ways of depicting the process.

Criteria	Priority	Weighting *	Alternatives							
			A		B		C		D	
			Raw score (RS)	RS X weight	Raw score (RS)	RS X weight	Raw score (RS)	RS X weight	Raw score (RS)	RS X weight
Total										

* Weighting equals priority divided by the sum of the priority assigned to all criteria

Figure 11.2: Decision matrix proforma

Note that the decision matrix is not a method of identifying or defining your alternatives, but rather a decision-making aid for analysing alternatives which are already apparent or visible to you. What uses can you see for all this in any decisions you or your colleagues may need to make in the library or information agency in which you work? Try it out on some decision which you, or someone you know, has recently made. Consider whether it might have affected the decision. Could the matrix be used, for example, as a staff selection or appraisal aid?

Decision-making exercise

Try the following exercise to test your decision-making skills, using the decision matrix method.

You are considering the purchase of a number of laptop computers for senior staff in your library at Wagga Wagga. They will be used for the following functions.

Functionality	Product/ purpose	Frequency
Word processing and desktop publishing	letters, memos	daily
	library annual reports	annual
	reports to funding body	monthly
	library publications	irregular
Spreadsheet	budget records	weekly
	membership statistics	weekly
	circulation statistics	weekly
Database	program budgets	weekly
	staff records	irregular
Internet	University intranet	daily
	information searches	daily
	email	daily

The laptops will be used in various locations in the library by senior staff, most of whom have experience with all of the software. They will also be taken home on a regular basis in order to allow staff to work on papers, access their email and undertake any other work-related activities that may be done from home.

Storage capacity on the laptops should be as large as possible to allow for the use of graphics software and the manipulation of digital images, and the ability to link the laptops via a network card to the main University network at work is also necessary. Processor speed is also very important to ensure the most efficient and effective use.

Internet and email access will require an in-built modem and the ability to connect to a broadband network is also desirable.

Four models of laptop seem to be appropriate and available, and you need to make a decision about which one to purchase. Initially it is anticipated that six machines will be acquired and ideally, we would acquire these as soon as possible in order to assist with the end of financial year processing.

The choices

- ABC – This is a widely available laptop commonly used in business and the education sector. Features include: standard operating systems and popular office applications software (that match those in use on the networked system), but only a mid-range not desktop publishing package. There is an in-built modem but to equip it for broadband access will cost extra. The machine weighs 2.5kg and has a larger than normal screen, a CD/DVD drive, 30Gb hard drive which is upgradeable if required and a processor speed of 1.3Ghz. It has an in-built mouse button but has the ability to connect an 'ordinary' mouse (this would be an extra cost). The machine is in stock and available for immediate delivery if accepted 'as is'. However to ensure the laptop can 'talk' to the main network in the library a network card needs to be installed which cannot be done for two weeks. It is also an additional cost. If anything goes wrong, the nearest servicing agent is in Sydney (500 kms away) and would require the laptop sent to them to do any work. Once the warranty expires, the machine can be included in the overall warranty covering all of these products held in the library for very little cost. The standard cost for the package is $2,500 with the broadband and network card and mouse an additional $700.

- MACIVER – This has the perfect software package for your needs, including high quality graphics and sophisticated desktop publishing software. While different to the software in use on the main system, it is claimed to be 100% compatible. Features include: a CD/DVD drive, 30Gb expandable disk, a 4Ghz processor speed but it appears very quick, a standard sized screen and in-built tracker ball. It weighs 2kg. Again, to enable the machine to connect to the network and accept broadband it will have to have appropriate cards and software installed at extra cost. It is a well-established product which has a niche market. Servicing is available in Canberra (250 kms away) and again, the machine would need to be sent away if anything went wrong. The warranty can be extended from twelve months for as long as required but is quite costly. Because the machine is not directly compatible with the main network, support cannot be included in the main network support agreement. The standard cost for this package is $2,400with the broadband, and network card an additional $300. These could be installed and setup within 24 hours. Warranty after the first year will be $250 pa.

- COBBER – This is a popular laptop with the home market. It is well-known for reliability, with servicing available in Wagga Wagga. It comes equipped with standard office software in a 'cut down' home version, including a modest desktop publishing package. All of this software should be compatible with the main system. It would need the broadband hardware installed as well as the network card to talk to the main network. This could be done in 24 hours. It has a CD drive, 30Gb drive and a processor speed of 1.5Ghz. It has a normal external mouse, standard screen and is fairly heavy at 3.5kg. The warranty can be extended from twelve months for as long as required and is relatively cheap. Because the machine is not directly compatible with the main network, support cannot be included in the main network support agreement. The standard cost for this package is $2,000 with the broadband, and network card an additional $300. These could be installed and setup within 24 hours. Warranty after the first year will be $150 pa.

- BANANA – This is a new, high end machine with sophisticated graphics handling capability. It comes with standard operating systems and popular office applications software (that match those in use on the networked system), and a highly developed desktop publishing package. There is an in-built modem and broadband access is included in the price. The machine weighs 2kg and has a larger than normal screen, a CD/DVD drive, 50Gb hard drive and a processor speed that seems lightning fast. It is supported from Sydney and would need to be sent away for repair. Enabling the machine to connect to the main network would be tricky but 'should' be possible. Total price also includes a three year warranty. A clever 'smart' mouse is also included. Total cost would $3,500 and delivery would be one month.

To do this exercise effectively you need to bear in mind the steps identified above:

- identify your alternatives (this step has already been done)
- establish selection criteria that will help in making an appropriate choice – to determine what features you will use to evaluate your alternatives you will need to look at what functions you need, and the situation/circumstances in which the laptop will be used
- assign a number to each feature or criterion according to its relative importance or priority (note that more than one criterion can be assigned the same level of priority)
- identify weighting factors – to do this you add up the numbers assigned to all the criteria, then divide the number assigned to each criterion by the total. To help here, have a look at the following:

Criteria	Priority	Weighting
Criterion A	10	10/30 = 0.33
Criterion B	8	8/30 = 0.26
Criterion C	8	8/30 = 0.26
Criterion D	4	4/30 = 0.13
Total	30	N/A

Hill and others (1979) give valuable guidance on how to select criteria and make judgements about the priority rankings and ratings.

Once you've determined the criteria, and the associated weightings, consider each alternative in terms of how well it meets those criteria. To do this, you need to design a scoring/rating system so that you are consistent in your judgment of how each option satisfies the criteria.

I have included my own ratings at the end of the chapter.

Problem-solving exercise: lost at sea

To give you some practice at problem-solving, the opportunity to reflect on what you have studied so far and some light relief, attempt the following exercise which is based on based on Nemiroff and Rasmore (1975, pp. 28–34). It is an oft-reproduced problem posed by the United States (US) Merchant Marine and as such requires a knowledge base which most, if not all, of you will not have. But you can use what knowledge you do have to go close to choosing the right items. And remember, people's lives are depending on you!

Instructions: You are adrift on a private yacht in the South Pacific. As a consequence of a fire of unknown origin, much of the yacht and its contents have been destroyed. The yacht is now slowly sinking. Your location is unclear because of the destruction of critical navigational equipment and because you and the crew were distracted trying to bring the fire under control. Your best estimate is that you are approximately 1600 kilometres south-southwest of the nearest land.

Below is a list of fifteen items that are intact and undamaged after the fire. In addition to these articles, you have a serviceable rubber life raft with oars, which is large enough to carry you, the crew, and all the items listed below. The total contents of all the survivors' pockets are a package of cigarettes, several books of matches, and five five-dollar bills.

Your task is to rank the fifteen items below in terms of their importance to your survival. Place the number '1' by the most important item and '2' by the second most important, and so on through '15', the least important.

Sextant	_____
Shaving mirror	_____
Five-litre can of water	_____
Mosquito netting	_____
One case of army 24 hour rations	_____
Maps of the Pacific Ocean	_____
Standards approved floating seat cushion	_____
Two-litre can of oil-petrol mix	_____
Two boxes of chocolate bars	_____
Fishing kit	_____
Five metres of nylon rope	_____
One litre of overproof Bundaberg Rum	_____
20 square metres of opaque plastic	_____
Shark repellent	_____
Small transistor radio	_____

When you have completed your ranking decision, compare it with the answers at the end of this chapter. In doing so, note the difference between your ranking and the number assigned by the United States (US) Merchant Marine in a comparable exercise. Then add up all those differences to find your 'score'. If your ranking is identical to the 'official' one for *all* items, you will score zero. If your ranking is exactly the opposite, your score will be 210. I suspect you will all score somewhere in between.

The problem involves both specialist and general knowledge, and which allows little room for flexibility. As noted earlier, the better problem-solvers are creative and flexible, especially in the area of unprogrammable decision-making. The list of problem-solving strategies suggests that you be flexible and attempt different approaches to solving problems.

Conclusion

Decision-making and problem-solving are activities which are undertaken every day by every person. They are constant activities in supervision and management. There are processes and strategies which can help in solving problems and making decisions whether they are small and simple, or large and complex. Simple problems deserve to be treated as such and solved quickly. Programmable decisions can generally be made on the basis of established rules, procedures and policies. More complex decisions require careful use of a process of logical decision-making, and the input of people who have the relevant expertise and experience.

The key to successful problem-solving and decision-making is to gain a knowledge of all possible facts, generate and consider a large enough range of alternative solutions, and to check the final decision to ensure that it fulfils the requirements of the organisation and the people whom it affects.

Answers to exercises: decision matrix

Rating of criteria

Criteria	Priority	Weighting
Software	10	10/68=.15
Price	9	9/68=.13
Compatability	8	8/68=.12
Portability	8	8/68=.12
Storage	8	8/68=.12
Processor	8	8/68=.12
Large screen	6	6/68=.09
Service/support	5	5/68=.07
Delivery time	4	4/68=.06
DVD	2	2/68=.03
Total	**68**	1.01

Judgments for ranking of decisions

Software:	It is assumed all office software is supplied. Desk Top Publishing is crucial – professional 10, medium 8, home use 6.
Base price:	All items multiplied by six: $12000 10; $15000 8; $20000 4.
Compatability:	Complete 10; demonstrated 8; needs extra 4.
Portability:	2.4kg or less 10; 2.5–3kg 8; 3.1kg or more 5.
Storage:	50Gb or more 10; 40Gb 8; 30Gb 6.
Processor:	Greater than 4Ghz 10; 3-4Ghz 7; less than 3Ghz 4.
Screen:	Large 10; standard 5.

Service/support: Local 10; Canberra 6; Sydney 5.
Delivery time: 2 days or less 10; up to 2 weeks 7; more than 2 weeks 3.
DVD: Yes 10; No 7

My answer, using the decision matrix method is:

Criteria	Priority	Weighting *	Alternatives							
			ABC		MACIVER		COBBER		BANANA	
			Raw score (RS)	RS X weight	Raw score (RS)	RS X weight	Raw score (RS)	RS X weight	Raw score (RS)	RS X weight
Software	10	.15	8	1.20	10	1.50	6	0.90	10	1.15
Price	9	.13	6	0.78	7	0.91	9	1.17	4	0.52
Compatability	8	.12	10	1.20	8	0.96	8	0.96	4	0.48
Portability	8	.12	8	0.96	10	1.20	8	0.96	10	1.20
Storage	8	.12	6	0.72	6	0.72	6	0.72	10	1.20
Processor	8	.12	7	0.84	7	0.84	4	0.48	10	1.20
Screen	6	.09	10	0.90	5	0.45	5	0.45	10	0.90
Service/support	5	.07	5	0.35	6	0.42	10	0.70	6	0.42
Delivery time	4	.06	7	0.42	10	0.60	10	0.60	3	0.18
DVD	2	.03	10	0.30	10	0.30	7	0.21	10	0.30
TOTAL	**68**	**1.01**	**77**	**7.67**	**79**	**7.9**	**73**	**7.05**	**77**	**7.9**

* Weighting equals priority divided by the sum of the priority assigned to all criteria

Figure 11.3: *Decision matrix answers*

Therefore, my choice of microcomputer would be the BANANA or MACIVER. How did your answer compare? Did we make different judgements about the priority of various criteria, or on how well each of the alternatives satisfied the criteria? Why? Was the exercise useful, and did it really assist in unravelling the complexity of judgements to be made in this case? Given that the same decision could have been reached on the sum of raw scores alone, do you think it is a useful decision making method?

Lost at sea answer and rationale

According to a survey of officers in the US Merchant Marines, the basic supplies needed when a person is stranded in mid-ocean are articles to attract attention and articles to aid survival until rescuers arrive

Articles for navigation are of little importance; even if a small life raft were capable of reaching land, it would be impossible to store enough food and water to subsist during that period of time. Therefore, the shaving mirror and the can of oil-petrol mixture are of primary importance as they could be used for signalling air-sea rescue.

Of secondary importance are items such as water and food, such as the case of Army rations.

A brief rationale is provided for the ranking of each item. These brief explanations obviously do not represent all of the potential uses for the specified items, but rather the primary importance of each.

1　Shaving mirror – critical for signalling air-sea rescue.
2　Two-litre can of oil-petrol mix – critical for signalling. The oil-petrol mixture will float on the water and could be ignited with a piece of paper and a match (obviously outside the raft).
3　Five-litre can of water – necessary to replenish loss by perspiration.

4 Case of Army food rations – provides basic food intake.
5 Twenty square metres of opaque plastic – used to collect rainwater and provide shelter from the elements.
6 Two boxes of chocolate bars – a reserve food supply.
7 Fishing kit – ranked lower than the chocolate because 'a bird in the hand is worth two in the bush.' That is, you have no assurance that you will catch any fish.
8 Five metres of nylon rope – may be used to lash equipment together to prevent it from falling overboard.
9 Floating seat cushion– if someone fell overboard, it could be used as a life-preserver.
10 Shark repellent – for obvious reasons
11 One litre of overproof Bundaberg rum – the alcohol content should be adequate for use as a potential antiseptic for any injuries incurred. Note: it will not keep you warm, and if drunk may lead to hypothermia and dehydration.
12 Small transistor radio – of little value since there is no transmitter. (Unfortunately, you are out of range of your favourite radio stations.)
13 Maps of the Pacific Ocean – worthless without additional navigational equipment – it does not really matter where you are, but where your rescuers are.
14 Mosquito netting – there are no mosquitoes in the mid-Pacific and it is too delicate to fish with.
15 Sextant – without tables and a chronometer, it is useless.

The basic rationale for ranking signalling equipment above life-sustaining items (food and water) is that without signalling devices, there is almost no chance of being spotted and rescued. Furthermore, most rescues occur during the first thirty-six hours and one can survive without food and water during this period.

Chapter 12
Team development and maintenance

> Coming together is a beginning, staying together is progress, and working together is success. (Henry Ford)

Introduction

While this aspect of supervision is often known as team management, for the sake of those who hear manipulative nuances in the word 'management', it is better called team building, or team development and maintenance. I prefer to use the latter term as a generic one to cover all aspects of the supervisor's role in teamwork. What, then, is a team?

A team can be defined as a group of people working towards a common objective. This will encompass sports teams, sales teams, production teams, and so forth, without really telling you what makes them a team and not just a group. A team can be further defined as 'a group of people who bring to their work a set of complementary and appropriate skills, and who hold themselves mutually accountable for achieving a clear and identifiable set of goals' (Hick 1998).

Dwyer (2000) differentiates between teams and groups as follows:

> The term 'team' and 'group' are frequently used interchangeably, since on many occasions they share almost identical characteristics. However, though a team can always be loosely classified as a group, a group may not conform to the more specific criteria for a team, which are as follows:
> - members operate according to a mandate
> - they are assigned specific roles
> - they consider the team is responsible for achieving specified organisation goals.
>
> A work team may form in various ways. The most common kind of team is set up by management. A team may, however, gradually evolve with its own particular structure and behaviours (2000, p. 157).

A team, then, is not just a group of people working together, or working in the same area. A good example of a group, as opposed to a team, is a number of people standing in front of a shop counter waiting to be served. They all have a similar objective, but they are not committed to each other and will probably not contribute to each other's efforts to be served. What makes the difference between a group of people and a team is that team members are dependent upon each other to ensure they achieve their common goals. This comparison applies in the library situation as well.

Teamwork is the ability to work together toward a common vision, the ability to direct individual achievements towards group objectives. It can enable ordinary people to attain extraordinary results.

Further additions to the definition are needed.

> A team is a working group of people who are jointly responsible for carrying out the tasks which they have been set. Their *commitment* to the task, their *willingness* to *participate in decision-making* related to the task, their *acceptance of* the group's *decisions*, and their *application* to the work involved, all indicate their *loyalty* to the group (Barlow 1989, p. 6 formatting added).

Note in particular the factors in *italics*. We can incorporate into this the notions that self-managing teams will often assign their own tasks rather than have them set by others and that a team with no diversity in it will be unlikely to work in an innovative fashion.

This chapter aims to consider the building, development and maintenance of teams from the supervisory point of view. Teamwork is no longer a new organisational method, and has gradually been introduced into, and understood by libraries. Most writings on the subject reflect the trials, errors and successes of implementing teamwork into a variety of library systems and organisations. Much of the material for the chapter has been excerpted from Hick (1998) and has been reproduced with permission.

Why teams?

Why do we work in teams? Why are teams worth the effort of building and maintaining?

> The organization will see tend to see team management as a means of distributing and controlling work, solving problems, making decisions, improving communication, increasing commitment, and resolving conflict.

> Individual library staff may see the team more as a means of satisfying social needs, giving them a greater 'sense of belonging' at work...staff who are well motivated have a real sense of wishing to share in the team effort to achieve common and agreed objectives (Bluck 1996, p. 1).

Teams come in a variety of shapes and forms, and can be permanent, semi-permanent or temporary. Some come together, or are built, to achieve a specific purpose, or a range of purposes, and then are disbanded. More importantly, there are ongoing activities or operations, and medium-term projects, which will benefit from building teams to accomplish them. The human development benefits of teamwork are such that many libraries use them as permanent units for providing basic services and operations.

Team organisation of work within library management structures is becoming increasingly common. This growth can be attributed to a desire on the part of staff and enlightened management to establish working environments that treat employees well, and that allow and practice participation in the planning, organising and controlling of work. Through teamwork, through formal work groups, people can be encouraged to see themselves as instruments of change, to work towards shared and relevant service goals, to be respected and appreciated, to be included and to participate in decisions affecting themselves and the library as a whole.

Teamwork often leads to increased job satisfaction, giving staff a chance to improve and widen their range of skills, especially when it involves cross-training and job rotation. Participation in work teams also increases job satisfaction by providing team members with unique opportunities that would not otherwise be available. For example, they will have the authority to make decisions and solve problems related to the tasks the team is charged with, they will have leadership opportunities, and the quality of decisions made should be improved because they will be able to view problems from a range of perspectives (Skopec and Smith 1997).

All of these factors must lead to improved productivity, improved individual and team performance, and therefore to improved goal achievement and customer service.

There is no precise formula for deciding when, where, why, and how to decide to implement team structures into the library's organisation. The experience of many libraries has shown, however, that the management of change, especially fast-moving and rapidly changing situations, is least successful within the traditional hierarchical and centralised organisational structure. It is also clear that the introduction of a TQM philosophy and its attendant processes will be enhanced with the adoption of team approaches to work. As one writer states:

> Certain conditions occur in the work situation that do underscore the limitations and weaknesses of traditional functional arrangements. Those conditions, which seem to respond effectively to team structures, are:
>
> - when one must attain a high quality end product in a limited period of time within specified budgetary resources;
> - when one attempts to solve new or complex problems;
> - when a rapid response to a problem situation or emergency is required, when consequences grow more serious over time, or when extremely tight deadlines must be met;
> - when experimentation with innovative ways of doing things is necessary;
> - when client satisfaction is an absolute must (Koteen 1997, p. 296; formatting changed).

Tom Peters (1988, p. 296) in his renowned work *Thriving on chaos*, suggests that the basic organisational foundation should be the 'modest-sized, task-oriented, semiautonomous, mainly self-managing team'.

He adds, in relation to strategies for ensuring the success of team building: 'train them; recruit on the basis of teamwork potential; pay them for performance; and clean up the bureaucracy around them' (Peters 1988, p. 297).

Hall (1999) outlined the results of research in which teams were found to be leader-focused and the most frequently cited examples of good teamwork tended to depend on attitudes rather than skills. Communication was seen as a key skill, but task-centred skills such as decision-making were more important in working parties than in permanent teams. Suggested areas for attention included leadership training, staff selection, communication with part-timers and open communication skills.

Teams are not always effective

Teams can be very effective. In many situations teams can achieve more than individuals working on their own. This is because teams can bring to bear a wider range of skills and experience to solve a problem. Teams also produce better quality decisions.

However, teams can be highly dysfunctional. They can develop a 'group think' mentality (where team members feel pressure not to disagree with each other) that can produce bad decisions. They can be disruptive, leading to arguments and discord in the organisation. They can be enormously wasteful of people's time and energy.

Teams are not for everyone, and some staff will baulk at the responsibility, effort and learning required in team settings. Staff who are forced unwillingly into a team situation may withhold their efforts and fail to perform their share of the work, or limit their involvement in the team's work. Team decision-making can be very time consuming, and this can be exacerbated when one or two team members dominate the team discussions (Shonk 1997).

In short, teams can be good, but they can also be bad. If the role of teams is to be positive, people must learn how to make them work effectively.

What is team effectiveness?

A team can be considered to be effective if its output is judged to meet or exceed the expectations of the people who receive the output. This is a question of the customer being right. If the team has been given some task to perform, the people who have assigned the task are the people who will judge whether the result is satisfactory.

The second criterion is that teams should still be able function effectively after they have completed their task. This means that even if the team has been disbanded, the people should have an enhanced working relationship that benefits the organisation.

Finally, effectiveness is judged by whether the team feels satisfied with its efforts. If the team members are pleased with their efforts, if the experience has been a good one, if time spent away from their normal work has been worth the effort, the team has most likely been effective.

What are the factors that contribute towards an effective team?

There has been a great deal of research into the subject of team effectiveness over the last decade or so and there is a consensus on what factors must be controlled in order to set up and run effective teams.

There are three areas of group behaviour that must be addressed for teams to be effective:

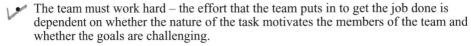

- The team must work hard – the effort that the team puts in to get the job done is dependent on whether the nature of the task motivates the members of the team and whether the goals are challenging.
- The team must have the right mix of skills – these skills include technical, problem-solving and interpersonal skills.
- The team must be able to develop appropriate approaches to problem-solving – this depends on developing strategies and using appropriate techniques for problem analysis.

What factors contribute to hard work, skill development and effective problem-solving strategies?

- The task itself should be motivating. One of the factors affecting the effort the team is likely to put into the job is the job itself. The characteristics of the job should provide motivation. The job should require a variety of high-level skills to make it interesting.
- The task itself should be seen as being worthwhile. It needs to be a clear and complete piece of work with a clear and visible outcome so that people can feel a sense of ownership.

- The outcome of the task should be perceived as being important. The end results of the team's efforts should affect others in the organisation and/or have a positive impact on the library's customers.

- The task should provide the team with an opportunity for self regulation. The team itself should have considerable autonomy to decide how the work is to be done.

- Feedback should be provided on the how well the team is performing. Effective teams regularly review how they are doing; and management has a very clear responsibility to provide regular and positive feedback.

- The team needs challenging goals which are clearly defined. For problem-solving teams the most important factor that fosters the hard work and effort necessary for success is having clear, measurable and challenging goals. If goals are unclear or too easy to achieve the team will not be motivated to make the extra effort that separates a high performance team from an ineffective group. When challenging goals are set the team will mobilise its efforts to find innovative ways to achieve feats that may have been considered impossible. Providing a challenging job is the most important motivator to sustain group effort.

- The team needs to be involved in the setting of the goals. In most cases a team has been set up to achieve a set of prescribed goals. Team members should spend some time discussing the goals and if necessary they should have the opportunity to negotiate the goals with management. They must have the opportunity to be involved in setting, and in committing to achieving, the goals.

- Rewards are important. Rewards reinforce the motivational aspects of having a well-designed task and challenging goals. People tend to be most effective when they engage in behaviours that are rewarded, so the rewards need to suit the personal characteristics of the people on the team. Rewards do not need to be financial – although they may be. Simply providing recognition for a job well done can be all that is required. Whatever form the reward takes, it is important that group effort be recognised, It can be de-stabilising and destructive to single out individuals from the group, when there has been a group effort.

- The team should have the right mix of skills. This is partly a matter of assigning appropriately experienced and skilled people, by reviewing the job to determine what skills are required, and by selecting staff so that the team has the right balance. Required skills include job-related (technical) skills, problem-solving and decision-making skills, interpersonal skills such as listening skills, and the ability to take criticism well. Training or coaching should be provided to make up any skill deficits.

Team activities are in fact a powerful vehicle for building skills. People learn skills from each other. They learn how other parts of the organisation function. Teams serve to build up a repertoire of skills in the organisation and this enhances the organisation in the long term.

Team members contribute specialist knowledge, but they should also be encouraged to be generalists in the way they behave in the team – opportunities need to be made available for individuals to take a time of leading, of contributing to team culture development, of generating new ideas, of training, and so forth.

- Agree on a code of conduct. At the beginning of a team project it is important to agree on a set of rules to ensure that team efforts are clearly directed and that all members contribute to the work. The most critical rules pertain to attendance, open discussion, using an analytical approach, not pulling rank over other members, planning the work and sharing work assignments. This will ensure that the work is done well and done on time.

- Contribute ideas and solutions. The willingness of all team members to draw on their own expertise and experience to contribute ideas and solutions is a vital factor in what makes an effective team. Team members should feel comfortable enough in the team setting to express themselves, and know that their ideas have value. Creative input from a variety of individual perspectives is the basis of effective problem-solving. Team culture must encourage contributions, not inhibit them.

- Support and trust. Ideally, the team can be an open, supportive, non-threatening environment but in reality there is often much at stake between people at work (personal rivalry, politics), which does not make deep personal exchanges with others an easy process.

  Trustful and supportive working relationships develop from positive orientations to others, from being helpful and endeavouring to understand the perception and difficulties of others. Support and trust can be observed from our behaviour and how we reveal our attitudes to others. There is no easy, idealised package of skills, but team members can examine their assumptions about others and work hard to offer non-judgmental and positive regard for individuals in the team, not allowing their own feelings to limit how they relate to others when working with them.

Garfield (1999, p. 5) offers the following insights into why people perform better in peak-performing teams than they would individually:

> Because they have coworkers with whom they can brainstorm and innovate. Most innovation is collaborative, despite the fact that we still believe that Thomas Edison, Albert Einstein, and a few chosen people in the back room are coming up with major breakthroughs all by themselves. If I have colleagues to brainstorm with, if I have people on whom I can rely for facts and strategies and tactics, and if we're all part of the same team pulling in the same direction toward shared missions and goals, then we'll see what I saw on the Apollo 11 project, one of the greatest collaborative efforts in history.

Team building

A team is a group of people working towards a common goal. 'Team building' is the process of enabling that group of people to reach their goal. It includes strategies such as bringing people together in formal group meetings for open discussion of broad-based issues. It means encouraging positive, informal interactions between group members. It means instilling an attitude of continuous improvement throughout the library. It means being alert to, and quickly trying to reverse, team-building problems such as jealousy, cynicism, and defensive behaviour.

In its simplest terms, the stages involved in team building are:

- ensuring that team goals are clarified and agreed, or committed to
- identifying factors which constrain the team from reaching their goals
- addressing those factors, removing or at least mitigating the constraints, and enabling the goals to be achieved.

Team building can also take a different form depending on the size of the team and nature of its goals and activities. In a project environment, for example, where team composition is continually changing, the emphasis must be on developing the skills in individuals to be effective team members. On the other hand, in teams where membership is static for a reasonable time, how the individuals within the team relate can have a major impact on team performance. If a member leaves, or another joins, the dynamics of the team can be changed greatly.

One of the key aims of team building is to change the behaviours and attitudes prevalent in the organisation, which are almost independent of who actually works there – new recruits who are 'different' often start behaving in accord with the existing culture.

Team building process

Staff selection

Team building begins while you are still selecting and recruiting staff for your library. It begins by hiring people who will work well together; it means beginning to develop a shared vision and commitment.

Agreed direction

To build effective teams, you not only need to show people where the library – and their specific team – is headed, but you need to get them to agree with and commit to that direction. We cannot expect people to support a team, or the library as a whole, if they don't agree with where it's headed or, worse, don't even know where it's headed.

Commitment and agreement is best built by meeting both team and individual needs to know and be involved with the library's vision for the future; management's strategy for getting there; why this is the best strategy; and by recognising every achievement that indicates the team is effective.

Meetings build teams

Part of building an effective team is having some group meetings. Meetings, or even parties or celebrations, with as many people as possible from the entire team, or even the whole library, help build a feeling of solidarity throughout the team and library.

It is also important to have everyone participate in smaller group meetings where some work is done or some decisions are made. This makes people feel that they aren't just part of some big group, but that they are an active, important part of a team.

For example:

- *do* have an interactive meeting once per week
- *don't* have meetings where people just make announcements and talk about the work that's been done and needs to be done
- *do* have meetings where everyone has an opportunity to give feedback on substantive issues.

Getting interaction

Perhaps the most difficult part of building a winning team is encouraging staff to work together in positive, informal interaction whether the team leader, or anyone who is 'management', is present or not.

For example:

- have team members take part in the selection process for new team members
- assign specific projects for two team members to work on together
- try to arrange for close proximity of work spaces, desks, offices, and so forth
- take your team off-site for formal meetings as well as casual get-togethers to build a sense of bonding;

Be aware of potential disruptions

There are limitless numbers of possible disruptions, and the worst are those which have the potential to affect the whole team. Some of these include jealousy, cynicism, lack of confidence. The team leader and team members need to have appropriate interpersonal skills to be able to recognise these problems before and as they occur, and be able to resolve them before they affect the whole team.

Review, feedback, measure

Be aware that team building never stops. Effective teams regularly review how they are doing. Without regular and constant follow-up, you cannot hope to get lasting behavioural change. Team building is sometimes viewed as being like staff training – if you just give people the correct knowledge, they will be able to apply it ever after. However, effective teams are constantly looking to improve – to further their potential.

Feedback is essential. Feedback provides the information needed to fix things that are broken and develop further those things that are effective. All team members should be encouraged to actively seek, and give, feedback. It is also important to translate feedback into positive changes, to ensure that the changes are acceptable to the team, and not to make change overwhelming by trying to tackle too many areas at once.

Types of Teams

From the perspective of organisational improvement there are three types of teams:

- the problem-solving team
- the work team
- the senior management team.

Work teams are often used as the basic organisational unit, problem-solving teams are used separately to improve the way the organisation performs in specific areas, and management teams are used to develop strategy and to drive the changes.

Problem-solving teams

Generally speaking problem-solving teams are established with a clearly defined task to investigate a problem and recommend a solution. The team is generally disbanded when the task is completed and members go back to their normal organisational duties, although they may sometimes be involved in implementing the solution.

There are two important issues facing problem-solving teams. One is getting started, and the other is handing over the recommendations for implementation. The key to getting started is to ensure that the team is committed to achieving an agreed set of goals. Goals serve to focus the team's effort.

Implementation is important. It will not just happen; it must be planned. Those charged with implementation must be brought into the solution stage so that they develop a sense of ownership towards the solution and buy into it. The best way to do this is to have the problem-solving team do the implementation.

Another approach is to phase those charged with implementation into the team so that the membership changes prior to the implementation. Whatever approach is used one should remember that the idea is to implement a solution and not to produce a report.

Work teams

Work teams are different in that they are a fixed part of the organisation. They have an ongoing function to control a set of activities that make up a discrete operation in the overall service process and need to focus on the critical factors in that process to ensure a quality product.

Their work is ongoing. There are no completion dates. They must think in terms of how they can constantly improve their work to minimise costs, reduce delivery time, or improve quality. One of the management issues is how to keep track of the performance of a large number of work teams to ensure that effort is focused on improving the performance of the key processes.

Management teams

At the senior level in an organisation there should be a team approach taken towards the effective implementation of the library's strategic planning initiatives. This implementation should include the achievement of a range of performance improvement goals. It is important to identify specific measurable business objectives and monitor the progress towards meeting them.

For the management team to behave as a real team they should be prepared to roll up their sleeves and help with the change effort. They should perform the higher level activities that support people at the lower level. These include communications, removing barriers to goal achievement, and providing support and encouragement to those affected by the changes.

John Smith, a county librarian from Cumbria England, provides a good overview of the effectiveness of teams in the work environment (quoted in Sanders 1995, pp. 128–132). In a summary of the core values influencing team development and behaviour, he notes the following issues that need to be considered:

- Team management is a skill requiring high levels of leadership ability. There is usually little hierarchy in team management – team leaders are expected to lead from the front but also be ready to share the leadership, delegate responsibility and encourage a critical, thinking approach within the team. In an established, mature team, this will help build a dynamic which will work to develop both the team and its individual members.

- Purpose and planning are essential to building a sense of direction for the team and clarifying its objectives. Planning will involve all team members and is a continual, integrated process to achieve broader organisational objectives. By including all staff in the process, a greater commitment is built towards goal achievement. In addition, team members have a clearer understanding of the work of their colleagues and how each of them supports the achievement of the whole.

- Leadership and 'followership' are key ingredients for successful teams. Leaders should aim to influence rather than tell, acknowledging the experience, knowledge and capabilities of team members. Good leaders will be future-oriented, trying to remain ahead of the ever changing situation.

- Team building and selection is another crucial variable in developing the successful team. Teams need to comprise a variety of talents, attributes and attitudes that may challenge each member and the team leader. Aim to build teams that will develop and stretch individuals while at the same time, show respect, understanding and acceptance of differing views, attitudes and approaches.

- Openness and criticism are important attributes of a mature team. As part of the developmental process, open questioning and positive criticism should be an accepted part of dealing with issues. They should also form part of the regular staff development interview aimed at identifying opportunities and considering future directions and career development.

- Good relationships and trust are all about good communication throughout the team. This is facilitated by building trusting, supportive relationships where team members are sympathetic to what is being communicated. As well, communication needs to be clear and simple – the meaning and intent should be obvious.

- Controlled change – evolution, not revolution, is the most effective manner in which change can be implemented without adversely affecting team productivity. Organised evolution, involving team members from the start and with clear objectives communicated to all, provides a sound basis for the successful implementation of change.

- Achievement and enjoyment are the hallmarks of effective teams. Being part of a successful team usually provides members with an environment where they have been stretched and challenged; where their ideas have been listened to and responsibility delegated, leading to a work experience which has grown them as individuals.

- Finally, a few practical issues directly impact on team success. Firstly, team size – anything less than three is not a team, more than twelve and it becomes difficult to manage and coordinate. Secondly, professional and clerical work is shared in teams. No one person gets all the 'drab' work, nobody gets to do high level professional work all day – tasks are shared taking into account the task, skill levels, aptitude and experience. Finally, teams do not work in a vacuum but as part of the larger organisation with its own culture, aims and objectives. This can impose constraints upon team effectiveness or may well provide impetus to team growth and development. It cannot be ignored and requires team leaders and managers to ensure that they stay closely connected to the broader environment in working towards organisational objectives.

Conclusion

In these days of client-focused library service, and at a time when quality management is becoming the key to ensuring that customer satisfaction is our paramount goal, teamwork is one means by which our chances of achieving that goal are enhanced. A conference paper by Pam Pitkeathly (1994) recommends from experience that leadership, trust, empowering of staff, flexible work systems, participative management and close attention to staff morale are the vital ingredients in team building.

Teamwork is a means of organisation in which participation and delegation are maximised. The building and nurturing of teams is a key supervisory function, requiring a range of skills to support and encourage the team. Teams are client-centred, goal-oriented, and through planned and coordinated activity will make effective use of human and other resources. Successful teamwork requires the kind of leadership which delegates responsibility, which inspires confidence and trust, which is open to experimentation and challenge, which allows risk-taking, and which helps team members develop to their full potential.

I trust that you can see that teams and teamwork can have a positive influence on organisational climate and the management of change, because the keys to a productive climate and successful change management – communication, participation and problem-solving – are equally vital elements of successful team development. Library supervisors and managers are ideally placed to create participative work environments, and to develop a team approach to service which meets the challenges of the future with its potential for vast and complex technological, social and economic change.

> Groups are like relationships – you have to work at them. In the work place, they constitute an important unit of activity but one whose support needs are only recently becoming understood. By making the group itself responsible for its own support, the responsibility becomes an accelerator for the group process. What is vital, is that these needs are recognized and explicitly dealt with by the group. Time and resources must be allocated to this by the group and by Management, and the group process must be planned, monitored and reviewed just like any other managed process (Blair n.d., p. 5).

Chapter 13
Conflict resolution

Let him who will not have advice have conflict. (Irish Proverb)

Definition

Everyone experiences conflict at some time. It occurs whenever two people, teams or groups have different wants or goals and one party interferes with the other's attempts to satisfy these. Differences in the way people interpret facts, differences in values, and the various ways people take action to satisfy their wants and needs can all cause conflict (Dwyer 2000, p. 100).

Many writers in the fields of psychology and of organisational behaviour agree that conflict in itself is not a bad thing. (As the old saying goes, 'only dead fish swim with the stream'.) In fact, conflict can be seen as an essential factor in the growth and development of successful business and public enterprises. Conflict can offer opportunities for change, for people to adapt and grow within the organisation. For example, in discussions about new policies and procedures within a team situation, challenging established ways can be seen as conflict when not everyone feels the same way. Yet that conflict can isolate the weaknesses in the proposals in time to correct them. It is therefore a useful part of the change process.

On the other hand, conflict can have negative consequences. If left unresolved, it can lead to feelings of mistrust, fear, resentment and anger, create a poor climate and result in weakened performance and loss of interest in goal achievement. It can also divert effort from the achievement of goals, affect people's work and health, and, if unresolved can lead to situations which will cause even more serious harm to staff and to the organisation (Rue and Byars 1999, p. 310).

Conflict in itself is not the problem. What does create the difficulties when conflicts arise at work is the way we handle the situation. Although conflict is often seen as a very negative concept, positive changes and new ways of doing things can arise from the resolution of conflict. If you think about some of the conflicts you have had recently, whether at work or at home, or with a lecturer or salesperson, how did you attempt to manage and resolve the situation? Some people naturally argue and fight, others attempt to defuse and pacify by capitulating quickly. Most writers on this topic assert there *are* ways of resolving conflict so that more than one of the parties will feel satisfied with the result.

We must learn to manage conflict in the organisation, to limit the negative aspects and emphasise the benefits that come from conflict. Therefore, it is important that supervisors and managers try to develop skills in the area of conflict management and conflict resolution, because the way we handle conflict can be either positive and constructive, or negative and destructive. The resolution of conflict uses skills in communication, motivation and negotiation. According to one source:

> …ineffective conflict resolution comes about simply because we have never been taught useful ways to handle conflict. Conflict management is a skill that can be learned. It is not the domain of certain intuitive people who automatically know what to do when disputes arise (Wertheim *et al.* 1992, p. 7).

The writers go on to outline the four major ways in which we respond to conflict. We fight (attempt to outsmart, argue, threaten), pacify the other person by giving in, avoid discussing the conflict altogether, or compromise (give a bit, get a bit). In each case the effect on us, on the other party, and on the relationship between the two parties will not be totally positive. To help get closest to the positive for all, Wertheim and others (1992) detail a number of basic skills which involve working out what you really want, sharing needs and concerns, expanding your options, considering your alternatives and reaching a winning solution.

Approaches to conflict resolution

It is worth bearing in mind, at the outset, that in some extreme cases it will be necessary to ensure that both or all parties involved in a conflict move from emotional mode to problem-solving mode. Taking time out, and making the decision to resolve the conflict later, may be a valid action.

The following approaches to resolving conflicts are offered as general guidelines to keep in mind as you work towards a resolution that will enable all parties to 'win'. The first four are general, the others more specific.

- Be creative, positive, and optimistic. Conflict is not necessarily damaging to the organisation, and may lead to change for the better.

- Try to understand the other party's point of view. Make a conscious effort to understand the motivations and needs of the other person or groups.

- Learn to listen actively. Focus attention on the other person or group, and try to comprehend what they are saying.

- Be appropriately assertive. Be assertive, clearly expressing your needs, feelings and ideas.

- Use statements which begin with 'I…' rather than 'You…' In a conflict we tend to begin with an accusation. The use of 'I…' sentences changes the orientation, especially in the beginning.

- Describe the offending behaviour, rather than criticising the offender, and say how you feel about it. This helps to separate the person or group from the offence.

- Invite the other party to do likewise. Now invite the other person or group to express their perceptions and feelings; listen carefully.

- Explore possible solutions. Negotiation towards an agreed solution may be a lengthy and complex process.

Strategies for dealing with conflict

Reece and Brandt (1993, pp. 355–359) explore a range of strategies for dealing with conflict:

> Some of the most common approaches used to resolve conflict include withdrawing from an actual or potential dispute, smoothing it over, compromising, enforcing a solution, and confronting the situation directly. These and other approaches can be grouped into three basic conflict management strategies.
>
> 1 The win/lose strategy. This approach eliminates the conflict by having one individual 'win' over the other.
> 2 The lose/lose strategy. This approach eliminates the conflict by having both individuals 'lose' something.
> 3 The win/win strategy. The conflict is eliminated when all parties accept a mutually satisfying solution arrived at through a step-by-step, problem-solving process (Reece and Brandt 1993, pp. 255–356).

The authors elaborate on the nature of each of these approaches, and the situations in which they are best applied. Their contribution is well worth reading.

Negotiation

In many cases of conflict, a solution cannot be found simply by having a discussion about it. A formal process of negotiation may be what is required to ensure that all parties involved have the opportunity for considerable input as the parties work towards a settlement of the dispute or grievance or conflict. It is necessary to negotiate conflict resolution because others have an issue which requires cooperation, even if the aims conflict.

Definition

The word 'negotiation' is defined in the *Oxford Dictionary* as: 'to confer (with another) for the purpose of arranging some matter by mutual agreement.' Leo Hawkins and Michael Hudson (1986, pp. 6–7) say that 'negotiation is a process of influencing behaviour.' Another definition they give is that 'negotiation is a process whereby parties with conflicting aims establish the terms on which they will cooperate.'

Clearly, the first step is to identify that a difference does exist. Each person's goals and desired outcomes can be discovered, possible solutions explored, and negotiation towards a desirable result (often a compromise) can begin.

Negotiation skills

Hawkins and Hudson (1986) also provide some guidance about the skills, such as communication, tactics, and concession-making, needed for successful negotiating. Their book provides a comprehensive step-by-step approach to the process with some more concise summaries which will be of use in less complex and demanding negotiation situations. Negotiating skills are also explored in Hiltrop and Udall (1995).

Probably the most useful and important point is that negotiation requires preparation. First of all, the subject being negotiated must be clearly understood, appropriate information gathered and distinct objectives must be established. Having a clear bottom line in mind, beyond which you will not go, is another important factor. The assumptions also need to be reviewed, and an attempt made to guess those of the party you are negotiating with. Researching all the facts and checking them is also important.

A further step is to define all the issues, including those in dispute and those which are common to both parties in the conflict. Then it is possible to decide your position, and to better understand the other party's concerns and objectives. This leads to a situation where the issue can be more fairly negotiated from a position of understanding. Finally, during the course of negotiation try to generate as many options as possible, work hard on the complex issues and ensure the other party fully understands what is being agreed upon (Dwyer 2000, p. 121). Thus the essential steps in the negotiation process can be summarised as follows:

Practical steps in the negotiation process

- Try to understand the other side's case and objectives before coming to the negotiation table.

- Assess strengths and weaknesses – yours and theirs.

- Have options in mind that may be helpful to move things forward.

- Talk less and listen actively.

- Ask open, probing questions. Asking questions gives control and allows you to steer the discussion.

- Avoid weak language – be positive but not aggressive.

- Avoid emotional comments, sarcasm, point scoring.

- Be aware of your body language and look to read it in the other party.

- Help others to concede without loss of face.

- Make small concessions and be clear everyone understands when a concession is being made.

- Summarise regularly, especially concessions.

- If necessary, spell out the consequences of failure.

- At the end, be very clear what has been decided and quickly put in writing.

Remember successful negotiation is about collaboration, it is not a contest. The aim is to meet both sides' needs.

Mediation

Mediation is the process of providing a connecting link between two parties for the purpose of reconciling them. As a further step from negotiation, mediation requires a third party as facilitator.

The following is a mediation process from the Conflict Resolution Network (2002) [<http://www.crnhq.org/>] which may be useful to anyone acting as a mediator in a conflict. In fact the whole Conflict Resolution Network website is a valuable resource in conflict resolution.

Attitudes for Mediators

These attitudes are relevant whenever you want to advise, in a conflict which is not your own. It may be a friend telling you about a problem on [the]telephone. It may an informal chat with both conflicting people. It may be a formally organised mediation session.

1 **Be objective** – validate both sides, even if privately you prefer one point of view, or even when only one party is present.
2 **Be supportive** – use caring language. Provide a non-threatening learning environment, where people will feel safe to open up.
3 **No judging** – actively discourage judgements as to who was right and who was wrong. Don't ask "Why did you?" Ask "What happened?" and "How did you feel?"
4 **Steer process, not content** – use astute questioning. Encouraging suggestions from participants. Resist advising. If your suggestions are really needed, offer as options not directives.
5 **Win/win** – work towards wins for both sides. Turn opponents into problem-solving partners.

Mediation Methods

Use the simple, yet effective rules from the "Fighting Fair" poster.

1 Define your mediator role as there to support both people "winning".
2 Get agreement from both people about a basic willingness to fix the problem.
3 Let each person say what the problem is for them. Check back that the other person has actually understood them.
4 Guide the conversation towards a joint problem solving approach and away from personal attack.
5 Encourage them to look for answers where everybody gets what they need.
6 Redirect "Fouls" (Name Calling, Put Downs, Sneering, Blaming, Threats, Bringing up the Past, Making Excuses, Not Listening, Getting Even). Where possible you reframe the negative statement into a neutral description of a legitimate present time concern.

Steps in Mediation

Open
    Introductions and agreements. Warm up, explanations, agenda if known.

Establish
    i   Overview: What is the matter? Each person to express their view of the conflict, the issues and their feelings.
    ii Details: What is involved? More details. Map needs and concerns. Clarify misperceptions. Identify other relevant issues. Mirroring if needed.

Move
    i   Where are they now? Identify areas of agreement. Encourage willingness to move forward. Caucus if needed.
    ii Negotiation: Focus on future action. How would they like it to be? What would that take? Develop options. Trading - build wins for everyone.

Close
    Completion: Contracting. Plans for the future, including appointed time to review agreement. Closing statements (Conflict Resolution Network 2002[1]

Dealing with difficult people

For most managers, dealing with difficult people – be they staff or clients, is part of the normal working environment. It can cause stress and anxiety for the inexperienced supervisor in particular and, as Watson found through interviews with new managers early in their careers (cited in Jordan and Lloyd 2002, p. 244) is seen as one of the most demanding parts of their job. Dealing with staff obviously requires a somewhat different approach than dealing with clients but some standard principles apply to both situations. Thus managers should keep the following points in mind:

- when dealing with difficult situations they need to develop a level of self confidence that will enable them to remain emotionally detached from the situation – with this self confidence comes the ability to be assertive as required and to accept that not all situations will be resolved with everyone happy at the outcomes
- if possible, prepare before the meeting and maybe even rehearse the situation beforehand in your head – this helps in preparing a strategy and foreseeing the problems that are going to be raise
- it is important to control your own emotions and not become angry in dealing with people who may be very upset themselves – while emotional detachment is important, it is also necessary to aim for a level of empathy to try and understand why the person is behaving as they are
- angry or upset people have probably been stewing for a while. (Let them have their say, do not interrupt and listen carefully. Acknowledge the feelings as well as the facts and show you respect their concern. Stay polite and calm yourself.)
- body language is important – watch yours and theirs
- take control by asking questions and repeating them if necessary to keep things on track
- remember that people are rarely being difficult just for the sake of it – usually there is a reason and this needs to be uncovered.

There is no easy solution to the issue of dealing with difficult people. But it is a very important part of a supervisor's or manager's job and must be handled accordingly – it is what they are paid for!

Conclusion

In any area of personal, professional or industrial relations, outcomes of conflict are affected by the personal style and self-esteem of the parties involved. If you ever find it difficult to communicate with your subordinates or supervisors, or if you find it difficult to say 'no' without feeling guilt, or if you find dealing with management and professional colleagues to be an intimidating experience, you are not alone! In fact, you are in good company. Many people find that low self-esteem, poor listening skills, inability to assert themselves are barriers which often interfere with their personal *and* professional lives. This is one reason that assertiveness training and communication skills training should be undertaken by all staff wishing to become supervisors and managers.

Part 3

Human resources management

Chapter 14
Introduction to human resources management

Introduction

As you study most areas of library management you will discover that a great deal of the theory is common sense. If so, then you should be successful in your staff relations. Indeed, the results of my survey of Australian library practitioners (Sanders 1993) confirm this. I asked respondents to indicate to what extent each of a number of factors was influential in providing them with the management skills and knowledge necessary for their current job. The following were the top responses:

- my own inherent abilities and common sense
- talking to other librarians
- experience in other jobs.

Induction to the job and reading management literature both rated lowly. Those issues are considered in Chapter 17.

The following material should confirm what your common sense tells you, and set you thinking about some principles and practices which will assist you in becoming a successful supervisor.

It has often been said, and most people in a supervisory or management position will agree, that the basic task of management is getting things done through people (some research to support this contention is summarised by Reynolds 1986). Attracting, selecting, training, maintaining and retaining the right people in each job are crucial to the success of any organisation. The tasks can be combined under the heading of human resources management, and this chapter aims to give an understanding of those tasks.

The following continuum is presented, not as a process that can be, or is, followed, but rather as a model or framework within which we can understand the needs of people in an organisation, and understand how people management activities depend upon considerable skills in dealing with people.

- You cannot retain staff unless you allow and provide for them to undertake training, *skills maintenance and continuing education.*

- You cannot train staff unless you know them and their performance well enough to *analyse their performance and training needs.*

- If you are involved in organising people, you must have developed skills in the area of *negotiation and mediation*.
- You cannot organise people before you *select* and appoint them to a position in your organisation.
- To select staff, you need to undertake *recruitment*.
- *Recruitment* is strongly dependent upon a thorough *analysis and description of the jobs* to be filled and performed.

This subject needs to be set within a context which has the greatest possible meaning and relevance for you. Use the following discussion as an exercise in personalised learning, relating what is said to your own work situation.

What is a job?

An understanding of what constitutes a job is basic to any study of people at work. 'A job should always be a planned entity consisting of assigned tasks that require similar or related skills, knowledge, or ability' (Stueart and Moran 1998, p. 175). A number of writers have outlined the important difference between a *position* and a *job*.

> A *position* is a collection of tasks and responsibilities which constitute *the total work assignment of one person*. Thus there are as many different positions in an organization as there are people employed there…
>
> A *job,* on the other hand, is *a group of positions* that generally involve the same responsibilities, knowledge, duties, and skills. Many employees, all performing slightly different work, may be classified under the same job title (Stueart and Moran 1998, p. 175; emphasis added).

For example, the reference librarians in an academic library are all seen to be doing the same *job*, but each has his or her own *position* of reference librarian. Similarly with cataloguers, serials staff and so on. (Do not confuse these with position or job classifications such as Librarian grade I, Library officer, Library assistant. Those are titles associated with job classification, and are tools for grading the work value of various positions in a library.)

Today, a job is more than merely a set of tasks, rather, you are encouraged to consider a job more as a suite of skills which when positively exercised will have a range of benefits which will help to satisfy organisational objectives. This alternative view of the job makes my previous definitions sound a trifle basic and lacklustre. As you read on, try to put this view into a library context.

Do you know your library's objectives?

How does your job help to fulfil some of those objectives?

Your work therefore becomes something which involves you and your personal attributes and skills – and realising this makes us re-think a number of traditional notions about work and jobs.

> If work is no longer seen as a sequence of events which finish at 5 pm but a cluster of communication, evaluation and decision-making skills – to name but three – then the boundary between work, leisure and family life diminishes (Hill 1991, p. 81).

I always emphasise to those who study library and information management the importance of communication and decision-making skills, and try to show that they are necessary to all workers, not just to supervisors and managers. This underlines the fact that people come into an organisation with values, attitudes, expectations and needs which are not all work-related. When you read about job analysis, too, refer back to this and compare the worker-oriented approach and the job-oriented approach in this context.

The role of the supervisor has been changing over time. Whilst supervisors clearly have a supervision responsibility, they also need to be part of a staff relationship which encourages constant development of the skills and abilities of those with whom they work.

- in what ways is the growth of your work skills ensured in your present position?
- does your organisation build this into your work?
- do you work as part of a team?
- is this teamwork intended and formalised in your job description, or do informal teams develop for particular needs and situations?

The growing need to be transparent in the quality of their services means that librarians need to be constantly developing and improving. And the relationship with the customer (both external and internal) adds further intangibles to the job description.

What does this mean? Are there really less personal development opportunities in the cataloguing, acquisitions and other areas? If your answer is 'yes', then you should consider whether or not the reference and other reader service librarians are the customers of the technical services staff.

Another clear change in the perceptions of work and jobs has developed from the need to develop sets of skills which will assist with promotion. Traditionally, librarians have been promoted to supervisory or managerial positions on the basis of their achievements in a particular professional or technical area. The skills of supervision and management have been secondary to that advancement in many cases.

The more enlightened library and information managers and supervisors now, however, are ensuring those latter skills are being acquired before promotion. Most library managers will agree that there is an inherent risk in training for promotion, and that is the possibility that the employee will go to another library for that promotion. This is one reason why many organisations are reluctant to train for promotion and are more likely to train to improve skills used only in the current position.

The final area of change has come about with development of strategic planning and the opportunity for individuals to recognise future directions and ensure they are able to develop the knowledge and skills needed as part of the organisation's development.

Are you involved in an enterprise that requires a business plan, encompassing an annual presentation of the service objectives of the library and the financial and other resource requirements needed to achieve those objectives? What is available in your library as part of the strategic planning process?

- statements of objectives?
- policies?
- strategic plans?
- budgets?

Think again about your job and its place in achieving the library's objectives.

- how do you know you are achieving goals?
- how do you assess your performance?
- how does your library assess your performance?
- is there any formal evaluation of individual performance?
- is there any formal evaluation of the library's performance, or of parts of the library?
- if you are lacking some skills which your job requires, or your future in the library may require, how does your library discover and cater for that?

The link between your current job, and where you want to be in the future, requires you to consider the complexity of relationships between you and your current job description, your supervisors, your colleagues, your customers, the organisation's formal planning processes, and probably a lot of other factors particular to your own situation.

> In short, each worker is a doer using his or her skills, a learner acquiring and expanding the skills that will open up opportunities for career development and a teacher assisting others to achieve their potential (Hill 1991, p. 81).

In what ways are you, in your present job, a doer? a learner? a teacher?

Much of the material in the remainder of this Part has its roots in the view of work and jobs expressed above, especially in the areas of staff development and appraisal. One of the aims is to encourage you to be a doer of the work, a learner of the subject, and a teacher, to others, of your own experience.

The changing nature of work

The work environment changed considerably over the last few decades of the twentieth century. Downsizing, outsourcing, 'casualisation', accountability, demographic changes, increased participation by women, rising educational levels, the loss of more traditional manual work and the growth in service industries, increasing levels of part-time work while at the same time, many are working longer hours than ever before, have all combined to create a far more complex employment environment than existed previously. For managers in particular, these and other changes have made human resource management a far more difficult and demanding area than it was in the past.

The trends in library and information work are no different as managers are faced with demands for increased efficiency – doing more with less. With staff costs typically comprising 50% or more of the total running costs for a library (Jordan and Lloyd 2002, p. 1), this is one area that gets close scrutiny in any cost cutting exercise. In addition to the organisational push to control or reduce staff costs, managers also have to deal with changing social patterns where staff want working hours to be more flexible, the work environment more supportive, career aspirations to be recognised and opportunities for personal development to be supported. Somehow, managers have to tread the middle ground of meeting both employer and employee expectations within a legislative, social and technological framework that impacts on all aspects of the work of an organisation.

The strategic management of human resources in order to meet both the needs of individuals as well as organisations, will become an increasing part of any manager's working life. As Nankervis, Compton and Baird note:

> Jobs are not static entities. As an organisation changes in response to economic, technological and market pressures, so jobs must change accordingly. Rising employee expectations for quality of work life, career programs and overall job satisfaction demand that jobs reflect not only organisational outcomes, but also the multiple needs of their occupants (2001, p. 203).

Chapter 15
Job analysis, design and description

As soon as you have finished a job, you start appreciating the difficulties.   (Chinese Proverb)

Job analysis

Job analysis is the *process* of examining a job by collecting and interpreting data about it. This is not to be confused with job evaluation, which itself is a systematic process to determine the relative value or worth of each job compared to other jobs in the organisation. Job analysis, then, is not a particular document, but it does give rise to documents such as the job description and the person specification. These documents are the product of the analytical examination of a job.

Many texts on supervision and management spend some time explaining why a job description is needed, and what it should contain, but few cover the methodology of obtaining the information – the job analysis. The brief coverage of some texts seems to sum up a general attitude towards job analysis: do it when necessary, and if it looks like too much work, get a consultant to do it. However, obtaining such important data is not necessarily as difficult and time-consuming as it may seem. The following guide to job analysis methods should facilitate the process in libraries.

Job analysis aims to acquire objective and verifiable information about the specific requirements of a position as it relates to the objectives of the organisation. It is fundamental to the process of building a workforce that best suits the needs of that organisation, and also provides a basis for performance appraisal and identification of training needs within that workforce. Its importance is noted by Nankervis, Compton and Baird:

 Job analysis is the process of determining the requirements of jobs – the data relating to duties and responsibilities, and the personal requirements to perform those jobs. It is the cornerstone of HRM because the information that this process collects serves all HRM functions (2001, p. 207).

From the supervisor's point of view, job analysis and the information it produces will be most helpful in evaluating training and development needs, and in job design. For those supervisors and managers involved in the recruitment and selection of staff, job analysis is often the first step in the process of acquiring the right person for the right job.

Job analysis methods

There are a number of job analysis methodologies which have been tried and tested with some success, and it is a matter of the individual library deciding which is most applicable to their own situation and to the particular job(s) to be studied. It is possible to study the job from two different perspectives. A worker-oriented approach will focus on the psychological and physical requirements of the job, while a job-oriented approach will involve direct analysis of the tasks being performed and the tools being used. It is important to combine the two approaches, to define the tasks undertaken, and to break them down into the knowledge, skills, abilities and tools that are needed to perform the job in a satisfactory manner.

The place to start is with the current job description, if one exists, because it will provide a summary of the duties and responsibilities of the job. However, if the job description has not been updated for some time, it may not provide a useful starting point.

Interviews, questionnaires, work logs and observation are the most commonly used methods of obtaining information about jobs. Job analysis is a complex process, and using only one method is generally not sufficient to provide comprehensive data about the job. So it is appropriate in many cases to used a combination of methods. For example, observation alone cannot provide enough data, since it cannot explain why particular tasks are performed; nor can it begin to explain the mental processes involved. But a subsequent interview could elicit that information. A daily log of tasks undertaken can be very useful, because it will indicate what individual tasks were performed and which tasks took precedence over others. However, while the log will provide one picture of the work flow, it will not indicate aspects such as the tools used, resources consulted or used for each task, or supervisory communication flows.

Questionnaires and interviews

Questionnaires and interviews are probably the most common methods used for job analysis. They can be comprehensive in their gathering of information, and can include questions about what the job involves and how it is achieved. Used in tandem – questionnaire first, followed by an interview – they can give a complete picture of the job.

The following checklist is a guide to the questions to consider including in a job analysis questionnaire or interview.

- Job title
- Salary or job code/Classification
- Department/Branch/Section
- Name of incumbent
- Date of questionnaire/interview
- Name and position/title of supervisor
- What is the general purpose of your job?
- What was your previous job, in which organisation?
- How long have you been in this job?
- To what job, or type and level of job, would you expect to be promoted?
- List those staff members you regularly supervise.

- Which of the following are part of your supervisory duties? Hiring/selecting; inducting; training; rostering; coaching; counselling; developing; budgeting; directing; performance appraising; promoting; compensating; disciplining; firing; other.

- What indicates the successful completion of your work? How is your performance assessed? What are the results of your work?

- List the duties of the job, and briefly describe what you actually do, and how you do it. Indicate those duties that you consider to be most important and least important. Note those duties that you consider to be most difficult. Divide the duties into daily, regular (for example, weekly, monthly) and irregular. What percentage of your time is spent daily, and/or weekly, on each regular duty?

- Are any of the above duties unnecessary? Describe, and say why.

- Are there any duties that you feel should be added to your job? Describe, and say why.

- What do you consider to be the minimum educational requirement for the job? How much previous experience is needed to perform the job?

- List any skills required in the performance of the job. These could include, for example, level of accuracy, precision in use of tools, personal skills, and supervision skills.

- List equipment, if any, that is used in the work, and indicates how frequently each item is used.

- Note any physical demands, for example, heavy lifting, cramped working conditions, excessive working speeds, queuing pressures, and any excessive requirements regarding hearing, use of computer terminals, reading, and speaking.

- Note any negative results of non-physical demands through contact with clients, close supervision, pressure of deadlines, queuing pressures, irregular activity schedules, working in isolation, excessive travel or other demands.

- What is the job environment? Consider such conditions as indoor/outdoor/below ground; lighting; temperature; ventilation; dust/dirt; fumes/odours/noise; dampness/humidity; comfort of furniture; other ergonomic features.

- Are there any health and safety aspects? Consider such things as fire or electrical hazards, insecure shelving, furniture, radiation, asbestos, and so forth.

After administering such a questionnaire or interview to the job incumbent, it is generally recommended that similar questions be asked of the staff member's immediate supervisor, to check the validity of the data. Certainly, questions about educational requirements and experience should be followed up, as the supervisor's answers are likely to be more objective.

Getting comprehensive answers to all or most of the above questions, by whatever combination of methods, should help in the preparation of a written and categorised set of data which will help to achieve goals in a number of other human resource areas, including recruitment, selection, training and development of staff.

You might like to compare the questions above with those outlined at the 'On-line position description questionnaire program' web site found at: <http://www.job-analysis.net/G908.htm>(hr-guide.com 2000).

Job design and motivation

To carry out the job analysis, using a combination of methods, it is useful to consider some basic principles which, if applied to the process, will help to give staff a real stake in their work and in achieving library goals.

The relationship of job design to job satisfaction and motivation is a crucial factor. As discussed in Chapter 10, high levels of productivity are most often achieved when the work that people do has meaning and significance. Work must be seen to be worthwhile and important, the person in the job must feel responsible and accountable for the work performed, and they must be guaranteed regular feedback on the quality and effectiveness of their performance of the job. That can be achieved by ensuring that the following elements are present in the job.

> *Skill variety* – the job requires a variety of different activities requiring the use of a number of different skills and talents that the individual possesses and values.
>
> *Task identity* – the job requires the completion of a whole and identifiable piece of work (i.e. doing a job from beginning to end with a visible outcome).
>
> *Task significance* – the degree to which the task has an impact on the lives or work of others in the immediate organisation or external environment.
>
> Personal responsibility for work outcomes is fostered when there is *autonomy* built into the job. Autonomy refers to the extent to which the job allows freedom, independence, and discretion in scheduling the work and determining procedures.
>
> Knowledge of results requires *feedback* in a direct, clear and timely manner (Scanlan and Keys 1983, p. 260, italics added).

Scanlan and Keys go on to say that in order to give worthwhile work, to ensure the person in the job can feel responsible and accountable for the work performed, and to ensure regular feedback, the job designer needs to combine tasks (*skill variety*), form natural and complete units of work (*task identity*), establish who is relying on the work and why (*task significance*), give some control over work methods and pace (*autonomy*), and allow open feedback channels (*feedback*). How these principles are achieved will depend upon the nature and level of the work to be performed.

If you become involved in job design, then you should read some of the more specific works in that area. The well-maintained web site referred to above is an excellent starting point.

Briefly, though, you should be aware that job design and job enrichment is a well-researched area. A number of strategies such as job rotation, job enlargement, and staff participation are being developed to help increase job satisfaction by changing aspects of either the content or the environment of the job.

Appendix 1 provides an example of a job analysis questionnaire.

Job description

Once the job analysis is completed you can then prepare a written and categorised set of data which will help to achieve goals in other human resources areas, including recruitment, selection, training and development of staff. The next step is to compile a series of documents which present an organised version of the data gained from the job analysis: the job description and the person specification. Detailed examples of these can be found in Appendix 2. What follows is a general outline of what they are, and what they should include if they are to be of use to managers, supervisors and staff.

A job description is a statement of duties and responsibilities which identifies simply and clearly what the person performing the job will be doing. It thus becomes a guide to the staff member about what they are required to do, and to some extent how, when and where they should be doing the job. It is also an aid to performance evaluation. One point to note carefully is that when indicating duties to be performed, a *specific statement* is much better than a general guide – the idea being to provide the security of a clear job statement without stifling the incumbent's initiative.

What follows is just one suggested format for a job description, but other ways of presenting the results of job analysis can be found in human resources management texts, articles, or your organisation's personnel department. Not every job description will include everything outlined below, but most of these headings should be considered.

Job description: what should be included?

Date – to be of any real use, a job description must be current. It must correspond to current requirements and present an accurate picture of what happens now.

Job identification – the name or title of the job, and the location of the job (for example, Department/Branch/Section).

Award classification – this may also include the salary range or, at least, the name of the salary scale and range.

Reporting/supervisory relationships:

- *Responsible to* –a statement to clarify reporting and authority relationships.

- *Responsible for/supervises* – a statement to clarify number, level and perhaps location of staff being supervised by the person in this job. Clarifies reporting and supervisory relationships.

Communicating and working relationships – a statement of contacts, liaisons required (for example, with other departments, libraries, suppliers).

Function – this statement gives the general purpose and scope of the job. It is a summary, and therefore should be succinct. The statement is necessary because there may be many other positions with the same title but quite different functions.

Key results areas – this is the most important item, as it should specify what tasks and activities must be performed successfully for the job to assist in achieving the library's objectives. These need to be linked with the required standard of performance in each case. For example, a key result area for a circulation desk assistant may be to ensure that all returns are checked in and desensitised within a certain time. The result and standard may be contained within the same statement, as in that example, or listed side-by-side for easy reference.

Statement of duties – this is the next most important item, since it should provide specific details on what is actually done. Specific duties are generally listed in order of importance, or priority, and often include the percentage of time to be spent on each task per week, or per day. These percentages are usually a guide to the average amount of time spent, and are not intended to be statistically correct. This and the previous section will make up the bulk of the job description.

Hours of work – this is useful for prospective applicants, and for planning training programs.

Special conditions – these may include a requirement to work extended hours (for example, evening shifts, weekends), to drive a van or bookmobile, to attend meetings after hours, to lift heavy objects, and so forth.

Resources used – these may include equipment (for example, photocopiers, computers, word processors), reference tools (for example, indexing and abstracting services, both manual and online), bibliographical aids (for example Anglo American Cataloguing Rules (AACR), Dewey Decimal Classification scheme (DDC.)

Person specification

The person specification is compiled, based on the job analysis and job description, to identify the sort of person required to do the job. The person specification should clearly identify the characteristics of the person most likely to succeed at that job, and include aspects such as education, training, experience, personal and physical qualities. There may be a strong temptation to overemphasise educational qualifications rather than specific abilities and experience needed to carry out particular duties. Resist that temptation: consider each specification or requirement and ask *why* each prerequisite, especially the educational standard, is necessary.

The concept of person specification presented here includes what others call a job specification and usually becomes the selection criteria against which prospective candidates for the position are assessed. The *job specification* specifies the skills and knowledge required to carry out each task, while the *person specification* specifies the experience, education, aptitudes and personal skills required of the person in the job. It is preferable to see the skills and knowledge included with the job description, and again with the person specification – there is really no need for a third document.

The person specification can cover any or all of the following areas. Make sure that it is clear, reasonably comprehensive, realistic and concise, and that it includes aspects of knowledge, abilities, experience and education required. The following list is not exhaustive but should serve as a guide.

Person specification: what should be included?

Knowledge – include here knowledge about particular professional materials, tools, routines, systems, issues, subject areas, languages, policies, procedures, terminology, rules, codes or schemes.

Abilities – include here oral and written communication, attitudes, interpersonal relationships, operation of equipment, training/teaching skills, specific or general organisational and supervisory skills, comprehension, receiving and giving instructions and feedback, cooperation, effective and independent work patterns, initiative, handling of pressure, flexibility, attention to detail, accuracy, reliability, ability to cope with/implement change.

Experience – in particular library departments or sections, in particular library types and sizes, length and extent of experience in each case.

Education – minimum/desired: secondary, tertiary, trade, professional recognition, specialised training courses or workshops.

Special requirements – driver's licence, demonstrated professional involvement, physical attributes, knowledge of local area, personal presentation, contract arrangements, interest in further study/training.

In each area, be sure to make it clear which specifications are essential, and which are desirable (and grades in between if necessary). That way the document, and the information it contains, becomes a useable guide, especially for staff involved in selecting the best person for the job.

Examples of person specifications appear in Appendix 2.

Conclusion

To carry out a number of human resources management functions effectively, one requires data on the nature and duties of jobs. Job analysis will enable the library to provide that data and ensure that each staff member has the necessary information to carry out their duties and responsibilities. It will also provide information to assist in the selection of new staff, because an up-to-date job description will help applicants to discover the true nature of the job, and the person specification will be of great assistance to those involved in deciding on the right applicant for the job.

Chapter 16
Recruitment and selection

His fellow employees would follow him anywhere…mainly out of curiosity.

(Source unknown)

Introduction

To a large extent, any organisation is only as effective as the people it employs, and that implies that selection of those people is a crucial part of the human resources program.

Choosing staff can, in some ways, be likened to punting on horse races: a decision to bet on a particular horse is a gamble; so too is a decision to employ one person ahead of other candidates. Both decisions are based upon predictions of performance among several choices, and are estimates based upon past achievements and present conditions. While the punter may consider such things as breeding, previous performances, track conditions, ability of the jockey and the odds on offer, the manager will base their selection decision on variables such as educational record, past performance and experience, exposed skills and abilities, personality and other characteristics. Each is trying to pick a winner, and in each case there are many poor choices and many disappointed people.

We cannot avoid some failures in selection but with effective selection techniques, we can at least improve the success rate. There are three main areas in the selection process: job description, person specification and, finally, recruitment and selection. A fourth area – induction – overlaps selection and staff training. In fact, as noted later, the induction of new staff begins as soon as the library publishes an advertisement for a position.

Job descriptions and person specifications were covered in Chapter 15. They are statements of duties, responsibilities and requirements which identify simply and clearly what the person performing the job will be doing, and what attributes they need to fill the job successfully. They are aids to selection.

Recruitment

Recruitment asks the questions:

- *where* do we find the right person for the job?
- *how* do we get him or her to apply for the job?

Recruitment sources

Common recruitment sources are:

- metropolitan daily newspapers
- local newspapers
- professional journals and newsletters
- campus interviews
- school, college and university noticeboards
- general employment agencies
- library employment services
- Commonwealth Employment Service (CES)/JobNetwork agencies
- in-house newsletters and noticeboards
- word of mouth or personal recommendation.

You need to consider which of those sources will provide you with the greatest number and widest range of suitable applicants for a particular position, at the least cost. Careful consideration will stop you from advertising in the Australian Library and Information Association's monthly newsletter, *inCite,* for a school leaver, and will discourage you from recruiting a chief cataloguer through the CES or a school noticeboard.

The advertisement

If you are not going to rely on word of mouth or personal recommendation then there will be a need to advertise the position. The wording of this advertisement requires careful thought: remember you are promoting your own organisation at the same time as you are recruiting new staff. They can also be expensive so you want the process to succeed the first time. Each advertisement should contain, at the very least:

- title and number to identify the specific position
- description of the job duties and requirements
- selection criteria based on the job and position descriptions
- conditions and benefits of service with this library
- how to apply
- closing date for applications
- name of contact for further information.

Again, remember that you are engaged in a public relations exercise every time you advertise; the advertisement must be factual and realistic if you want to avoid attracting unsuitable applicants and bad public relations. Attracting the right applicant through an advertisement is achieved regularly, but time, effort and skill must go into its preparation. Libraries in some locations, for example, may feel the need to promote the attractions of the area when they advertise for staff. Some jobs (for example, unusual or newly created positions) will need to be explained in more detail than is normal. One way to improve your advertising skills is to get ideas by regularly reading the advertisements which appear in the recruitment sources listed above.

Some examples of advertisements appear in Appendix 3. Consider how they meet the criteria mentioned in the preceding section. How could you improve on them? Could you use some of the ideas for your own library?

The application

Applications should include a letter of application and a résumé which includes the details listed below. If a candidate fails to provide any of the details you will need to assess whether this is important or not and raise the question at interview. For most positions age, sex, religion or marital status are immaterial and questions regarding these can be considered discriminatory (as well as unnecessary). However, occasionally, there may be situations where such questions are relevant and exemptions are allowed under anti-discrimination legislation. For example, an advertisement in the *Canberra Times* (17 Jan 2004) from a boarding school asking for a resident tutor noted that the position involved responsibility for female boarders aged 12 to 18, and thus they were seeking only female applicants.

- name
- address
- present position
- previous work experience
- educational qualifications
- professional qualifications and achievements
- list of transferable skills and abilities
- names of people to whom reference can be made to confirm what appears in the application
- other relevant details in support of application (for example, career aspirations, outside interests)

It is normal practice for applicants to supply a separate document in which they specifically address the selection criteria for the position.

Selection

These days some organisations outsource the recruitment and selection process, and in libraries which are part of a larger organisation the process may be managed by a human resources management team not the line library staff. However, the process will still usually involve someone from the line area – after all, they will be working directly with the new recruit and will therefore want to have direct influence on who is selected.

The selection process requires a range of skills and abilities, and a great deal of effort if it is to be successful. Some of those skills can be learned, but many of the most successful staff selection people have a natural ability to weigh up highly complex variables and select the right person. Objectivity cannot be instilled easily, but a few comments on how to avoid the subjectivity traps in interviewing and selecting will not go amiss. Note that there has been considerable debate over many years over the validity of the interview as a selection method. However, for virtually all positions, it is still considered a worthwhile exercise that provides one, but not all, of the major inputs to the selection decision. The following, from a recruitment management consultancy, highlights the importance of the interviewer in making the process as useful as possible:

> What is required during the job interview in particular is interviewer discipline. Discipline to work out what it is that the interviewer (or more appropriately what the organisation) is looking for and why is he looking for it; to consider how he will recognise it when he sees it; and how he will judge whether it is there in sufficient quantity; and to assess each new candidate strictly in terms of the qualities and attributes he has described, rather than in terms of his own likes and dislikes (Accel-Team.com 2003).

The selection interview

The objectives of most selection interviews are threefold:

- to determine the candidate's suitability for the position

- to ensure that the candidate is clear about what is expected of the successful applicant and about the kind of work he/she would be expected to undertake
- to ensure that the applicant feels they have had a fair hearing.

Despite all its possible defects, the interview is still the most widely accepted practice in selection, so how can we make it as effective as possible?

Probably the single greatest fault in interviewing is a lack of planning. Careful and systematic planning must take place. A number of steps can be noted:

- receipt (and acknowledgment) of all applications
- evaluating the applications by comparing the organisation's requirements (job description and person specification) with the individuals' attributes
- considering possible interviewees, and discard unsuitable candidates
- re-reading applications
- deciding on interviewees
- arranging interviews
- organising the pattern of the interview, noting especially any information needed which was not in the application or 'suspicious' areas which need probing.

It is important to allow sufficient time for the interview, to allow time at the conclusion to write down your comments, and to ensure there are no interruptions during the interview. The physical arrangement and conditions of the waiting area and the interview room are important, both to give a good impression of the organisation and to help the interviewee to feel at ease. As indicated in Chapter 17 on staff development, the interview is part of the induction process, and the initial impression gained of the organisation can be a very important part of your welcome to the organisation.

Ensure that the interview room is private, and that the interviews will not be interrupted. Make sure that each interviewer has their own set of materials relating to each interview. Adequate time needs to be allocated for each candidate. Use the time before and after each interview to discuss the previous candidate, record important notes, and prepare for the next. The selection panel must meet in advance to plan the pattern of interview, discuss and decide on questions to be asked, and by whom they are to be asked, and determine the amount of information to be given so that all applicants are treated the same.

A great deal has been written on the subject of interview structure and style, and I suggest that you read something from that literature. The following is a suggested pattern of interview which can be modified to suit particular levels of job and types of library.

- Greet the candidate by name.

- Introduce the candidate to panel members so that they know who is conducting the interview – this helps to break the ice and put the candidate at ease.

- Begin with socialising questions or comments to ease any tension, for example, comments on the weather, travel to the interview, or the environment of the library.

- Start with a brief summary of the position and of the conditions of work or service.

- Questions about the candidate's education and qualifications:
  What subjects did you enjoy most? why?
  How do these studies equip you for this position?

- Questions about motivation and commitment:

What attracts you to this job?
Why are you contemplating a change of job?
What do you know about the job/this library/the parent organisation?
What do you like most about your present job? what do you dislike most?

- Questions to find out about the candidate's ambitions and suitability for this job:
  What expectations do you have of this job?
  How will you feel about not being able to use certain skills?
  How do you see your future with this library?
  What do you perceive as your training needs for this position?
  What plans do you have for your own professional development and further studies?

- Questions on the candidate's work experience:
  Outline the duties and responsibilities of your current position.
  What are the most difficult/troublesome aspects of the job?
  What improvements could be made to the work you are doing at present?
  What has your previous experience given you that will help in this position?

- Questions to assess problem-solving skills, the ability to apply previous experience to problem-solving, and the ability to think creatively:
  How would you deal with such and such a situation?
  What would you do if...?

- Questions to probe the candidate's personal characteristics. Evaluation of answers to such questions requires some caution; subjective answers are likely as candidate tries to give the 'model' answer.
  What are your interests outside work? why?
  How do you feel about lazy staff members?
  What is your work philosophy?
  What do you consider to be your own strengths and weaknesses?
  What qualities do you think are essential for this position?

- Questions relating to the candidate's interest and flexibility:
  How do you feel about working split shifts?
  How do you feel about working overtime or at weekends?
  How would you feel about working at different branches/campuses?

- Give the candidate the opportunity to ask questions.

- Inform the candidate how and when they will learn the results of their application.

- Thank the candidate for attending.

Note especially:

- If the interviewer does most of the talking, he or she is *not* interviewing.

- Questions which will *not* aid the selection process are: questions which can be answered 'yes' or 'no'; antagonising questions which raise the defences you may earlier have lowered; leading questions which either give or suggest the 'correct' answer; questions which have discriminatory connotations.

- Discover the non-verbal language of interviews. (See also Chapter 9, on communication.)

- Do not forget that, while the interviewers want to discover whether or not the applicant is suitable, the candidate is at the same time assessing whether the organisation suits him or her!

- Let the interviewees know when they can expect a decision.

- Prior planning of the interview strategy, tactics, and questions is very important.

- Generally you should not ask a question without having an aim in mind – make sure you know *why* certain questions are asked.

Interview questions should be designed so that all applicants are treated the same, and so that each applicant gets the opportunity to put their best foot forward in the interview and give the interviewers the chance to assess them fully in relation to the position being sought. Using an interview-based candidate rating or review form is one way of comparing the various candidates.

A useful web site worth exploring for further ideas on a variety of recruitment tests, different types of interview, and which includes 2000 interview questions, can be found at: <http://www.hr-guide.com/selection.htm>.

One writer suggests that it may be more productive to choose staff who can evolve as the needs of the organisation change. Change, after all, is the only constant. So what personality traits should you seek in staff? Below is a list of qualities that might be considered essential in a new staff member, but of course no single individual will have all of these qualities. The list was developed in relation to the digital library situation, but it can be been adapted to suit any recruitment in the modern library. A candidate for a modern library position should clearly have several of the following qualities:

- the capacity to learn constantly and quickly
- flexibility
- an innate scepticism
- a propensity to take risks
- an abiding public service perspective
- an appreciation of what others bring to the effort and an ability to work with them effectively
- skill at enabling and fostering change
- the capacity and desire to work independently
- the capacity to work cooperatively with others under little supervision
- the desire to learn (based on Tennant 1998, p. 10).

An interview rating chart and associated forms should be used with caution, and as a means to compare candidates rather than as the sole decision-making aid.

Finally, to remind you of some of the key points to watch for when planning your interview, Figure 16.1 depicts some simple guidelines for the interviewing process.

Stages of the interview

Welcome, introductions, environment, interview opening

Non-threatening surroundings and positioning. Give name and relevant position for each interviewer. Put interviewee at ease. Ask general questions to begin with.

Body of interview

Wording of questions, probing for information, interviewee should do most of the talking, show interest, planned approach to interview.

Termination

Indicate how and when a decision will be communicated, finish within allotted time, discuss that candidate before the next interview.

Figure 16.1: Stages of the interview

Once the interviews have been completed, make the decision as soon as possible, while the applicants are still making an impact on your sensory devices. Let the successful applicant know as soon as possible, preferably by telephone and follow-up letter, and advise the unsuccessful ones by first available mail. In other words, finish the exercise with a public relations flourish!

Experience will also tell you that the requirements for notifying candidates of their success, or otherwise, is often guided by formal and strict organisational policies and regulations. This will also apply to the need to contact referees to verify a candidate's claims before completing the process.

The following comments from Vicki Williamson, former librarian at Curtin University stress the importance of careful recruitment and selection, and highlight the need for training in the skills used by successful selectors.

> Employees are the most valuable asset of an organization, and an organization can only be as good as the people who work in it. Good recruitment and selection processes, coupled with an on-going, targeted and responsive staff training and development program and planned human resource management places any organization in a position of competitive advantage. 'Don't you forget it' is the most important message I could ever give anyone, regardless of the level at which they work in the organization.
>
> Recruitment and selection are an important component of any human resource management plan, and they are part of the life cycle of an employee.
>
> Progressively, government regulation and legislative involvement in our workplaces require those managing recruitment and those participating in selection to have a working knowledge of legislation covering diverse areas such as equal employment opportunity, affirmative action, occupational health safety and welfare, and training. Keeping up-to-date is sometimes difficult if you are not a person dedicated solely to human resource work. Many of us who work in libraries have involvement with a range of duties and it is really only the very large libraries that can afford a dedicated human resource department with specialist staff.
>
> The associated issue for large libraries which do have a human resource department is to ensure that it has in place processes that link human resource plans with the library's strategic or corporate plan.
>
> Delegating recruitment and selection responsibility either to junior staff and/or to a technical process such as testing is also no guarantee of success. Without the

involvement of managers there is no guarantee that your recruitment and selection process will match your library's strategic plan and direction. Equally, involving only senior managers might not ensure a balanced approach. For example, the selection panel members might not appreciate the nature of the work and the knowledge, skills and competencies needed to undertake that work. Establishing selection teams that comprise a balance between senior managers and representatives from the work teams ensures a balanced view. After all, recruitment and selection are all about building teams of people who can bring to the work team required core and complementary skills.

Recruitment and selection involve dealing with people, and require those undertaking the recruitment and selection to have good people skills. You have to be good with people, interested in people, and to like and be good at recruitment and selection.

When participating in selection panels it is important to know about the role and responsibilities of panel membership. What are the organization's rules and regulations about confidentiality? What information could you be required to provide if there is an appeal against the decision of a selection panel? These are just two examples of the sort of information that participants in selection panels need to know and find out about before leading or participating in a selection panel. A good selection panel convenor will always ensure that all panel members are fully briefed before interviews begin.

The importance of documenting and recording how decisions are made by selection panels is becoming increasingly important.

Finally, remember that all applicants for positions in the library who participate in the library's recruitment and selection processes are your clients and, as such, they deserve a quality service. For example, even unsuccessful candidates should receive advice about the outcome of their application.

On the other hand, in the case of the successful candidate, the employer's handling of the recruitment and selection process and the quality of service provided during the recruitment and selection phase of the employee's life cycle could determine whether the successful candidate accepts the offer of employment. If they have not received quality service during the recruitment and selection phase, they may decide that your organization is not for them and therefore decline the offer of employment! (Williamson 1995, quoted in Sanders 1995, pp. 167-168).

An interesting example of keeping up-to-date as per Williamson's first point is found in a recent article which indicated that disabled candidates were often frustrated that they were never directly asked how their disability would affect their work performance, or what specific assistive technology they might require. Most were apprehensive about raising the matters themselves. Candid discussion about the needs of candidates with disabilities lets both parties know what to expect and averts misconceptions and fears (Rodriguez and Prezant 2002, pp. 38–42).

Conclusion

As you may have realised by now, there are no hard-and-fast 'how-to' rules in the recruitment and selection process. Experience goes a long way towards combating the problems inherent in the selection of the right person for the job. For those just learning to select, using common sense, a knowledge of the common pitfalls (as noted above) and a sense of fair play will, on their own, ensure a better than even chance of success.

Chapter 17
Staff development

It is what we learn after we know it all that really counts. (Source unknown)

If you want creative workers, give them enough time to play. (John Cleese)

Introduction

Staff development is a continual concern of library supervision and management, and in a climate of change and innovation it becomes even more important. In fact, no library has a choice of whether or not to develop its employees. When a new employee starts work, they are never perfectly fitted to the organisation and they will require some orientation to the job, to the library, to the rules and policies of the parent organisation, and to their new colleagues and supervisors. Some education and training must take place.

As indicated in Chapter 2, no library is entirely static, which means that continuing staff training is needed to provide new skills and knowledge in a specific job, or education to increase the continuing employee's general knowledge and understanding of the library's full environment.

As ALIA (the Australian Library and Information Association) note on their web site, there is a joint responsibility between staff and institutions to foster continuing professional development (CPD) in order to better cope with the dynamic environment of the library and information sector which requires staff to be open to life long learning. They go on to point out that CPD is intended to:

- maintain and improve member's technical knowledge, professional skills and competencies;
- assist them to remain flexible and adaptable; and
- provide reasonable assurance to the community that they are keeping themselves up-to-date through such activities as professional reading, participation in seminars, courses and conferences and workplace learning (ALIA 2003).

Staff development encompasses a wide range of formal and informal activities that stimulate communication, improve morale, address professional issues and prepare staff for challenges in the workplace. For example, in any one year, a large library might plan for and undertake new staff orientation, regular staff seminars, job rotation programs (within library), vendor sessions (for example system training), in-house training courses run by external or internal groups, and external conferences, seminars and workshops.

Most organisations work with staff on an annual basis to develop Personal Development Plans (or similarly titled documents) that spell out in detail the training and professional development directions that suit both the needs of the organisation and the needs of the individual. As Jordan and Lloyd note:

> Ultimately, training and development are the responsibility of the individual, and an effective organisation is one which recruits and supports staff who actively want to learn. For staff to realise this aspiration, there needs to be a commitment to training from the top down. A training culture cannot exist without the support of senior managers (2002, p. 185).

This emphasises the dual responsibility for training and career development and suggests that a considerable amount of time should be spent on this activity.

In-service training is treated here as a work-related exercise. The responsibility for this type of training should rest with the employing library. Conversely, continuing education is primarily concerned with the individual and as such is provided by professional bodies outside the library, for example, ALIA and through various ALIA-accredited program . However, there are considerable overlaps between the two functions. Thus, if you wish to develop an in-service training scheme that is concerned with, say, automated circulation systems, and another body is running a seminar on such a topic, then this could become part of your training program. But the distinction should be borne in mind, as too often libraries rely on outside bodies to provide training on topics which fall clearly within an in-house scheme.

This chapter begins with two aspects – orientation and in-service training – which are to some extent related, and which overlap in their operation. The importance of staff development will become even clearer as you complete this topic, but as one text points out: 'Human resources are too valuable for any institution to fail to invest in the training programs needed for upgrading staff' (Stueart and Moran 1998, p. 199). A great deal of the theory of human resources management relates to common sense. As always, you should attempt to apply the theoretical knowledge outlined in this chapter to practical situations in your own work.

Orientation

Most of us at some time or another have entered a new work situation. It can be both an exciting and an intimidating time. There are new people to be encountered, names to be remembered, positions to be memorised for future reference. In a large building, just finding your way around, even from workplace to toilet to staffroom and return, can be the sort of problem which detracts from gaining a favourable impression of the new job and organisation. Many of the problems encountered in the first days in a new position can be avoided by implementing a planned orientation program. Human resources management theory stresses the value of a sound induction program.

Definition

Orientation involves a range of activities, and the delivery of information, aimed at familiarising the new staff member with:

- the workplace and how it operates
- health and safety aspects of the library
- conditions of employment
- the work of the staff member's section and/or teams.

The orientation program aims to introduce the library and its parent body to the new employee, to relieve the new employee of any worries about the new position, to inform the new employee of their responsibilities, and to provide basic 'hygiene' information (such as lunch times, pay dates, and rosters). Depending on the level and nature of the position, induction may involve a few days, or may continue over several weeks.

A good orientation program has been found to make the new employee a great deal less anxious about starting work in their new library, and also has the beneficial effect of ensuring that staff are more likely to remain with the library. An unwanted result is to have new staff questioning their decision by the first day. If a library makes a negative first impression, it may take months to overcome an employee's initial frustration. Poor orientation programs can also impact future recruitment efforts. During your first week or so in a new position everyone you know 'how's your new job?' Unfortunately, if the response to the question is 'It's not what I expected' or 'I'm not sure I'm going to fit in there', this can result in negative feedback which could discourage others from applying for a position in the organisation.

Design of an orientation program

Before embarking on the design of an orientation program, it is necessary to clearly establish some general and specific objectives. Below is a list of general objectives. These are by no means comprehensive, and when you design your programs, you will have to deal more specifically with the needs of the library in question.

Objectives of an orientation program

The main objectives of an orientation program are:

- to introduce the library to the new staff member
- to help the new staff member identify with both the total library system and the more specific area in which they will be working
- to relieve the new staff member of any worries or anxieties about the new position
- to inform the new staff member of the exact responsibilities and requirements of the position
- to provide basic information to the new staff member, for example, pay dates, hours of work
- to communicate to the new staff member opportunities and support provided for development and promotion within the system.

These objectives are not listed in order of importance, but rather are of relatively equal importance. However, the overriding consideration of an orientation program should be to ease the new person into the organisation. As one source emphasises:

> Through a properly conducted induction program, new employees become socialised to an organisation. Socialisation is the process through which new employees acquire the knowledge, skills, and attitudes that make them successful organisational members. Since most new employees have a natural desire to succeed and 'fit into' the organisation and work unit, induction programs become an effective socialisation procedure. When organisational socialisation is effective, there is a uniting of individual and organisational goals. If new hire socialisation is ineffective, the result may be a rejection of the organisation by the new employee (Nankervis, Compton and Baird 2002, p. 318).

When you design a program, you should keep that statement in mind and be aware that you are trying to reconcile those goals. My approach to the design of orientation programs encompasses three stages in the process: preliminary, initial, and follow-up.

Preliminary orientation

Many orientation programs suffer because the program is not implemented until the new employee actually commences work. Yet the period between job application and work commencement can colour a new staff member's attitude to the library. In fact in some cases I would go one step further back and consider the role of the job advertisement in the induction process. The common factor with the preliminary program is that we do not yet know the identity of the new employee. For the sake of simplicity, we can consider this stage in three phases.

- The *job advertisement*, from the point of view of induction, is the first step in the process. It should carry the usual information relating to the position (see Chapter 16) but it should also clearly establish the name of a contact person whom potential employees can contact for further information about the library, the parent body and the job itself.

  The contact person fulfils two roles. First, the person should be informative about all aspects of the position being advertised. Second, the contact person should remain constant throughout the whole selection and hiring process until the new staff member has taken up duties. In large organisations this is not always practical, but some emphasis is placed on this aspect of the program.

- The *application phase* covers a variety of steps, but, depending on the level of appointment, some or all of the following should occur. The applicant should receive amplification of the advertisement, for example, advancement prospects, salary levels, conditions of appointment, and a detailed job description covering the duties and responsibilities of the position. Some information about the library, its role, the community it serves, and its achievements, would also be useful now.

  Many librarians question the need to supply information at this stage. They prefer the interview or even the pre-employment period to impart much of this basic information. However, the applicant needs some of the information to perform at their best in the interview, and the orientation program is better served if the dissemination of information is spread throughout the process.

- The *interview* is the third phase. Some libraries conduct pre-interview tours and introductions to the library and sectional heads, but this is time-consuming and costly and is best used at more senior levels. The interview itself is another step towards obtaining integration and agreement of the goals of the library and the goals of the individual. (We are concerned here with the interview only as a phase of the orientation program.) The philosophy of the library should be restated and the job description discussed, so that the applicant becomes more familiar with the requirements of the library and of the job.

  The interview completes the preliminary orientation stage. Once the job offer has been accepted by the successful applicant, the second stage commences. The second stage will build on and develop from the information supplied in stage one.

Initial induction

- *Pre-employment*. The initial induction stage covers the period from acceptance of the job through to the first days in the job.

  If the applicant is at a professional level, the employing library should begin immediately to acquaint the new employee with the workings of the position and of the library in general. Reports, details of policy, statistics, and the like should be forwarded to enable the new staff member to gain historical and current perspectives of the situation before arriving on the first morning.

  This 'involvement' method would generally not be used for more junior staff, but all staff should receive basic information relating to the first day on the job. Such information includes where and whom to report to; when to arrive; how to travel there; where to park; how to get into the building; and details of the orientation program itself. Some libraries display a comprehensive approach to providing information at this stage. Thus, rather than wait until the new staff member has taken up the position to give such information as general background to the library, names of colleagues, list of club and social activities, and so on it is sent in an advance package of information.

  The approach has much to recommend it, because a new employee is usually very receptive to such information before they begin. Likewise, it assists with acquainting the new employee with the whole system as soon as the job has been accepted.

- *Commencement of duties*. The planning and detailed organisation of this phase of the orientation program will depend very much on the nature and size of the library, and on the availability of staff. Some larger libraries use a batch method of appointing junior levels of staff so that orientation can be batched according to levels and groups. Smaller libraries cannot avail themselves of this method and will tailor their programs to each individual.

  This is the crucial period for the orientation program. All the good work of the preliminary orientation period can be wasted if this stage is not well planned and executed. You should refer to your objectives to see if your program is meeting them. There should also be regular feedback sessions (daily at first, then weekly) to monitor the progress of both the new staff member and the program itself.

  The other crucial factor in this initial period is information overload. Some programs are so intense, and the new employee is subjected to such a plethora of new information, that total confusion and anxiety can result. Remember, we are trying to avoid that! Spreading the information through the preliminary period will help, but in designing your program, consider ways of providing variety and allowing time to absorb new tasks and ideas.

Follow-up

This final stage is one that is often neglected. The follow-up to orientation will overlap to some extent with your in-service training program, but its role in induction should be recognised. During the follow-up stage the library should evaluate:

- the success or otherwise of inducting the new employee
- the effectiveness of the orientation program itself.

The timing of the follow-up stage depends upon factors unique to each library and each program, but six months after appointment (often coinciding with an end of probation period interview or evaluation) would seem to be the maximum date for evaluation. Ideally, the follow-up should consist of a meeting between the new employee and the librarian in charge, or the librarian responsible for the program. Evaluating the success of orientation in general should occur regularly, probably on an annual basis.

Supervisor's role in orientation

While the library manager or some other executive will normally cover background information about the library, its role and services, its overall policies (for example on flexible working hours, leave, and so on) and procedures, the supervisor must cover these if senior management does not. An effective program will have sorted this out in advance.

The supervisor's informational role does cover:

- a welcome to the section
- tour of the section and/or larger department
- introductions to fellow workers
- tour of library and staff amenities
- hours of work, breaks, rosters
- review of job description/contract
- health and safety requirements
- introduction to the new job.

Overall, the supervisor should cover information that is of most immediate relevance to the new employee before proceeding to more general information; and that requires an assessment of priorities when planning the program. It is up to the supervisor to make the new employee feel welcome, and begin to help them to feel part of their new work environment. In a team environment, this may also mean explaining the purpose of the work group, its goals, why the job is so important, group norms relating to job rotation, training, leadership, and so forth.

In-service training

Too often libraries have a well-developed orientation program but fail to build on its benefits with ongoing staff training. The reverse happens too. Buying material for a staff library collection and circulating library journals among staff do not constitute a training and development program.

Training makes an important contribution to the operational effectiveness of the library. Among the benefits accruing from successful training programs are improved job performance; the acquisition of new skills; better staff and public relations; improved motivation; increased support for organisational goals; and the provision of a pool of staff skilled beyond their present job requirements who will be available to fill future vacancies. Individual staff members also benefit, resulting in greater job satisfaction, mobility and interest in the job and the library. In turn the library benefits with higher quality staff and service, and greater staff stability and retention rates.

Job training

The most common form of training, and the one which can be seen in operation every day, in every library, is job training. Learning how to perform a particular task can be undertaken in groups or individually. What is important is that the staff member understands *why* a certain task is performed in a certain way, *why* it is performed at all, and how that task meshes in with other tasks and procedures related to it.

Initially, job training involves the supervisor in training the new employee in the specific tasks of the job. If the supervisor does not do the training, then they must ensure that someone else does. Any training given to an employee should be carefully planned, and should adhere to the following basic principles:

- teach the simple tasks first
- break down each task into simple, basic components
- teach only the correct procedures
- keep teaching sessions short, and reinforce the learning through practice
- help develop skills through repetition, practice and feedback
- be aware that the trainee needs to be motivated.

Job training is most useful to teach skills and knowledge that can be learned in a reasonably short time, such as circulation desk routines, bibliographic verification and copy cataloguing. Getting someone trained for reference work, and other less routine jobs, may involve seminars, lectures, simulated work exercises and other off-the-job programs.

ALIA accredited packages such as QILS (Quality in Library Service) are also extremely useful in assisting managers and supervisors implement training programs for more junior staff. The purpose of the QILS program for instance is to:

- focus staff on agreed service expectations and client satisfaction
- provide staff with the skills and support needed to achieve and maintain identified service standards
- identify and address skill gaps
- extend the competencies of inexperienced and experienced staff
- emphasise teamwork as an essential extension of individual competency
- integrate electronic with print resources, and document delivery with in-house resources
- obtain staff input into policies and procedures
- encourage lifelong learning in staff (Burrell and McGrath, 1999).

With such pre-packaged training materials available, managers are able to develop general competencies in staff without a huge commitment of in-house resources to the process.

Job training is the bridge between orientation and continuing in-service training. Like all training, it needs to be planned. When preparing a training plan take note of the following:

- be aware of the possibility of information overload
- training objectives should be clearly stated
- feedback should be welcomed
- flexibility should be in-built and encouraged
- training should move from the basic and general to the specific
- attitudinal or behaviour guidelines should be considered.

Many jobs may also require the person to become familiar gradually with other aspects of the library's work, in order to be rostered onto a variety of tasks. This could be part of a job rotation scheme, or part of the intended job description of the new staff member. The following gives an example of the detail that should be covered in training a new library assistant in a public library:

- circulation routines – for example, loans, returns, fines, statistics, customer relations
- shelving
- membership – for example, registration and renewals, filing, enquiries
- overdues – for example, notices, accounts, blacklists
- processing – for example, repairs, end processing
- enquiries – for example, directional, quick reference, referrals
- other services – for example, housebound, special clients, special equipment.

Note in particular the need to:

- prioritise training needs
- review progress regularly
- break jobs down into readily taught, complete tasks
- include a framework for regular training in any plan
- develop and plan a training program in advance.

Continuing staff training

Continuing staff training occurs as specific training needs are identified for both new and more established employees. The supervisor has a very clear role in recognising these training needs, and in ensuring that employees have the opportunity to grow in their jobs and become ready for advancement opportunities as they arise. The general aims of continuing staff training are to:

- tenable staff to be better equipped to meet their responsibilities within the organisation
- provide benefits to the organisation from this increased staff awareness
- enable staff to be in a better position to gain advancement within the organisation
- encourage staff 'in-house' in order that they will seek self-improvement programs by taking advantage of continuing education opportunities.

Training, then, plays a part in determining the effectiveness and efficiency of the library. The supervisor, by playing his or her role in training, can assist in the major contribution of training to:

- reduced learning time for new employees to reach an acceptable level of performance
- improve current employee performance
- achieve support for organisational objectives
- obtain better cooperation and greater loyalty
- aid in solving operational problems such as low morale, poor service to patrons, excessive waste of materials
- fill staffing needs
- benefit employees themselves, as they increase their knowledge and skills and thus increase their marketability and earning power.

Training and education should be encouraged as a matter of policy, and that policy must be endorsed by all managers and supervisors. Specific training needs must also to be identified. The library should have established the design and requirements of each job and by continual evaluation of the work of staff be aware of training needs. Training needs to be evaluated to see if the specific requirements are being met.

Training needs analysis and evaluation of training

It has been said that training within the work environment is the most useful and relevant training that can be undertaken.

Perhaps that is because it is under the control of the employer, and is most readily tailored to the needs of the organisation. It is seen clearly as the responsibility of the organisation, rather than of the individual staff member. The difficulty with in-service training is achieving that fusion between the needs of the organisation and the needs of the individual employee. In addition, finding staff with the requisite expertise and time to undertake the training is a challenge in most organisations. Thus clearly defining needs and the resources to meet those needs is an essential step in any work based program to ensure that, in addition to meeting the training goals, valuable resources (trained staff) are not used in an inefficient manner.

Training needs analysis

Training occurs as specific training needs are identified for both new and more established staff. The library should have established the basic operations and procedures of each job, and by continual evaluation of work performance and output be aware of any performance deficiencies and thus training needs.

Feedback from performance evaluation and appraisal is perhaps the most common source of data used in assessing training needs. Other sources include job analysis and redesign; surveys of training needs; active solicitation of (and unsolicited) feedback from staff, users and other 'clients' (for example, book suppliers, equipment and service providers, accountants); consideration of future developments in the library's planning continuum (for example, planned introduction of new services); new legislation or policies from the library's funding body; and, of course, feedback from the participants and trainers in current training programs (including orientation checklists). (All senior staff must be sensitive to this kind of feedback, and regular communication between those responsible for planning and producing training and those supervisors in closest contact with staff is essential.)

Nankervis, Compton and Baird (2002, p. 591) highlight another area which has become well-established practice – the use of 'exit' interviews. These combine closing off administrative issues such as computer sign-ons, security passes etc. together with a level of fact finding about the reason the person is leaving and their attitude towards the work place. They may be asked for their opinion on working conditions, communication issues, things they consider could be improved upon etc. From this process, the organisation may gain valuable feedback on its overall functioning and may be able to identify problem areas. The important point in this context is that if the process is in place, it can be another means for highlighting training needs.

Evaluation of training

Training objectives can be developed when training needs have been established. To assess the achievement of those objectives, some kind of evaluation must take place – whether formal or informal.

In some libraries, evaluation is a low priority activity because of its degree of difficulty. Those areas which are most commonly evaluated include the content of courses or programs, and the appropriateness of an activity to the organisation. Evaluation of courses and activities for appropriateness and content is done in various ways. In-house courses are often evaluated at the end of the session and from informal discussions with participants. Other courses and activities are evaluated through comments from those who attended and through reports which participants are required to write for their senior management, their supervisors, or even for presentation to those who could not attend but who will benefit from the feedback. As Jordan and Lloyd note:

> Evaluation is important if the quality of training is to be improved, and if it is to be made clear that it is the effect of training that matters most of all. In times of diminishing budgets, training needs to be good value, but even where cost is not an issue (if such a place exists!), training which delivers what it sets out to achieve should be identified and valued, whereas training which fails to meet the stated objectives should be redesigned, or in the case of external training, avoided (2002, p. 230)

The following are based on items in *Staff Development in Australian Libraries* (1988) and highlight the difficulties of measuring the success of staff development programs while giving some ideas on how to evaluate the benefits of staff development.

The first comments reflect on what staff development really is, in terms of the tangible and intangible benefits for the library and the individual concerned.

> For some library programs, such as new staff orientation, staff seminar day, participants are asked to provide feedback. While this does offer some evaluation, it is to a large degree a subjective measure. Special sessions in particular subject areas…may have noticeable effects in a demonstrated ability to assist particular groups of [clients].
>
> Sessions of this type, however, raise another issue – to what extent should they be regarded as developmental? Where does training end and development begin?
>
> Staff are also entitled to some study time…[which] might also be rated as staff development time.
>
> The other side of the staff development coin to the time that an institution contributes is the time individuals are prepared to spend themselves in study, or attendance at evening or weekend meetings and seminars. It would be a measure of a less than effective development program, particularly where professional staff are concerned, if the time, money and effort is contributed totally by one party (Knox 1988, pp. 5–6).

Isabella Trahn (1988) has this to say about a library whose formal staff development program and function has the brief to establish staff development needs; to establish a program to meet those needs; and to draw up an agreed staff development policy.

> The evaluation techniques to be used for staff development…[are] a combination of the traditional formal feedback sheets for specific activities, formal follow up sessions with supervisors, and informal feedback. Statistical measures of level of use, locations and numbers of participants, levels of complaints…[are also used.]
>
> Because of the involvement in the library planning process and the spelling out of goals, objectives, priorities and performance measures, evaluation is, to a considerable degree, a normal part of planning; however, evaluation could be done better…
>
> To some extent, the breadth of staff development goals makes effective evaluation difficult. Developing the skills and improving the performance of over 200 individuals and in particular in the library as a whole is no mean feat and involves so many variables outside the ambit of influence of the Staff Development librarian that the prospect is daunting; however, meeting the specific objectives of a one year plan is less so and that is where the energies are generally directed.

> Planning is the key...It defines what you are trying to achieve and sets out your priorities, so that evaluation is given perspective and proportion (Trahn 1988, pp. 6–7).

For staff training courses (for example using Kinetica or new databases) and specialised subjects (for example, occupational health and safety issues) it is possible to use a one-page evaluation sheet. This can not only ascertain the quality of the course, (for example, how good was the facilitator? how well was the course presented? how relevant was the content?) but can also get the participants to consider their own learning outcomes and how they intend to use the learning in their current job.

> The real evaluation occurs on the job from supervisors and colleagues. Staff should perform better, make fewer mistakes and supervisors should theoretically supervise more effectively. Some of the training literature suggests three-way evaluation after course attendance – from supervisors, colleagues and staff. This is very time intensive, but one idea which works towards this is an Annual Staff Development Review. The supervisor of each section interviews staff about their work, any training/development needs, and if they perceived any benefits from post training/development activities. It is considered less threatening than performance appraisal and can be a useful tool for supervisors, who follows up any staff development suggestions (Newnham 1988, p. 9)

Continuing education and career planning

Most library managers would agree that *continuing education* is a matter for the individual to pursue. 'Continuing education consists of those learning opportunities utilized by individuals in fulfilling their need to learn and grow following their preparatory education and work experience' (Conroy 1978, p. *xv*). The goals of the library and the goals of the individual staff member do not necessarily coincide in a continuing education program. However, if the employing authority is conscious of the value of an aware and interested staff, it should actively encourage staff participation in continuing education. Such staff self-development may include activities which are common to the library's in-service training program, and will include for example, specialised seminars, staff interchanges, and staff visits to other institutions. The employing library can encourage the development of its staff by providing funding and by providing a forum for staff to transfer their new knowledge and understanding to other staff, and to inform their colleagues of new developments in their fields of interest.

Allied to this is an issue which has generally been placed in the 'too hard' and 'not our responsibility' basket by library managers. *Career planning* is still very much a necessary consideration for those concerned with the growth and development of their professional staff because managers, supervisors and staff must plan their work lives. A person's career is not summed up by the decision to pursue librarianship as a profession. Career planning is a conscious determination to grow and develop, and to promote self-esteem and competence. Individuals can approach this by addressing their career goals and plans through assessment of their own life, values, interests and aspirations, bearing in mind that their work and career may be only one part of their total life which includes family and social aspects as well.

The library can approach each individual's career aspirations as well. Managers and supervisors should be concerned with the careers of their staff, and providing career enhancing programs and activities can help improve job satisfaction and a variety of organisational relationships. The library that assists with career development may also benefit from an individual's development of further job-related knowledge and skill. This is another reminder that first level studies are just the beginning of lifelong learning.

In the following excerpt from comments by Veronica Lunn for the 1995 edition of this text, Veronica suggests the kinds of benefits that come, in practice, from an organised and ongoing program of staff development. She clearly indicates the vital role of communication in this, and shows that client-focused libraries must continually allow their staff to develop.

In a client/provider relationship the moment of truth occurs at every point of interaction.

Each organisation seeking to develop and focus the energies and skills of their staff meets this moment of truth daily from the time of initial contact with a new staff member. Orientation begins at the first point of contact, where a series of questions may or may not have been addressed: What information has been provided about the organisational culture, the position, career paths, and plans for development, and what are the mutual expectations?

Most organisations conduct formal staff induction programs, which should ideally take a global perspective, incorporating not only the library, but introducing the new employee into the corporate body. Each new employee should have the opportunity to meet the Corporate Manager, and to understand the aims and objectives of the organisation and the specific roles of other departments. This approach inculcates a sense of belonging to the corporate team.

Similarly, a global orientation in the library provides for longer-term benefits. Specific on-the-job training is more effective once placed within the larger context. Encouraging and acting on feedback from the orientation program fosters a sense of involvement in the process and facilitates a dynamic and relevant mechanism. The orientation program should provide a clear road map, not only of the organisation but also of the individual's path within the corporate body.

Integral to such an understanding is an appreciation of the opportunities available for the individual and the organisation to maximise the potential of the labour resource. All employees should have a clear understanding of the ongoing program for staff development. Continuing education programs, training needs of staff, and the skills and information needs of the organisation must be constantly reviewed. The program should reflect the existing and projected needs of the organisation, and staff should feel that they have played a significant part in its development.

An annual training needs analysis should not only incorporate course availability, but also should assess the need for placement of staff in other sections or libraries. A staff exchange or placement program is a valid component of staff development. Similarly, networking, both formally and informally, should not be overlooked: cooperative training and education projects between libraries maximises resources and shares costs.

One aspect of staff development that is often neglected in the focus on formal programs is the need for managers and supervisors to inform and educate their staff in forums other than in-service programs. An effective communication and feedback environment is an invaluable factor in staff development. Short briefing sessions, regular professional and technological updates, shared information on projects, and discussion about planned projects create a scenario in which staff have a desire to be informed. This enhances self-development and a positive response to programs initiated.

Skilled, well informed and highly motivated staff are the single most valuable asset in any organisation. Productivity gains and enhanced job satisfaction are the inclusive product of staff development programs that are well planned, effectively monitored, conducive to change and, most importantly, geared to excellence (Lunn 1995, quoted in Sanders 1995, pp. 186–187).

Organisational climate and change

Every library can, and in fact should, create a climate in which people are motivated to extend themselves and to perform at their optimum level most of the time. Staff development aims to expand staff understanding of concepts, procedures and techniques, encouraging staff to take new approaches and risks in reaching solutions. It should also develop confidence in reassessing patterns of thinking and acting.

For all of that to take place, and for staff to be able to put their new learning into practice and continue to learn on and off the job, the working environment must be supportive. Most writings on staff training and continuing education at least mention this need:

> ...organizational climate and leadership style, in particular those encouraging participation, will help encourage attitudes, relationships, motivation and morale conducive not only to training and development processes but also organizational change and innovation (Saw 1989, p. 17).

Chapter 2 provided an introduction to organisational climate, which might be useful to re-read at this point.

Performance appraisal

Definition

Performance appraisal is the systematic evaluation of the performance and future development of individual staff members.

Performance appraisal systems have been adopted by most Australian libraries, often as a result of their implementation within the broader organisation. Appraisal is not new, but its introduction into many libraries has been handled with kid gloves in the knowledge that it can be uncomfortable, and that it can be damaging. However, supervisors and managers are, inevitably, appraising their staff every day in informal ways. Performance appraisal is introduced as a supplement to, and not a replacement for, that informal appraisal.

For example, the University of South Australia promotes the following outcomes for effective performance management:

- A clear understanding of the purpose and goals of the organisation
- Clarification of roles, tasks and outcomes expected of individuals and teams
- Fair recognition of the contribution of individuals and teams
- Systematic provision of development opportunity
- A positive approach to the management of people and increased job satisfaction. (Ranieri 1999, quoted in Luther 2000).

Performance appraisal is also seen as an opportunity to strengthen the relationship between the corporate goals of the funding body and the role of individual staff members. Thus, the goals of the funding body should be related to the library, and then to the team in which any individual staff member operates. The individual's position within the team can be then considered in terms of the broad range of tasks required by their position, and what their focus should be for the coming year (Luther, 2000).

Each individual staff member needs to know what is expected of them, how well they are doing, some idea of what the future may hold, that assistance in development is available, and that their contribution to the library will be fairly rewarded. The library, in its turn, needs to know how well its staff are performing, and how it can help if necessary. The library also wants to know who can take on added or different responsibilities, and how and when to prepare staff for those.

A formal appraisal system will run its cycle on a six-monthly or annual basis. Many libraries will appraise staff after a six-month period (sometimes this can even be a trial or probationary period of employment), with annual appraisals thereafter. The following is a general outline of the process as adopted by many libraries. Individual differences occur, especially in the methods of evaluation.

- The staff member being appraised and his or her supervisor complete a performance appraisal form.

- Each then reads the other's comments.

- The staff member is interviewed by his or her supervisor and another more senior staff member. Other supervisors may be involved if the staff member being appraised has more than one supervisor. This is vital to gain a complete picture of performance.

- The comments from appraisal forms are discussed.

- The staff member's performance goals for the next year are then agreed. Goals, along with any staff development needed or desired, are programmed into an action plan for the staff member.

- All the participants in the performance appraisal sign the assessment form and action plan.

- A formal letter or memo is sent to the staff member summarising the interview, goals, further training, action plan and intended means of evaluation.

The methods of evaluation of performance will vary from one library to another. Whatever method is used, it must be valid, and it must be reliable. To be valid, the method must include factors which accurately evaluate the performance of the staff member. There are many criteria that can be used, as the following list indicates:

- volume of work
- quality of work
- interest
- initiative
- job knowledge
- cooperation and contact with other staff
- judgment
- work habits
- reliability
- adaptability
- ability to train others
- responsibility
- exhibition of specific skills
- ability to learn
- leadership
- accuracy.

Not all of the above will be applicable to every job. For example, leadership can be assessed in a person with supervisory responsibilities, but not in a person who has not had the opportunity to lead others. In the latter case, only leadership potential can be assessed.

People tend to work, learn and achieve more if they have clear goals, are involved in setting tasks and goals and have reasonable feedback about how they are performing in terms of those goals. The job or position description (discussed in Chapter 15) can be a real aid here. Ideally, the job description will outline a standard of achievement of tasks which the incumbent is required to fulfil. This outline, along with key result areas and targets, if regularly updated, helps to ensure that both supervisor and staff member are fully conversant with all aspects of the job and its goals. It also forms a basis for mutually beneficial and informed discussion both during the formal appraisal and at other times if problems arise.

A successful appraisal scheme depends on frankness and objective comments from all participants. Staff must be assured that they need not be afraid to be honest, and that they will suffer no recriminations from open comment. Staff have a right to express a point of view which is their own and which may differ from that of their supervisor. They should feel free to question the comments of their supervisor if necessary. Another of the keys to successful appraisal is the relationship between feedback and involvement.

Supervisor's role in performance appraisal

The supervisor will generally be involved in assessing a number of staff each year – both informally and formally. Performance appraisal allows supervisors to identify and develop staff members with different potential to meet the challenges faced by the library. Many supervisors will feel uncomfortable sitting in judgment of others and find the form filling to be complicated, difficult and time-consuming. However, if appraisal is seen as a continuous process rather than as an annual event, then the benefits can be realised. Closer working relationships, opportunities to motivate, uncovering of problems and establishing training and development needs are all potential benefits from well-considered and delivered appraisal.

Supervisors should have the most in-depth knowledge of the work of the staff for whom they are immediately responsible. When considering the performance of a staff member, the supervisor will use a number of their skills, especially those in communication and listening:

- be open minded
- avoid being judgmental
- learn to listen and understand
- practise patience
- be open and honest
- be responsible
- maintain confidentiality.

With the above essential behaviours being practised, the supervisor needs to know the answers to the following questions:

- Can I describe exactly and precisely what performance characteristics concern me?
- Do I know what they view their job to be?
- Do I know what they feel is lacking to make them a good performer?
- Have I communicated my concern in a helpful non-threatening manner?

- Are there policies and procedures which might be blocking them?
- Have I acted to support them and how do they feel about that?
- Have I offered, or given, them all the help they need?
- Have I given them all the information they need?
- Are they in a job for which their education, training, skills and experience fit them?
- Are there outside situations which may be affecting their performance?

Many of these questions will be answered in an informal manner during the everyday working situation. Supervisors should be gathering information constantly throughout the year, making clear notes of relevant job performance data for reference during the annual appraisal. Opinions based on the memory of distant events are likely to develop bias, whereas your notes will indicate highs and lows of performance over the year.

> There's also a cultural issue. Despite various inputs and shared discussion, one person appraises another. It highlights a power imbalance with which Australians are not particularly comfortable, at work or socially. Performance appraisal flies in the face of the Australian notion of egalitarianism.

> Many managers handle this poorly, by distancing themselves from a direct leadership role in preparing for the process or engaging with it. Staff are told to go away and prepare their yearly goals, do a preliminary rating of their past performance and think about what training courses they might like to do (Simons 2000, p. 50).

In such a situation, and it sounds very familiar, staff could feel that their supervisor is not happy in their leadership role, and yet, staff will be expecting leadership and guidance about how they should focus their work and development. For a performance appraisal system to have satisfactory outcomes, supervisors and managers need to overcome any concerns they have about the personal aspects of power, and need to be skilled at exercising and communicating many aspects of leadership.

It is still very clear that there is value in having the above questions confirmed formally through the annual performance review form and interview. On the other hand, all employees need to hear feedback regularly, and certainly more frequently than once a year, whether there are problems or not. Good feedback motivates employees, and problems will get fixed sooner rather than later. Even if it is not a formal performance review, employees should receive casual but specific face-to-face feedback on their performance on a monthly or quarterly basis.

In a personal, but well-considered, view of the performance appraisal process Losyk (2002) identifies the biggest challenges and rewards of effective performance appraisal. In particular, he highlights the need for the supervisor/manager to understand the potential role of bias when evaluating others' performance – an issue we have briefly explored in other areas of this text. Losyk also identifies the need to clearly define the job and expectations before embarking on performance appraisal; the appropriate structure of an appraisal interview; and the complimentary roles of the manager and employee in effective performance appraisal. Indeed, most of the points Losyk raises are issues discussed throughout this text. He concludes with a comment on the need to maintain communication to achieve best results:

> Finally, work on keeping communications open until the next appraisal interview. If you are doing a good job as a manager, and if you are getting your employees to perform well, then you will not be feeling all this tension and stress the next time you need to evaluate someone. Your employees won't be feeling it either. Instead, you can look forward to effective, productive face-to-face meetings that will give you and your employees a chance to achieve greater job satisfaction, improved morale, and higher productivity (Losyk 2002, p. 11).

One of Australia's leading human resources experts, Les Pickett, has said that performance appraisals too often concentrate on the past, and that nothing takes the place of open communication on a daily basis.

> To a certain extent, retrospective reviews are a waste of time because the problems that come up – or outstanding achievements – should have been addressed at the time…the real issue should be focusing on the future direction of the employee – their objectives for the year and what skills they need to achieve them. (Pickett quoted in Vincent 2002)

Conclusion

All categories and levels of library staff have a need to learn, a need to be trained, and a need to be developed. Human resources represent the most expensive ongoing costs of any library, and while training takes time (and therefore adds to the costs of human resources), it is important for libraries to realise that they need to develop their staff. Not to do so can lead to low morale, low performance, poor public relations (through mistakes, complaints, and so forth) and staff turnover.

Training and development often plays a role in the achievement of objectives set in strategic plans, and prepares the organisation and its employees for future direction by building skills and competence. However, if formal training and development programs are not as prevalent in libraries as assessment activities, this may suggest that senior management may pay lip service to the implementation of human resources planning without allocating the resources (or the commitment) to middle managers to follow through. The gathering of human resources data through assessment and appraisal becomes a futile activity when that data is not used to train and develop employees in line with library plans which (if fully integrated with the overall strategic plans of the organisation) in turn will aid in the achievement of the organisation's short and long term objectives.

People are the library's most valuable resource, and training and development, linked to regular and ongoing performance appraisal, will help retain a skilled and motivated group of staff who will in turn help to achieve the library's goals most effectively.

I would like to give the last word on staff development to Cyril Houle, with whose thoughts some of you may well agree (despite the fact that he voiced them over thirty years ago), although I hope that is not the case. I believe one of the points made here is that your initial study and training are not fully retained beyond a few years, and that continuing professional education is a must!

> The voice of the aggrieved alumnus is always loud in the land and, no matter what the profession, the burden of complaint is the same. In the first five years after graduation, alumni say that they should have been taught more practical techniques. In the next five years, they say they should have had more basic theory. In the tenth to fifteenth years, they inform the faculty that they should have been taught more about administration or about their relations with their co-workers and subordinates. In the subsequent five years, they condemn the failure of their professors to put the profession in its larger historical, social and economic contexts. After the twentieth year, they insist that they should have been given a broader orientation to all knowledge, scientific and humane. Sometime after that, they stop giving advice; the university has deteriorated so badly since they left that it is beyond hope (Houle 1967, p. 263).

Chapter 18
Personal and interpersonal skills

Time management

> You will never have any more time than you have today. (A gem from the desk diary)
>
> Work either expands or contracts in order to fill the time available. (Parkinson's Law)

Definition

> …time management principles provide methods of planning and organizing work, both in the library and at home, to achieve those goals that you consider important. Time management focuses on effectiveness (doing the right job) rather than efficiency (doing a job right) (Cochran 1992, p. 9).

Cochran goes on to debunk a few myths about time management. For example, time management is not actually the management of time as the phrase suggests, but rather is the management of one's work and other activities in relation to time. Time management is also not about working longer hours or working harder. It is, however, about making more effective use of one's time, delegating when necessary and possible, making decisions about what is important and concentrating on those priorities, preventing the wastage of time, and achieving goals set (Cochran 1992, pp. 9–11).

Supervisors and time management

It is in the nature of professionals – and librarians are no exception – that they take a pride in providing the best possible service, even if sometimes it means taking more time in trying to serve some or all clients to a very high standard. However, time management suggests that sometimes priorities must be decided, for reasons of service, economy, even politics. We are also having to understand and develop within an environment where information needs and sources are growing daily. Keeping pace becomes difficult, and juggling priorities, managing our time, seems to become equally difficult. As we move from 'mere employee' to supervisor, from being managed to managing, we find that more and more of our time is being spent doing 'management' activities such as planning and leading, and less and less of our time is being spent on doing what some may see as 'real' professional work.

How do supervisors and managers spend their time if it is not poring over AACR or DDC, or sitting at the information desk with a welcoming smile?

A recent Australian survey indicated that managerial tasks involving information seeking, decision-making, problem-solving, and knowledge, staff and financial management occupy the largest share (39 per cent) of a manager's time (Durant and Morley 2002, pp. 7–9). Much of this takes place through meetings (both planned and unplanned), reading and writing reports and reading mail. Other common activities included writing letters and memos, reading journals, and making and answering telephone calls.

Hence not only do we have to use our time effectively, but also we need to be constantly aware that a percentage of the work we do will be related to professional work but will be, in reality, management work. And I'm sure that a similar survey amongst library managers would tell us that email reading and writing will be a growing if not dominant category.

The danger here is that we can become so involved in meetings, report and email writing that we lose sight of our real work and individual goals. We must always be sure that those supervisory and management activities are goal-related, and not being undertaken just for the sake of it. When you read the next section on meetings, you will understand that they are one of the great challenges to time management.

I know my own major barriers to effective time management are interruptions, and the email. As an example of time management techniques in action, I have summarised below the way Cochran (1992, pp. 50-52) suggests you handle the time management challenges of *interruptions*, and them some guidelines on how to control your *email.*

Interruptions

Interruptions provide one of the biggest challenges to librarians. Past management studies have identified visitors as a serious time management problem, or have discovered that the average manager is 'interrupted' every few minutes, but one must be careful to define what really is an interruption. After all, managing is about dealing with people and resources, so it should come as no surprise that an important part of time management involves dealing with 'interruptions', and indeed, deciding what are and are not interruptions.

Librarians can use many techniques to deal with interruptions. Some techniques discourage or prevent interruptions. Others help librarians cope with interruptions to lessen their sometimes negative effects. Some of the less helpful ones I have read of include:

- rearrange your office furniture to discourage casual conversation from people passing
- stack papers or books in the chairs in your office to discourage visitors from sitting
- use non-verbal and verbal clues to discourage long interruptions for example, 'I won't invite you to sit down; it will save your time and mine'
- use planned interruptions to keep other interruptions short. for example, 'I have other matters on my schedule today that I must attend to now'
- use hideaways.

And then some more helpful ones:

- remember that a librarian's job often consists of interruptions
- anticipate the request (using guides, handouts, signs, and so forth)
- close your office door for a short period if necessary to meet a deadline (but discuss with staff first) – difficult if you do not have an office of course!
- be honest about when you can complete a client's or staff member's request
- cooperate with co-workers in having some time available to everyone with limited interruptions
- limit your interruptions of other staff members

- train staff members to carefully consider their interruptions (Cochran 1992, pp. 50–55).

Email

Some days it seems our worklife is driven by our email. Email has become the most common form of work communication in many information enterprises, and libraries are no exception. We need to constantly review how we deal with the huge quantities of email which have the potential to prevent us from achieving the goals of our work.

There are a number of versions of a 'Ten commandments of email', and a paraphrase of Tom Spring's reported version (which comes to about 20, in fact) is enlightening (Spring 1999). These are all general guidelines, and of course do not apply in every situation. And you will notice that nearly all of them are not specific to the technology of email – they mostly emanate from, and apply to, all communication means.

- it is all right to ignore an email the same way you might any communication
- make your messages short and informal
- emails cannot replace a phone call
- take care with sending and receiving attachments
- delay sending emails in response to something which has angered you – like letters and phone calls, wait for a calmer moment to respond
- try to avoid sending an email when a personal encounter is required – especially when it comes to reprimanding, rewarding, hiring or firing
- use the features your email program offers – particularly spell check!
- beware of what you say, it is so easy to send an email to the wrong recipient; if you would hesitate to say it in person, don't send it
- remember the hierarchy when it comes to communications. If it's an important message that can't be said face-to-face, then pick up the phone, or leave voice mail. Many times, email is the last resort
- be aware that misunderstandings can occur, because punctuation, spelling and grammar can be lost in the transmission (Spring 1999).

These are the kinds of helpful tips you can find when you read further in the area of time management, or undertake a course, or workshop on the subject. Like most topics in this book, and in this chapter in particular, you are provided with an introduction only, and you must read further to gain the benefit of a wider range of experience.

Meeting skills

> Time spent on any item of the agenda will be in inverse proportion to the sum involved.
> (C. Northcote Parkinson)

Interruptions were referred to above as but one example of why time management skills are so important. Meetings are another example of an activity that we feel obliged to be part of and which we encounter frequently, but which pose problems for our time management. Meetings can seem to be a waste of time, and indeed sometimes are.

> Oh, give me your pity, I'm on a committee
> Which means that from morning 'til night
> We attend, and amend, and contend, and defend,
> Without a conclusion in sight.

> We confer and concur, we defer and demur,
> And reiterate all our thoughts.

We revise the agenda with frequent addenda,
And consider a heap of reports.

We compose and propose, we support and oppose
And the points of procedure are fun.
But though various notions are brought up as motions,
There's terribly little gets done.

We resolve and devolve, but we never dissolve
That is out of the question for us.
It would be such a pity to end our committee,
Where else could we make such a fuss?
(Source unknown)

Those of us who are actively involved in organisations, associations and clubs outside work will certainly have an idea of the difference between a good meeting and a bad one. However, meetings do have a purpose, and they do have a role in the decision-making and communication areas of the supervisor's role.

Meetings serve a number of purposes.

- They can be held to inform staff about decisions made, or policies established in a way that gives them a feeling of being involved that a noticeboard or memo announcement cannot.

- They may be called to gather information, ideas, points of view about issues or practices that affect those involved. Again, it is a more personal way of gaining such input that a survey or circulation memos cannot achieve.

- They are called to discuss items of interest to those who attend.

- They are used to help solve problems and make decisions.

One of the greatest benefits of meetings is the opportunity they give for discussion and instant feedback on the items being raised and talked about. No other device of communication has this advantage. Few librarians learn in library school how to run an effective meeting, but meetings constitute a significant portion of most librarians' time at work. Because of that, research indicates that meetings comprise one of the largest time management problems for librarians.

While some time management experts recommend categorically not to call meetings or attend them, most librarians cannot, realistically, follow that advice. Most librarians must attend meetings regularly for a variety of reasons.

First, of course, your supervisor may require your attendance. Staff meetings called by the library director, for example, would be difficult to miss.

Second, you might need to attend a meeting to get correct information for handling a particular situation. In a crisis, for example, it may be necessary to distribute information to the staff as a group so that everyone gets the same information at the same time.

Third, if you are involved directly with the goal of the meeting, you should attend, of course. Groups assigned with the planning and implementation of specific library projects must meet regularly to keep the project moving smoothly.

Fourth, the politics of your job may require you to attend certain meetings. Increasingly, librarians work to develop good public relations for their libraries, and this may require the presence of the librarians at certain meetings (Cochran 1992, pp. 57–62).

There are some techniques which when practised will help librarians to minimise the time-wasting effects of any meetings that they call or attend.

- consider alternatives such as a memo, telephone conference call, email, or a video conference
- start the meeting by agreeing on a definite finishing time
- keep the meeting as short as is reasonably possible
- produce an agenda in advance, invite contributions to the agenda, stick to it, and don't have an item called 'any other business'
- ensure that any audio-visual equipment is set up and working *before* the meeting starts
- if you are chairing the meeting, have an active and moderating role.

Supervisors and meetings

The role of the supervisor in meetings will vary, depending upon whether they are leading the meeting (for example as chairperson or facilitator), or whether they are a participant without an obvious leading role. In all cases, however, it is the supervisor's role to ensure that they participate fully, listening carefully, speaking clearly and appropriately, contributing with ideas and opinions, and assisting with the formulation and making of decisions. All of this needs to be done while attempting to ensure all have an opportunity to contribute, because meetings are about communication and interpersonal relationships, and effective relationships cannot develop if staff are silent (or silenced!) during meetings and then make their real feelings known later in the tearoom or workroom when it is too late. Techniques such as small group breakouts and brainstorming can help to ensure contributions are encouraged without anyone feeling put upon or inhibited.

Being prepared (at the minimum, having read the agenda and thought about, or researched, any areas in which you can be expected to have an interest) is another part of the supervisor's role in meetings. Meetings can assist with team building, organizational climate, motivation and morale, and can help bring about cooperation and commitment among staff. The supervisor should have thought about who will be attending, what they might be expected to contribute, who may need some encouragement and assistance with putting their point of view, and generally facilitate the positive benefits of meeting.

Report writing

> Writing crystallizes thought and thought produces action. (Source unknown)

The aim of this section is to introduce you to some ideas on the writing of reports, and to provide a basic method from which to work when writing reports. The method outlined here is not the only way to proceed but it will serve as the basis for you to find your own best method. By using these ideas in conjunction with further reading as suggested at the end of this section, you should be able to produce a written report which will inform, persuade and require action from its readers.

Nature and purpose of reports

Reports are an extremely important means of communication within any organisation. They are written in order that the ideas expressed in them may be used as a basis for action or a decision of some sort.

Always write your report with this in mind:

- that you know the purpose of your report
- that you are able to provide all the facts and ideas on situations
- that someone else who may or may not know the total situation is going to be reading it, commenting on it, discussing it and ultimately making some decision based on it.

Your report is important for the organisation for which you work. Properly used, it may play an important part in some area of policy-making, presenting and using information in such a way that management has a basis for decision-making. Equally important is the effect of the report on its writer. Because your report is read by your peers and your seniors, it is going to reflect creditably or otherwise on yourself. A good report is very good evidence of ability.

Reports come in a wide variety of shapes and sizes, from a one-page submission on a minor problem through to the annual report of your organisation. It may be a regular monthly report from a departmental head, or a one-time major exercise reporting on a user survey. Whatever it is, it must always clearly provide all the information necessary to allow it to serve as a basis for discussion, deliberation and decision. A good report which shows the qualities of accuracy, orderliness, precision, clarity, persuasiveness and so on is achieved through methodical, solid work. The quality of the report reflects the amount of time and sweat expended on it.

Method

As noted, the method outlined here is just one way of going about writing a report. Above all make sure there *is* some method to your report writing. Planning anything helps prevent it from being second-rate. The method outlined below is based on the Australian Public Service handbook on communicating and writing (Walsh 1989). Many other sources are available, and many other methods can be found by reading in the field. This particular one is useful because it is simple to understand, and it is Australian.

Aim of the report

First, always consider the aim of the report: what is required of you, what you have been asked to do, what is the purpose of the report, what is specifically needed. If the instruction is vague, go to the person to whom you are to report or to the person who has issued the instruction and have it clarified. Find out who the report is for, why they require it at this particular time, and whether it is purely for information, or whether action will be taken upon it. Make sure you have a definite notion of what is required in the report. Consider who is going to read it.

Plan your approach

Decide what you will do and how you will do it; how you will gather information, what work needs to be done. Will you need to read files, run a questionnaire or survey, visit specialists in the subject and ask questions, observe the situation for a few days or hours, will you need the help of other people? How much time will you need?

So, before you gather information for the report, always work out your plan of action, based on the requirements of the report.

Gather your information

You will need to gather information from two main sources. *Primary sources* are your interviews, questionnaires, checking records, files, manuscripts, letters, minutes, acts, statutes, material that you must analyse and interpret, which you derive from experimentation, observation and first-hand sources. You will also use *secondary sources*: printed and published material which will give you extra background, ideas and stimulus.

A point to be aware of: when using other people, beware of bias, prejudice, emotion, misunderstanding and self-interest. Always check on the absolute reliability of your material before placing absolute faith in it. If you cannot check it, say so in your report and make it clear whether it is an opinion or a fact. Don't allow your carefully designed evidence to be coloured by an easily checked wrong fact.

Organise your information

Now you begin to organise and arrange your material. Edit it as necessary to avoid duplication and repetition, and arrange the material into broad divisions, grouping it within each division. These broad divisions can give you the basis of your writing plan. You can use a card system for this, or spread it out on the floor in groups. Perhaps now is a good time to allot subheadings to the groups.

Analyse your material

Study your information in detail, in conjunction with your terms of reference. If you do have statistics, for example, a questionnaire or a survey, work out what they mean. Interpret the results of your research and begin to evaluate. What does it all mean? The answer to that enables you to identify recommendations and draw conclusions.

Decide on your conclusions

Any conclusions you reach should be based on analysis of the material. Summarise your main ideas on what your findings revealed, making sure any conclusions you draw are supported by your findings.

Decide on your recommendations

Any recommendations must also be seen to proceed logically from the previous arguments. It is, of course, ridiculous to have recommendations which suddenly appear in your report with no apparent connection to what has gone before, although it does happen. Your recommendations must make sense against the backdrop of facts and arguments presented in the body of the report. In fact, anyone reading your report must be able to foresee your recommendations before they actually read them, because they are a logical extension of the arguments presented.

Make a writing plan

The idea behind a writing plan is to guarantee a systematic and controlled approach to writing. You should now have a command of your material, so don't blow it all at this stage by not thinking clearly before you start writing. Plan your report now, even if it is only a list of paragraphs or subject headings. It will also give you some confidence, and then you will be ready for the next step.

Writing the draft

You now have all the facts and arguments prepared, your conclusions drawn, recommendations decided, in fact a complete plan of the report. Writing the draft is the cumulation of all these things, and there is no special technique involved. However, your report will normally contain the following main items or sections: title; table of contents; summary of main findings or recommendations (sometimes called an 'Executive summary' or 'Abstract') introduction (for example the aim of the report, statement of the problem, background information if required, and so on); method of investigation; findings (your findings are the body of your report); conclusions and recommendations; and appendices and a bibliography as appropriate.

You may write the draft in one sitting, if you find that fluency and continuity come easiest that way. You may prefer to write slowly and painstakingly, checking and re-writing as you go, and still gain the desired fluency. You will find the way that suits you best.

Edit the draft and prepare the final copy

Don't skimp on this part at all – it is vital. No matter how tired you are, no matter how tedious it now all seems, the report is still not quite finished. It doesn't seem quite right to submit a third-rate report after all your research just because you have failed to check the draft carefully. Be highly critical when you do check it, go over it with the proverbial fine tooth comb, looking for false or inaccurate statements, unsupported opinions, bad logic, irrelevance (this is especially important), imprecise and unclear language, and longwindedness. Take a real pride in presenting an excellent report.

Summary

In summary, the ten stages of this method of presenting a report are:

- consider the aim of the report and who will read it
- plan your investigational approach
- gather information
- organise the information you have gathered
- analyse the material
- decide your conclusions
- decide your recommendations
- plan your writing
- write a draft
- edit and prepare the final copy

Should you wish to gain more ideas and insights into report writing, delve into some of the numerous texts on business communication, and report writing handbooks. Some stimulus on language and style can also be gained from these.

Final thoughts: your report will be a bad one if it is confusing to read or follow, if it is illogical, if it is unsupported with evidence, if it is hesitant or non-committal, if it is unchecked, if it is inconsistent or if it is unwieldy. Try to make your readers' task interesting and easy.

Stress management

Stop worrying – nobody gets out of this world alive. (Clive James)

Introduction

Stress, we are told, is a normal and natural part of our lives, and is a factor in the management of our lives at work and elsewhere. Stressful situations cannot be avoided, but their frequency and effects can be controlled and, generally, minimised. But we are told that the frequency and the duration of stress are both increasing. Economic pressures and the pace of change are two of the culprits.

For all of us, stress has become an issue, whether it is us, our families, or friends and colleagues who are affected. For example, family and other relationship concerns can create difficulties and problems that are brought to work as the person is still thinking about, and trying to solve, those problems. There are few people who can say honestly that they completely switch off from their non-work life once they enter the library for work each day.

Interest in stress as an issue has also come about because we have a renewed concern with the human factor at work, a genuine and growing concern that the quality of people's work lives is important. There are, in libraries, attempts to develop more psychologically healthy work environments. You could say that one of the aims of this book, in emphasising supervisory and people-centred skills, is to encourage the development and use of skills and techniques which will help to prevent stress. As Bryson notes,

> It is an important management role to ensure that the physical setting, health and safety practices, work relationships and job structures do not create unnecessary stress for individuals. The ability to assist individuals to manage their responses to stress and minimise the stressors in the workplace will also result in a happier and more productive (1999, p. 321)

Definition

> Stress is sometimes referred to as the modern epidemic – a widespread condition that makes life extremely unpleasant, and a pathological disease that needs to be cured (Eunson 1987, p. 203).

> Stress is defined as any demand made on a person from the environment. Stress can occur as a result of both pleasant and unpleasant situations, for example, a promotion can be as stressful as being fired. Stress, in moderate amounts, enhances performance but is damaging in large quantities (Queensland Government Workplace Health and Safety 2000, p. 10).

Causes of stress

Our ability to cope with stress and its consequences will depend on the quantity and the quality of the stress we experience. The death of one's spouse or child or parent is among the greatest stressors we can experience. Yet people handle these in a range of ways. Major changes at work, or in family circumstances, or in living conditions, or in financial state will cause stress, generally to a less extent than stress arising from the death of a loved one. Even lower on the stress level scale are events such as getting a driving or parking infringement notice, preparing for Christmas or holidays, and going on a diet.

However, our response to the event and the amount of stress it causes will depend on a number of factors, including our environment (for example our job) and our personality.

The supervisor and manager can have some influence on the former by understanding the nature and design of jobs, and by understanding the motivational factors of work. They cannot have the same influence when stress is heightened by personality, although recognition of the symptoms of stress and careful preliminary counselling of staff will be possible and often desirable.

In terms of the nature of jobs, two factors emerge from research: job demands and job control. Eunson (1987) reports on a model of job-related stress developed by Karasek (1981).

> One of the conventional wisdoms of stress on the job is that managers have the greatest stress, while other workers, for example assembly-line operators, have the least stress. Karasek acknowledges that many managers and professionals have high *demands* placed upon them, but they also have a fair amount of *control* over those demands, or in the ways in which they can respond to those demands. In other words, increased responsibility usually means increased power to handle those responsibilities. In contrast, many workers with high demands placed upon them have little control over those demands or the way in which they can respond to those demands; these would include people whose work routine gives them little freedom to move physically or to alter circumstances, such as assembly-line operators. It was this group that Karasek found experienced the highest levels of stress (manifested as exhaustion, depression, etc.).
>
> Thus, Karasek asserts, the most stressed people on jobs are those in high demand/low control jobs; the next most stressed are those in high demand/high control jobs; the next most stressed in low demand/high control jobs; and the least stressed of all in low demand/low control jobs (Eunson 1987, p. 208).

All of this would seem to imply that a sensitive organisational climate, careful job design and more participative planning and decision-making in the library will tend to ease or prevent the incidence of stress. This, however, assumes that all staff will be happy to participate and have more control, and that is not so. Many people prefer not to be burdened with the kind of job enrichment that requires them to take more responsibility for decisions that affect others as well as themselves.

> Stress can manifest itself in many ways and each individual reacts to it with varying responses. Some staff find stress a stimulus, whilst others react distressfully or by exhibiting fatigue or an inability to cope with the public and other staff. Stress can lead to excessive sick days which places undue pressure on other staff as they continue to provide a service.
>
> An additional source of stress in public libraries today is the intensive change taking place in both technology and the social structure. The automation of public libraries has boomed over the past eight years in Australia…At the same time as they are adjusting to the new technology, staff can also be faced with social changes in their private lives. Given the higher divorce rates, more single parent families, higher unemployment, teenage pressures and an ageing society, many staff are coming to work having left a home situation which may be less than satisfactory. There is no doubt that more public library administrators are dealing with staff who are suffering from stress in their private, as well as their work, lives. (Poustie 1992, p. 126).

Queensland's Workplace Health and Safety Guidelines for people working in libraries note some generic causes of stress identified in the library environment:

- work flow (too much or not enough)
- conflicting work demands

- lack of recognition of work achievements
- lack of control over work
- conflict with supervisors or colleagues
- working with difficult or abusive clients
- lack of social support (eg. family, co-workers, friends)
- aggressive behaviour
- monotonous, repetitive work
- poorly designed or inadequate workplaces (Queensland Government Workplace Health and Safety 2000, p. 10).

This list shows that many of the causes of stress radiate from changes that have taken place within the profession, within society, and changes that have been imposed upon libraries and their funding bodies. Those who work in libraries will not agree with a statement made in 1984 which placed them in the occupation which exhibits the lowest stress levels. Research shows that change creates stress, and that change is endemic in libraries. However, the impact of that change in terms of stress can be managed and ameliorated.

Stress management strategies

There are many strategies, some of which libraries are developing, or have had in place for some time, for dealing with stress in the library. In fact, as in many life contexts, prevention is better than, easier than and preferable to, the cure. Those strategies upon which supervisors and managers can have some influence are covered in some detail elsewhere in this book. The following will give some idea of the importance of the role of the manager and supervisor in reducing stress in the workplace.

Organisational climate, communication (especially feedback), positive performance appraisal, job design and enrichment, motivation, participative planning and decision-making, time management, supportive behaviour and interpersonal relationships, and teamwork will all have considerable impact on the prevention of stress in any organisation. Many of these must be pursued with the personality, characteristics, ambitions and values of the individual in mind if we are to prevent stress from becoming a major factor in the work lives of staff. Training for the library manager or supervisor must include a knowledge and understanding of those kinds of factors if stress management is to be part of their library's successes.

Whether we are relatively stressed or non-stressed at any particular time is mainly determined by the individual. Therefore, the prevention of stress is an individual enterprise as well. Relaxation techniques, diet, exercise, massage, meditation and time management are all well documented methods of stress prevention.

Conclusion

Stress is an issue for study and research in order to give us some further insight into the behaviour of people, and the effects of that behaviour in the library organisation. Stress does appear to be linked to staff performance and job satisfaction, and anything the organisation can do to enhance the general health of the workforce has performance implications. Managers and supervisors can prevent some of the stress caused by changes to work and to the work environment by involving staff in the change process, by communicating clearly and regularly during planning, and by dealing with the work environment of individual staff to ensure they can achieve the balance of demand and control in their jobs that is appropriate for them.

Personal relaxation techniques, diet, exercise, massage, meditation and time management are all well-documented methods for stress prevention. From a supervisory viewpoint, to reduce job stress in the workplace, management needs to give top priority to organisational change.

> But even the most conscientious efforts to improve working conditions are unlikely to eliminate stress completely for all workers. For this reason, a combination of organizational change and stress management is often the most useful approach for preventing stress at work (National Institute for Occupational Safety and Health 1999).

The National Institute for Occupation Safety and Health (NIOSH) report *Stress at work* goes on to outline a stress analysis and prevention program that bears repeating here.

Step 1 – Identify the problem.

- Hold group discussion with employees.
- Design an employee survey.
- Measure employee perceptions of job conditions, stress, health and satisfaction.
- Collective objective data.
- Analyze data to identify problem locations and stressful job conditions.

Step 2 – Design and implement interventions.

- Target source of stress for change.
- Propose and prioritize intervention strategies.
- Communicate planned interventions to employees.
- Implement interventions.

Certain problems, such as a hostile work environment, may be pervasive in the organization and require company-wide interventions. Other problems such as excessive workload may exist only in some departments and thus require more narrow solutions such as a redesign of the way a job is performed. Still other problems may be specific to certain employees and resistant to any kind of organizational change, calling instead for stress management or employee assistance interventions. Some interventions might be implemented rapidly (e.g. improved communication, stress management training), but others may require additional time to put into place (e.g. redesign of a manufacturing process).

Step 3 – Evaluate the interventions.

- Conduct both short- and long-term evaluations.
- Measure employee perceptions of job conditions, stress, health and satisfaction.
- Include objective measures.
- Refine the intervention strategy and return to Step 1 (National Institute for Occupational Safety and Health 1999).

Further useful information on job related stress can be found at the American Institute of Stress main website <http://www.stress.org/job.htm> and numerous Australian government, educational and health related sites. See, for example, the National Occupational Health and Safety Commission <http://www.nohsc.gov.au/OHSInformation NOHSCPublications/factsheets/stres1.htm>; the Victorian Government Department of Health <http://www.betterhealth.vic.gov.au/bhcv2/bharticles.nsf/pages/Work-related_stress>; and the University of South Australia's Work and Stress Research Group <http://www.unisa.edu.au/workstress/main.html>.

> Possibly the healthiest thing about the whole phenomenon of stress is that it is now socially acceptable to discuss it as a normal phenomenon. Previously, many people believed that life was a rat-race, which you either survived or did not survive. Those who didn't survive were labelled 'crazy', or had 'nervous breakdowns', while those who did survive saw nothing

remarkable in lifestyles that embraced little exercise, over-eating, self-medication through alcohol, tobacco, caffeine and pills, insomnia, ulcers, heart attacks, short concentration spans, aggression, submission to mutilating roles, psychologically and physically hazardous jobs, and distorted styles of thinking.

Approaches to stress management let us see that

1   susceptibility to stress is not an either/or phenomenon, but rather a continuum, and
2   where we are on that continuum is largely up to ourselves to determine (Eunson 1987, p. 230).

Political qualities and skills

One of the penalties for refusing to participate in politics is that you end up being governed by your inferiors. (Plato)

Introduction

You may well be thinking that this is the arena of senior management and all that goes with it – difficult decisions to consider, new fields to learn, different skills to develop, while all the time trying to be a leader and manager to your staff. This topic unlike most others in this book, takes a view from the top, of managers and supervisors looking out on, and being imposed upon, by their funding body or parent organisation. However, you should be able to relate this topic to your own organisation or situation as you read and respond to what follows.

This topic considers political and leadership qualities in the context of managing a library. The aim is to gain an understanding of the politics of library management, as a basis for understanding the sources of power in publicly and privately supported libraries. Today's library and information managers, like all managers, need to be a fully functioning element of their political environment. Why? Because…'Politics is the management of power and influence. As we all know, without power and influence managers are unlikely to achieve anything' (Griffin 1991, p. 134).

Definitions

What, then, is politics? John McDonough (1985) offers the following perspective.

What does political in an organization sense mean to you?…When I have asked this question of fairly diverse groups of people, here is what they have replied, in essence:

It is the amount of effort over and above doing the job it takes to get recognized and valued; or, shortcircuiting the established processes of organization for personal gain. The last time I gave a talk similar to this, a woman got up and said, 'Politics is knowing who is in charge and whom you have to please.'…these are representative of the way people define politics.

There are a couple of lessons for us. One is we tend to use the word politics as a catchall for all those subjective and irrational forces that are out there that we don't have sufficient understanding of and control over. Two, we tend to define it in a way that politics are practised by the other people. Almost nobody ever writes down anything that puts him in the center of politics in the organization. (McDonough 1985, p. 54)

Yet that is what the library and information manager must do. Forget the negative connotations of the word. Undertaking the kinds of political activity that are suggested in this topic is not a sign of weakness. The role of power and politics in management is as inevitable and necessary as is our participation in the wider political process.

What is meant by the library's political environment? As an introduction to the topic, you can do no better than to read a paper given at the ALIA Biennial Conference in Perth, 1990, by Eric Wainwright, called 'Why some libraries succeed'. It sets the scene for this topic with its emphasis on innovation and change in the context of the management of libraries and information agencies. In summary, Wainwright (1990) makes a number of points which are most pertinent to this topic:

- Funding bodies of libraries are influenced by their constituents (for example, taxpayers, ratepayers, shareholders, consumers), which makes the funding body examine the library in terms of its performance.

- The ability to undertake innovative change is an ingredient of success in improving service delivery and performance to target clientele.

- Constraints on innovation in public organisations include fear of the political and personal consequences of failure, the size of the organisation, and structural and bureaucratic barriers.

- That an appropriate organisational climate is critical to the promotion and acceptance of innovation.

- That despite the limitations of their political environment, libraries and information agencies must encourage change and innovation, through their human resources, in order to meet their client-centred objectives most effectively.

All decisions have a political component

Richard De Gennaro wrote an article which is nearly 20 years old, but it is well worth reading before you study library and information supervision and management. The following excerpt is designed to whet your appetite for the whole article, but also to highlight another context within which we study such topics as this. That context is the real world of library and information management.

> Because a library operates in a political environment and nearly all the really important decisions that are made at the highest levels have an overriding political component...

> In the library world, as in education, business, and government, few major program decisions are made solely or even largely on the basis of careful studies of needs and costs. Consider, for example, decisions to build a new library building, to open a new departmental or branch library, to achieve excellence in some special subject discipline, or to embark on a major automation program. These program decisions are usually the result of an initiative or vision by an imaginative or powerful person, perhaps a library director, a dean, a president, a mayor, or other official. They are political, emotional, or even personal decisions – justified, rationalized, and perhaps implemented with the assistance of various kinds of analyses and studies, but seldom derived from them.

> It is important that librarians understand how and why these really critical decisions are made so that they will not be disillusioned or discouraged when they discover that the 'best', the most efficient, or the least expensive solution frequently loses out to the one that is the most politically expedient or attractive. (De Gennaro 1978, pp. 23–24).

Is this, in your estimation, a cynical and reactionary statement of the case, or is De Gennaro correct in his assessment? If you read on, you will find that it is a not unrealistic assessment of the politics of library management, and that his comments are just as valid today as when they were written.

The nature of politics in library management

The best writers on the political environment dwell mostly on the ways and means of appropriate and effective political action, and least on an outline of the acts, laws, rules and regulations of governing bodies and governments. Library and information managers must be acutely aware of the environment within which they operate, and that includes a knowledge of how they are controlled from outside or above. However, the most important skills in management are those which enable the manager to work and act successfully within that environmental context.

Qualities for political achievement

Success, then, is related to the management style and abilities of the library manager. Let us now take the advice of one of Australia's most politically astute librarians. At the 1991 New Zealand Library Association Conference in Auckland, Warren Horton, the former Director-General of the National Library of Australia, spoke on libraries and politics. He indicated that lobbying, for a long time one of the mainstays of political activity, is in essence a reactive process. The real key to success is the proactive building of government relations.

He went on to outline the following golden rules for successful participation in the political process, many of which are echoed in the above readings.

- have vision and a long-term view
- have effective plans
- communicate, and develop an informed profession
- be realistic
- cut your losses when necessary
- seek allies
- use professionalism judiciously
- timing is essential
- trust your leaders
- leaders cannot hide from responsibilities
- be brave (Horton 1991).

Apart from personal qualities and skills, the library manager must ensure that the funding body, and in particular the senior management, is constantly aware of, and encouraged to support, the library.

The following view, from Dorothea Brown, on the politics of dealing with senior management, presents some very practical and realistic ideas on the topic. Dorothea (the former Libraries Manager, Canterbury Public Library, Christchurch, New Zealand) wrote this as a 'Practitioner View' for the first edition of this book, and has granted permission to reprint it here.

First, an observation about *paid* as opposed to *elected/appointed* officers:

Paid officers have the real power long-term. They have and manipulate the information on which the elected/appointed officers make their decisions.

Elected/appointed representatives come and go: paid officers watch them.

Elected/appointed councils and boards change in make up, so their policies and priorities will change.

Paid officers get a second, third…chance to put forward their pet projects: they can afford to retreat and bide their time.

United, paid officers would be an irresistible force, if only they realised it.

Second, library managers are often located apart from head office. As a result, we often do not or cannot share the informal but powerful networking of corporate staffrooms and offices, nor readily plug into the corporate grapevine. That is why our corporate colleagues should be looked upon as an influential client group and be treated with at least the same respect as that which we show our 'external' clients.

Interest in and respect for their goals, and understanding of their problems. Senior officers get little praise and recognition, and are just as pleased to be stroked as the rest of us.

Good manners with all corporate colleagues. The person you insult or put down today, you may need tomorrow.

Quality service when they depend on your contribution for their performance; meeting their deadlines, writing good reports, providing accurate information.

Ask for advice. Recognise and exploit the wealth of professional skills and expertise which is available for the asking. In any case, people love to feel needed.

Use corporate colleagues as a sounding board for the community. They are a significant and influential group in it, and they each have their own networks and represent every grouping of age, opinion, needs and interests.

Apologise early and often. There is nothing more disarming than an apology. Share your feelings and your fears.

There are times when I feel more strongly supported by my corporate colleagues than by my own staff, simply because they are more in tune with the prevailing political pressures and compromises, and understand more clearly the conflict between professional principles and political expediency. It is in my own interest to cultivate my corporate relationships so that I can get – and give – such support when it is needed.

Third, my corporate survival rules:

All of the above, plus…

Don't embarrass the corporate manager or chief executive. Keep them informed about real or potential disasters, the sort of stories that will get headlines in the morning paper: don't let them read about it over breakfast.

Establish your parameters: your level of authority, autonomy, and financial accountability. Determine their expectations of, and your obligations for, information and reporting. Establish your access to and relationship with the elected/appointed representatives.

Accept that you operate in a political environment, that politics is the art of the possible, and that you will have to compromise if you want to survive.

Meet their personal and private library needs; accept that they will want favours.

Share good news stories. Copy every letter of thanks to your corporate manager and to your committee chairperson.

Invite your corporate manager and your committee chairperson to your external and in-house activities, make them feel involved and part of your work culture and family. They will turn into your supporters and, in time, champions.

Accept that their priorities may not be the same as yours.

Do your homework. Argue from data, not emotion. If you haven't got the data, then get them.

Be prepared to be challenged. Identify and ask as many of the why or negative questions beforehand.

Be prepared for delays, to wait.

Accept failure as graciously as you can; you may get another chance, so in the meantime analyse why you failed and learn from the experience.

Safeguard yourself with the written word. Confirm verbal agreements, instructions, discussions, etc. with written memos and reports. Always keep copies, and keep your handwritten informal notes.

And last, but most importantly:

Keep your sense of humour and perspective, and don't allow your sense of self-worth and confidence in your ability to be affected by negative experiences.

No, I don't apply all of these all of the time, but I know from experience that they do work. I just wish I'd remember them in moments of high stress! I do my share of apologising instead (Brown 1995, quoted in Sanders 1995, pp. 221–223).

Conclusion

Building effective political relationships requires all of the qualities mentioned by Dorothea Brown (1995) and Warren Horton (1991). The supervisor who wishes to grow and develop within their library and within the profession should take note of their advice. I suggest, too, that you improve your abilities and skills, be prepared to have your own performance appraised, demonstrate that you are an effective supervisor, and become accountable for all of your decisions and actions.

Part 4

Financial management

Chapter 19
Financial management

Can anybody remember when the times were not hard and money not scarce? (Ralph Waldo Emerson)

Introduction

Libraries in the late twentieth and early twenty-first centuries continue to experience economic difficulty caused by increasing competition for funds in the public sector, which are subject to increasing scrutiny. Most libraries, as public services, are non-profit agencies and are supported through the tax and rates systems on the basis that they provide a 'social good'. If they are to attract financial support, especially in times where there is keen competition for public funds, service agencies must be able to demonstrate both their effectiveness in providing that good, and their efficiency and responsibility in handling public money. Libraries in the private sector face very similar challenges.

The overwhelming and rapid changes in information technology over the last two decades have challenged the traditional role of the library, its services and the processes used to provide those services. Economic and financial conditions thus require that library administrators seek management information and methods which will facilitate informed and justifiable decisions about the allocation of existing resources as well as enhancing the provision of support for the library operation.

> The very existence of libraries poses fundamental questions of a financial or economic nature. How much should be spent on libraries? What proportion of national expenditure should this be? How may such expenditure be allocated to different kinds of library, or to different libraries of the same kind? What contribution do libraries make to national wealth which justifies expenditure on them? How much should be spent within a particular library on its different and competing elements of provision and service? Can contrasting patterns of financial support for library activities be related to effectiveness or efficiency in those various activities? (Hennessy *et al.* 1976, p. 137).

Although written more than thirty years ago, those words are still appropriate to today's libraries. Increasingly, librarians find themselves confronting fundamental micro- and macro-economic questions like the ones posed above. There is a growing demand for performance, accountability, efficiency and rationality, and these now provide a forceful impetus for the librarian to consider basic concepts of financial management and applied economics. This chapter aims, in the context of managing a library or information agency, to explain the basic principles of financial management and accountability. These are vital issues for library supervisors and managers who are responsible for the management of people and resources, who must be part of the political process, or who wish to develop and sell services in a competitive environment. Library managers need to have the financial and political acumen to understand the budget documents, as well as to understand the environment and context within which the budget must be planned, justified and operated.

> All libraries, whether in the public or private sector, operate in a competitive arena. They compete with other organizations for finite and scarce resources in a zero-sum game. Unfortunately, there are winners and losers. The losers ... are often the organizations least prepared to express their value and contribution in terms understood by their funders (Penniman 1990, p. 4).

Budgeting

Introduction

A budget is a summary of planned income and expenditure for a specific period of time, usually one year, and reflects the goals and objectives of an institution in monetary terms. Its formulation is part of the process of planning; while its execution over the time period it covers acts as an important control device, being one measure of performance towards planned goals (Bryson 1999, p. 96). Budget systems can be of a number of types, including line item, lump sum, formula program and performance. Many variations of these types are possible, and in practice they are frequently used in combination. Whichever method is used, however, the aims of the budgeting process remain the same: to translate diverse activities and outcomes within the organisation into a common measure, ie. dollars, and to provide standards against which such activities can be measured to enable corrective or other action to be taken (Bartol *et al.* 2001, pp. 533–535). A well-planned and justified budget will help ensure that these aims are met. Good financial management is essential for libraries: the value of the library's contribution to its community is always under question, and one which is part of a larger organisation will always be in competition for funds.

Definition

Budgeting is a managerial planning tool which assists with decisions about the allocation of resources, and which is used to monitor the results of those decisions to ensure they conform to the plan. Note that budget development and strategic planning go hand-in-hand.

Budgeting methods

Line item and lump sum

The traditional methods of library budgeting are either the line item or lump sum systems. The line item is the most common approach, with expenditure broken down into categories such as salaries, books, periodicals and equipment. On this basis, the annual library budget is usually simple to compile.

In the past, 'current' allocations remained relatively unchallenged and the argument for the budget focused on explaining why increases in appropriations should be made. The method shows how the funds are spent and, only vaguely, how the library manager manages various sections of the library. Many library managers are required, or decide on their own, to submit a detailed report with their annual budget estimates justifying past, current, ongoing and new items of expenditure.

This method of allocation has the potential for conflict when the funding body earmarks particular funds for particular projects that may not necessarily match the library manager's proposals. That poses a real problem for library managers: do they argue against the project and run the risk of losing the funds altogether, or do they accept the funds and at least be sure of some support?

The lump sum budget (sometimes referred to as a one-line budget) confers a greater degree of freedom to manoeuvre among various aspects of the total library budget. This system involves the allocation of a fixed sum to the library management, who then make allocations within the total amount given.

Some organisations use a combination of both line and lump sums. Here certain items are fixed, and the remaining part of the budget is a sum that the library manager can allocate according to need.

The above methods don't require any sophisticated forms of evaluation of expenditure to be carried out. Indeed, both methods are more likely only to record expenditure. Using this rather simplistic approach to budgeting makes proper evaluation of the success or otherwise of a particular budget allocation difficult or impossible.

Formula

Another approach to budgeting is to use a formula, and formula budgets are generally found in academic libraries. This method involves the establishment of weighted criteria which then become the basis upon which funds are allocated to the library.

Some are based on the manpower required to complete library operations of various kinds in different situations. Characteristics such as holdings, acquisitions, equivalent full-time student users, actual number of students, equivalent full-time academic staff, and selected professional staff may be used and weighted against factors such as time taken to undertake certain activities. Another simple method of, say, allocating resources would be based on the number of students in a particular award program and the average number of class/credit hours taken by each student.

Weighted measures present certain difficulties in relation to the problem of establishing a library budget. What the measures do is to make the library management very conscious of the tasks performed, and if they achieve nothing else, then at least that is a plus. Formulas may also have a place in the allocation of the library budget once the total funds are known. The library manager who is aware of formula funding could well use the technique in allocating funds among competing needs.

Factors to be considered might include the number of students enrolled in a particular course, weighting of courses by type (for example, science or history), or number of database searches done in science as against sociology. By being aware of the various factors involved, usage and so on, the manager could arrive at a suitable means of allocating resources over time. It would be important for the manager to be aware of trends and changes in demands, and adjust the formula allocations accordingly.

There are problems with the 'traditional' forms of budget, and the following statement points out some of the reasons why program and performance budgets became so widespread in the late 1990s.

Budgeting strategies are better known and used more often than are training strategies. Even though the power of the purse is used more, it is not necessarily used better. One very valid criticism of public budgeting is that it impedes change and improvement and thus assures preservation of the status quo. New programs typically fare poorly in the budget process, while many less worthy and obsolete activities are allowed to continue year after year with little critical examination.

Budgets also tend to occupy an inordinate portion of the manager's time. Budget making has become over-elaborate to the extent that questions are being raised about the cost effectiveness of many public budgetary processes. Public budgeting, since its United States advent in 1922, has followed an accountant's model, with emphasis being placed on economy rather than effectiveness and productivity. Typical object-of-expenditure budgets have only remote connection with the program activity of an organization (Gardner 1979, p. 46).

Program budgets

Program

The program budget focuses attention on, and is based on, the activities which are to be funded in order to achieve library goals. It bears a direct relationship to the functions and services of the library, and each service unit should have considerable input to the budgeting and controlling processes. A program budget looks at the goals of a particular unit or service division (for example, interlibrary loans, or specific branches), and considers what specific activities are required to achieve those goals. It looks at the level of that activity as well and its priority within the strategic goals of the organisation. Then the resources needed to undertake those activities are costed, and a budget submission is prepared. This process is carried out for all functions or units of the library, and involves supervisors of units, sections, and so forth in the budget process.

While the finished product of this budgeting method may be in line item format, the key point is that each area, department, section or unit of the library will be initially budgeted separately.

In order to arrive at a program budget the branch librarian, or supervisor, needs to have decided upon the goals and program objectives of the branch, with input from staff and users, and based on a knowledge and understanding of the total objectives and strategic plan of the library service. They will have planned any major new activities for the coming year and have costed those activities. Items like major capital works will have been decided at a higher level, but the branch librarian will (one hopes!) have had considerable input to that decision, and indeed may even have initiated discussion of needs in that area.

Some of the figures will be determined by ongoing policy. For example, branch librarians may be allowed to attend one conference every second year. Items like rates, insurance, office maintenance may be an apportioned amount, as a contribution to a service-wide cost based on the size, nature and level of activity of the branch. Other items of projected expenditure are based on expected usage, and past usage is often used as a guide. However, in determining the future expenditure on these items, the branch librarian will also need to consider any new activities beginning during the year and any past activities that will no longer be undertaken. The branch librarian will have consulted a variety of people, including other branch librarians, the branch supervisor, the city librarian and other central management staff.

A program budget necessarily includes a large number of staff in its preparation and formulation. Key skills of communication, teamwork, participation (and numeracy helps!) will be required for the program budget process to succeed in its aims of articulating goals and plans with expenditure of funds.

Planning, programming, budgeting system

The technique of planning, programming, budgeting system (PPBS) developed in response to increasing concerns among public authorities about the high cost of library operations. PPBS is a management and financial system focusing on the accomplishment of stated goals by the establishment of programs of services selected from alternatives on the basis of cost effectiveness and goal fulfilment, rather than stressing objects of expenditure.

In essence, what this system of budgeting demands is management's emphasis on outputs rather than inputs into the library. This is a reversal of the traditional approach to the library budget. In theory at least, it enables a clearer quantification of the costs and benefits of any program (or collection of activities) in order to better assess how well money is being spent.

PPBS appeals to the administrator because it seems so rational; however, in practice there are many problems associated with its implementation (Bryson for instance notes that it does not act as a useful operating tool for line managers and is time-consuming and complex to construct (1999, p. 103). It may be that the library administrator can learn a lot from understanding PPBS, and, in a modified form, the basic principles could be used with considerable effect alongside traditional budgeting methods.

Zero base budgeting

Zero base budgeting (ZBB) is also a form of program budgeting. It was developed to overcome the limitations of incremental budgeting, aiming to force organisations to critically review proposed expenditure against outcomes in order to better understand the impact of this activity on the organisation as a whole. Anandarajah and others define it as:

> …a budget [being] prepared for every activity is evaluated on its own merits, and each item of expenditure is critically reviewed for its effect on the whole budget. No item of expenditure is included in the budget unless it is absolutely necessary to the operation of the organisation. The ZBB approach eliminates budgeting for unnecessary expenditure (1998, p. 18)

Thus each activity (program) is fully costed and its objectives quantified as far as possible. All programs can then be compared and prioritised against corporate objectives. Prioritising can be difficult in large or complex organisations as managers need to have to have a good understanding of all the programs proposed in order to determine their priority and allocate funds. It is also a time consuming technique that requires managers to undertake considerable training in its operation and implementation. A zero base budget can provide a number of costed increments for each program, in order of priority, whereby management can decide which activities to fund and at which incremental level. The provision of increments allows management to know where to spend when extra funds are available, and where to cut when money is short.

PPBS and ZBB comparison

ZBB incorporates the essential features of PPBS, including objectives identification, analysis of activities and alternatives, and their relative cost/benefits, but goes beyond the demands of PPBS in terms of justification and analysis. ZBB incorporates two major steps, the identification of organisation-wide decision packages and their ranking in priority order following goal attainment, and cost effectiveness calculated each time without reference to previous budgets. The final product is the presentation (from department managers) of several layers of service – in fact several budgets – for consideration by top management. This amounts to statements of what the organisation as a whole can accomplish, the means necessary and consequences foreseen, given specified objectives and external conditions. Decision packages are identified on the basis of activities performed at the lowest level of the functioning of the organisation, and then ranked in successive stages of the organisation's echelons.

Maximum involvement of managerial staff improves the understanding of the interrelationships of various activities to the functioning of the total system. ZBB deals with activities in specific sections as well as cost centres which cover the whole library. PPBS and other program budgets deal with activities and programs without considering how the library is formally organised.

Cost analysis

Cost analysis is an important part of any financial planning process. For managers, gaining a clearer understanding of the actual costs involved in any activity provides a foundation upon which more sophisticated measures of benefit and effectiveness can be assessed. Taking into account fixed costs (those that cannot be altered over the short term, eg. building/insurance costs, water rates etc) and variable costs (those directly related to the level of work done and thus easy to manipulate in the short term, eg. costs associated with overtime, book purchases etc) managers can develop a 'true' picture of the real costs associated with the program and assess this against its deliverables. Stueart and Moran (1998) make the good point that cost benefit analysis is concerned with the cost, cost effectiveness with the value – an important distinction (p. 353)

Pestell and Lihs (1992) describe a unit cost analysis study undertaken by the Public Libraries Division of the State Library of Queensland. It is still worth reading to get some understanding of the amount of effort involved in producing such management information. They provide some rationale for the undertaking:

> A thorough understanding of the specific financial inputs to modern library systems is essential…In order to make rational, objective decisions managers need to know the financial implications of their actions. Relating financial data to non-financial information allows the assessment of the viability of specific services, the relative costs of different types of services, and productivity and performance costs.
>
> This vital management information can indicate where economies may be made, where greater efficiencies may be required, whether particular services or service levels are cost effective, which services or service levels are over- or under-funded, or what the development or the introduction of services would cost. A cost analysis should not be regarded as a means to justify cost savings or reductions in services but as a positive management technique to improve the effectiveness of the library's services, provide the best value for money and provide the essential information necessary to gain a greater share of the funding body's revenue (Pestell and Lihs 1992, p. 277).

The information collected, along with the results of the study, led to decisions being made about 'expensive' or non-cost-effective methods and services, and to decisions being made about the economy, efficiency and value for money provided by those parts of the division that were covered by the initial analysis.

Cost accounting is a management tool. Management information systems today are capable of providing sophisticated reporting of all aspects of an organisation's business, including financial information. Thus salary costs can be broken down against material processed, increase/decrease over previous accounting periods highlighted, warning 'bells' sounded if variations go beyond certain ranges etc. Anandarajah and others (1998, p. 88) discuss the usefulness of operational performance reporting systems that enable top management to assess progress towards strategic objectives through detailed reporting measures aligning strategic and budgetary plans and reporting accordingly.

In reality, cost accounting is related to, and in many libraries supports, the management of a PPBS. As with most systems, cost analysis has some problems. For example, how is administrative cost apportioned, how are overhead costs spread over various activities? Cost analysis is of considerable value to the library manager when it comes to a question of library expenditure justification. However, there is a price to be paid in the sense of better management and the diversion of resources in order that better records can be kept. An element of cost analysis should be part of the library manager's information gathering system.

An important 'cost' to consider is depreciation. Items in the library are given a useful life and then their cost is depreciated over that life. Depreciation is a factor that appears to be ignored in the library context: if anything, it is taken for granted. It is assumed that certain items of library stock, carpets, buildings, etc. will ultimately wear out and will be replaced. Many library managers do not prepare for this until the event becomes inevitable. At that point costs become significant. If depreciation were taken into account, perhaps long-term planning for libraries would be put on a more solid foundation.

This section has attempted to look at some general principles associated with library budgets. It has shown that good budgeting procedures are difficult in the library context. By the same token, this does not mean that nothing should be done about it. Various techniques have been discussed, and in reality most library managers practise at least some, if not all, aspects raised on library budgets.

Analysis of items in a library budget

The basic budget can be divided into a number of clear areas:

- buildings: development and maintenance
- salaries
- resources, materials
- other costs
- special projects
- enterprises.

The first two items are generally fixed costs and can come to the library as tied grants or be withheld from the library's operating budget and be paid by an administrative section of the funding body. In the latter case the library has no control over the expenditure or otherwise of these budget items, and in some cases the library's management does not even know what the amounts are.

Buildings: development and maintenance

From the time of completion, library buildings incur recurrent costs that must be a fixed, or variable, cost against their continued occupancy. The costs include rates, electricity, gas, insurance, and repairs and maintenance. There should also be allowance for depreciation for fittings like shelving.

Salaries

In Australia, salaries are usually determined by an industrial award that can vary from state to state, and from one type of library to another. The only times the library manager has control over salary costs are at the initial point of hiring and in the area of promotions. At each time, a starting salary is determined, and thereafter any salary increments are generally determined with reference to the particular award. Apart from salaries and wages, costs to be decided here include workers' compensation payments, superannuation, leave loadings, shiftwork and overtime, casual and short-term relief, and perhaps even certain expenses associated with the hiring of staff such as travel and removal expenses. Salary costs are not readily changeable in the short term – staff cannot be summarily dismissed. They are therefore fixed in the short to medium term and have to be treated as such – any changes have to be budgeted for and planned over the longer term.

Resources, materials

These costs consist of the amounts paid to acquire the materials required to satisfy user needs. Basically they consist of books, serials, newspapers, various non-print materials, costs of bindings and repairs, and perhaps equipment needed to use some of the non-print materials.

All of these costs are recurrent, variable costs, and the level of funding can change from year to year depending upon the budget allocated to library services, internal library policies as to how much will be allocated to each, and the ever-rising costs of serial subscriptions.

Other costs

These are associated with the administration of the library and its various sections, and consist of postage, stationery, staff development, travel costs, telephone and other electronic communications, maintenance of equipment and computer systems.

The first four of these costs are fairly straightforward. However, many library managers 'gamble' on how much they will allocate to maintenance of equipment. Certain items should be maintained, as breakdowns can be costly. The manager hopes that little will go wrong and knows that the items have only a limited life anyway.

Maintenance of equipment has tended to become a costly item of expenditure. Many larger libraries now employ a trained technician responsible for maintaining all equipment, while smart managers or the funding body ensure that service and maintenance contracts are realistic in terms of what they cost and what they cover.

Computer systems costs include establishment costs, costs associated with maintaining software and hardware, and network costs if the library is involved in such activities.

Special projects

Many libraries receive special grants for particular projects that are attractive to the people determining how the library will allocate its finances. A feature of grants is that the library has to set up a separate activity code to handle the monies allocated. It may also mean a diversion of money away from other projects just as crucial to the library's well-being and its ongoing activities. There are arguments for and against special allocations. In a situation in which resources are scarce, many library managers are not prepared to argue against any financial grant, no matter what its source or purpose.

Enterprises

Many libraries engage in projects where it has active trading accounts. Some of the most common are:

- photocopying,
- sale of materials,
- rental of materials.

Such activities are usually set up so that they are self-funding and indeed may make a profit. Separate account codes are usually kept, and in some Australian states this is mandated by audit requirements. Many managers look upon these activities as outside the normal library functions, and they can be expensive in terms of labour costs. Some larger libraries, especially academic and state libraries, run a separate photocopy section which operates as a trading enterprise (or profit centre), the profits from which are used for special projects and for improving services to users. Others may even outsource to a commercial supplier.

In the previous sections a brief account of the types of activities that make up a library budget has been given. The library manager requires a certain amount of accounting expertise if he/she is to understand what is involved and be able to argue the case for finding sufficient monies to maintain existing programs and indeed increase them where considered necessary. Increasingly library managers find it necessary to devote considerable energy to this aspect of their total charge. The next section gives an introduction to some of the principles and skills involved.

Management accounting

Introduction

Once the library has decided on a budgeting method (or had a budgeting method thrust upon it), how can we keep a record of what is happening in the budget, how monies are being spent, how much is left in various accounts.

Definition

Management accounting may be defined as the effective planning and use of all the information and records available to an organisation in order to measure performance, assess the current situation, and plan future activities, as an aid to effective management.

An adequate accounting system is vital as the means for control and management of the budget. In other words, the library management need to be able to see, at any time, how much has been spent in any area, how much is committed for expenditure, and what balance is still available for expenditure. Similarly with receipts, the management decision-makers need to be able to see how various items of income are meeting expected levels – this can have an effect on whether the budget is balanced or not. Monitoring and inspecting accounts means that decisions can be made from a controlled basis.

What is needed, then, is a system of accounting for income and expenditure, and a means of reporting that to those who need to know – all levels of management, all those who need that information in order to make decisions. The system should provide information to staff to indicate how the budget is progressing, and, as a by product, produce reports which can be used for constructing future budgets. As the section on budgeting indicates, there is no direct provision or demand for good accounting systems within the budgetary methods themselves.

From the library's point of view, accounting is really a secondary, support activity, and so long as accurate records of disbursements, commitments, income and balances are maintained, then a system can be developed to reflect the structure of the budget.

This system may be set up within the library, or the library may have to use one which is set up at higher levels in the organisation – the city financial director's department, for example. If the latter is the case, then you will be dealing with clerks and accountants who may use strange jargon. The following is supplied to allow you to feel more at ease in dealing with these people.

> If you want to become part of the modern world I recommend you become an accountant more or less immediately. First of all, let's just see if you're aptitudinally suited to this lofty calling. I'd like you to be so good as to answer the following questions:

> Can you count to three? Of course you may use a calculator during the final stages of your working, although it's probably better to lease one than to buy one, because the leasing of business machinery can be deductible at full rate, whereas purchase price, although deductible through charges against the current account and again advantageous through depreciation it is ultimately going to show up as an item of capital expenditure, and the opportunity cost of such utilisation of funds is obviously going to be the possible write-back to standard value of any books purchased before balance date and held subject to sales tax exemptions provided by the vendor with monies other than those already earmarked for consideration as possible year one and year two input figures for an automation development programme with installation at year one plus five.

> Secondly, can you lean back in a chair, look out the window and demonstrate what's meant by the term 'a sharp intake of breath'? This is to be done whenever a non-accountant attempts to count to three, so it's got to be mastered fairly early on. Of course, if you want to be a cost accountant or auditor you'll also have to be able to put your hands together as if you're praying and tap your incisors with the nails on your two forefingers. But that's really fairly advanced and should probably be left till later.

> Finally, and this is the real nub of the matter – can you draw a line down from the top of a piece of paper to somewhere near the bottom and can you count to three on both sides of the line? This is the very lifeblood of accountancy and if you can do that you're not only halfway there, you're halfway back as well. (Clarke [1979], p. 13.)

Accounting and the library

What is the function of accounting in the library?

- To find the truth.
- To report the truth in a way everyone can understand.

Clearly Fred Dagg's experience with accountants (as related by Carey [1979] in the quote above) has been with individuals who have not fulfilled the above functions! Someone once said, and I apologise for not having the reference to it now, that 'Accountancy is the language of management.' I have to disagree with such a bald statement, especially in its application to library management, but I am certain that an effective library manager needs to know something of this language and of its principles.

The importance of the above statements to the busy librarian, troubled by rising book prices and salaries, fluctuating exchange rates, and other rising costs is that recognition of the overall purpose of accounting can be lost in the pressures of coping with daily crises. A knowledge of basic principles might help reduce those pressures.

Elements of an accounting system

A number of desirable elements to be found in an accounting system include:

- clarity
- simplicity
- relevance
- brevity
- topicality
- reliability
- authenticity
- auditability
- reportability
- comparability

The best financial reports for the library staff who are making management decisions will be *clear*, *simple* and *relevant* to the needs of the library.

It is possible that one system can cater for the information needs of several different groups within the one organisation. (By 'the one organisation' here I mean the city council, or the company, or the university, or the school, of which the library is a department or section.) In some organisations the setting up, by individual departments or sections, of independent ways of accumulating data on financial activities will result in a great deal of duplicated time and effort. The umbrella organisation should have an integrated accounting and reporting system that can reduce duplication and at the same time provide each section with data which it can then analyse and make use of in individual ways. The use of spreadsheets and more sophisticated software has enhanced the library's ability to keep accurate records of expenditure in a quick and relatively simple manner.

Topicality is important, and ensuring it can be a major problem for library management, especially when the library is part of a large organisation. There may well be a case for the library setting up its own internal system of accounting to serve as a check on the accounting system of the parent organisation whose reports to the library may be months behind the fiscal reality. Worse still, those reports may be as basic as a bank statement or a list of cheques drawn on the library's accounts. Management need up-to-date and accurate fiscal information in order to make reliable and effective decisions.

Reliability, authenticity and *auditability* are achieved through any basic system if the records provide evidence that all of the entries represent proper transactions, which are initiated with the correct authority and which are properly recorded. Your controlling body should have in place a system which is set up in accordance with the auditing requirements of the overall organisation, and those requirements will be embodied in the laws and regulations which govern the organisation's existence.

As stated earlier, *management accounting* is the effective planning and use of all the information and records available to an organisation in order to measure performance, assess the current situation and plan future activities, as an aid to effective management. It involves the provision of data from the accounting system to the library management, keeping them regularly informed about targets, commitments and attainments, through financial and statistical reports. The emphasis here is on service to management to assist decision-making. This is where the *reportability* and *comparability* of the accounting system are important and clearly go beyond recording receipts and payments.

Management accounting at work

From the library's point of view, *management accounting* will assist with the following.

- Focusing attention on the few exceptional items where performance is not up to expectations, when actual results do not meet budget plans. This could be called *management by exception*. Where there is a major difference between estimates and expenditure, library management can concentrate on taking corrective action in that area, perhaps even by altering a number of other areas of the budget to help correct a budget imbalance.

- Monitoring and controlling overall organisational performance by contributing information to the control function of the *management by objectives* continuum.

- Meeting the need for information about achievements (and failures) by individual sections, or even by individual people. This is part of responsibility accounting, and the accounting system will be classified so that such information is readily available. For example, the materials vote can be divided by type (for example, fiction, non-fiction, biography, reference, serials, non-print) – and further, each of these could be subdivided by level (adult, children's) or by subject areas (such as humanities, social sciences, science and technology, travel, sport, art and literature).

- Meeting the need for information about gross income or net income from specific sources. This is contribution accounting, and again a simple classification of the accounting system enables specific sources of income to be recorded separately.

- *Commitment accounting.* This is especially relevant in libraries where large sums of money are committed to the purchase of books, serials and other library materials. Serials are a prime example of the need for this part of a management accounting system. Existing needs have to be evaluated and expressed in money terms, showing the amounts required for each particular serial and exactly when each amount should be available. The budget will show the total amount required, and the accounting system should provide reports on the spread of this demand throughout the year. Provision needs to be made for unpredictable price changes and unforeseen changes in publishing policy in respect of existing orders, as well as for new publications.

The final element of an effective system of management accounting is that it should allow *comparability*. That is, the system should provide the following information to facilitate comparisons, both internal and external:

- comparative figures for specific items of income and expenditure for the library for this year and for several past years
- similar information about similar libraries for the same periods: interlibrary comparisons
- trends in costs of books, serials and other library materials over the same periods
- immediately available data for the library itself showing the total budget for the year, total of expenditure to date, balance of budget still available, total of current commitments.

Comparisons between libraries are especially useful. The adoption of inter-firm comparison services in the private sector many years ago proved beyond doubt the value and benefits to be gained when different units in an industry adopt uniform accounting methods and reporting formats. Libraries could do well to adopt such a scheme, even if only on a regional and informal basis. Be aware that there are the same dangers inherent in these comparisons as there are in interlibrary comparisons of book stock and circulation figures gained through statistical publications; there is no substitute for knowing your own community, its needs and translating that into your own distinctive planning and action. However, the political value of interlibrary comparisons can be substantial if the right comparisons are produced to the right people at the right time.

Conclusion

Library budgets and budgetary controls have become more complex as society demands more accountability from public institutions. Library managers must take the initiative and show they are capable of not only understanding, but also preparing and controlling a budget in a responsible fashion. Even in a library where the accounts are all paid, and the budget is controlled by a central division, there is a need to monitor and control expenditure that is within the library's own managerial environment. The library's budget is its most political activity, and the more you know about its preparation, execution and outcome, the greater will be the validity and credibility of your relationship with your colleagues and your funding body. It is unlikely that new services can be sought or increases in budgets gained without your accountability showing.

It is in the area of financial planning and control, at least as much as by the services provided, that the library and its management will be judged by the funding body. Library budgets that are well researched, accurate and carefully monitored, can be a management asset. One of the biggest challenges for library managers is to be able to understand, and then use, the information contained in the budget and associated financial reporting data to meet the needs of their communities.

Appendix 1
Job analysis questionnaire

The following job analysis questionnaire is reproduced with the kind permission of the Human Resources Office, James Cook University, Townsville, Queensland. (Some formatting changed.)

General staff position document

The information provided in this document should give an accurate description of the position and its requirements, and be based on the general staff classification criteria.

General information about the job

This section is intended to provide general information about the job, such as where it is located, what decisions have been made about it and who is currently occupying it.

1 Position number

If you do not know this, please contact the person in your Division/Office responsible for staffing matters or Human Resources Office.

| |
| |

2 Local title of the job

This should arise out of, and be consistent with, the description of the main purposes of the job below.

| |
| |

3 Where is the job located?

Faculty/School or Division/Office

| |
| |

4 **Has this job been previously assigned a HEWLevel?**

Please tick one

No ☐ **Go to question 6**

Yes ☐ Please specify the Level, from 1 to 10, of present grading_____

5 **Is the job currently occupied?**

Please tick one

No ☐ **Go to question 6**

Yes ☐

Name of Occupant:

Staff Number:

6 **Main purpose(s) of the job, (focus):**

This should be a short statement of 1 to 5 sentences explaining why the job exists

Statement of duties

7 **List of tasks or duties:**

List the most important or time-consuming tasks or duties first. The list is assumed to include the general requirement 'Any other duties, consistent with the employee's classification/qualifications, as directed by the supervisor' and this need not be written in.

	% of Position

Organisational relationships

These questions ask about <u>direct</u> and <u>indirect</u> reporting relationships. If another person is supervised by you, they report <u>directly</u> to you. Those they supervise report <u>indirectly</u> to you.

8   Organisational Relationships:

Please complete a diagram below which shows where the position fits in the work unit, that is the title of the positions directly above, below and next to the position.

9   Describe the position/s which report directly to the position described in this document?

Please tick one

N/A   ☐   **Go to question 11**

Yes   ☐   How many positions?   ☐

Please list them:

Staff directly supervised	Continuing staff	Non-continuing staff	Casual staff

10 **Are there any other jobs which report indirectly to this position?**

Please tick one

No ☐ **Go to question 11**

Yes ☐ How many? ☐

11 **Please provide a written response in relation to the positions impact and reporting relationships with other areas of the University and outside organisations.**

Supervision received and level of independence

12 **Level of supervision:**

Please tick the definition which most closely matches the level of supervision which is/will be provided **to** the occupant of this job.

☐ Clear and detailed instructions are provided. Tasks are covered by standard procedures. Deviation from procedures or unfamiliar situations are referred to higher levels. Work is regularly checked.

☐ Direction is provided on the tasks to be undertaken with some latitude to rearrange sequences and discriminate between established methods. Guidance on the approach to standard circumstances is provided in procedures, guidance on the approach to non-standard circumstances is provided by a supervisor. Checking is selective rather than constant.

☐ Direction is provided on the assignments to be undertaken, with the occupant determining the appropriate use of established methods, tasks and sequences. There is some scope to determine an approach in the absence of established procedures or detailed instructions, but guidance is readily available. Performance is checked by assignment completion.

☐ Direction is provided in terms of objectives which may require the planning of staff, time and material resources for their completion. Limited detailed guidance will be available and the development or modification of procedures by the employee may be required. Performance will be measured against objectives.

13 Independence required in the job:

Independence is the extent to which a staff member is able (or allowed) to work effectively without supervision or direction. Please provide typical examples.

14 Funds Control:

If this position is responsible for the control of funds, show the size of the budget for which you have authority to commit expenditure:

Operating budget:	$_____
Petty cash:	$_____
Research funds:	$_____
Faculty funds:	$_____
Other funds:	$_____
TOTAL:	**$**_____

Judgment and problem-solving

15 Judgment and problem-solving required in the job:

Judgment is the ability to make sound decisions, recognising the consequences of decision taken or actions performed. Please provide typical examples.

Problem-solving is the process of defining or selecting the appropriate course of action where alternative courses of action are available. Please give examples of the more complicated problem solving required in this job. Please provide typical examples.

[ ]

16   Recourse to higher level

Please give examples of the level at which the incumbent is expected/able to refer, or seek advice/assistance on, problems to another person. Please provide typical examples.

[ ]

Training and qualifications needed to do this job

17   Formal educational qualifications and skills and knowledge required to do this job:

Care should be taken to list educational qualifications which are really needed to do this job – i.e. those without which the job could not be done. Specifying unnecessary qualifications is likely to discriminate against EEO groups who are less likely to have such qualifications. Desirable qualifications may be listed but the absence of these will not prevent an applicant from being appointed. Definitions of formal educational attainments are attached at A. Also include skills and knowledge genuinely required to do the job.

Essential
Desirable

Prepared by: _____ ___/___/___
(Date)

Supervised by:_____ ___/___/___
(Date)

Approved by: _____ ___/___/___
(If applicable)　　　　　Director / Head of School　　　　(Date)

Authorised by: _____ ___/___/___
(Mandatory)　　　Executive Dean/Pro Vice-Chancellor　　(Date)

Occupant: _____ ___/___/___
(If job currently filled)　　　　　　　　　　　　　　(Date)

Attachment A

Definitions of educational qualifications

Year 12: Completion of Year 12 of secondary school.

Trade certificate: Completion of an apprenticeship normally of four years duration, or equivalent recognition.

Post-trade certificate: A course of study over and above a trade certificate and less than an advanced certificate.

Advanced certificate: A two year part-time post-Year 12 or post-trade certificate, or a four year part-time course for those who have only completed Year 10 of secondary school.

Certificate: A two year full time or four year part-time course, without a Year 12 prerequisite.

Degree: A recognised degree from a tertiary institution, often completed in three or four years, and sometimes combined with a one year diploma.

Postgraduate degree: A recognised postgraduate degree, over and above a degree as defined above.

Note: The above definitions also include equivalent recognised overseas qualifications.

Attachment B

James Cook University

Guidelines for position document writing

For general staff positions only

1 Aims

The aim of this document is to provide staff, supervisors and heads with information about the preparation of position descriptions, and the general principles of job evaluation.

2 What is a position description?

A position description (PD) is a document that provides detail about a job that exists within the University environment. PDs can be used for a number of purposes, for example:

- clarification of job structure and requirements;
- as a recruitment tool to send to applicants;
- training purposes; and
- to assist in determining the appropriate classification level.

A PD should provide the reader with a clear idea of the prime purpose of the job, the major tasks required, the amount of freedom available to make decisions and the level of knowledge and skill required. It should include information about the challenges and constraints of the job and an organisation chart indicating its position within the organisation.

3 Why are jobs evaluated

Jobs are evaluated to establish internal relativities, to assist in job design and to determine the appropriate classification level within the award, which in turn establishes the salary range.

Jobs can be very different to one another. How do you compare a Carpenter with a Librarian, a Human Resources Professional with a Financial Accountant, or a Chemist with a Secretary?

By looking at a range of components that comprise each job, we are able to measure their relative contribution to, and impact on, the University.

4 How are jobs evaluated

By using a PD that has been written according to the standard format and includes information on the seven dimensions against which a position **must** be evaluated. Of these, there are five primary dimensions:

- training level or qualification
- task level
- judgement and problem-solving
- level of supervision and independence

- organisational relationships.

There are two dimensions used as cross-checks after an assessment has been made:

- typical activities
- occupational equivalent.

Each position is rated at the level of best fit for each dimension. There is a consistency in language between dimensions so that a decision made for one dimension should be reflected in the other dimensions at the same level. If the evaluator finds that they do not see this consistency across the dimensions when they are interpreting a PD, then clarification is required. This is usually done through the supervisor.

5 Important factors in job evaluation

5.1 Organisational context

Jobs do not exist in isolation, they interact with other positions around them. Job evaluation looks at each job in relation to the reporting structures, the communication networks, how the position relates and interacts with other positions within the University, and how the position impacts on the organisation.

5.2 Jobs belong to the organisation

Jobs exist because they contribute to the attainment of the University's goals. Individuals come and go as their career needs change but the work they do still needs to be done.

Jobs will be evaluated, not the people who fill them. They measure job requirements, not the experience or ability of the position holder.

5.3 The job now

Jobs change and evolve according to new technology, procedures, regulations, structures and funding. Few jobs remain the same over a long period of time. In writing a PD the aim is to capture a picture of the position as it is at a given point of time.

5.4 What is in a name?

The PD should not contain any reference to a job's current classification level, as this may influence evaluators. Even a job title can evoke pre-conception in some people's minds. However, it cannot be omitted as it assists in identifying the job. Evaluators undergo comprehensive training in the use of HEWL Dimensions and in the principles of job evaluation in order to reduce the risk of imposing any prejudice or bias. It is not unusual for two positions with the same title to be evaluated differently due to different levels of responsibility and requirements for knowledge and skills.

Supervisors should take the time to create a title that is relevant to the major function of the job rather than using a title that was established using old criteria.

6 Pitfalls

To avoid some common pitfalls in preparing a PD and to ensure an appropriate evaluation please consider the following helpful hints:

- Ensure that the content and language reflect the level of responsibility expected of the position. A common problem is that PD's are overwritten or claim responsibilities and knowledge that are not consistent with the level of the position.

- Avoid gender-specific language, e.g. 'He manages ....', 'She is responsible for...........', as the PD should describe a job regardless of the current incumbent.

- Avoid the over-use of words such as 'Assists' or 'Co-ordinates' unless you are going to qualify the depth of involvement in the task. The impression is that the person 'assisting' has a secondary involvement and, therefore less accountability for the outcome. Consider carefully whether this is a true reflection of reality.

- Avoid describing the specific skills and qualifications of the current incumbent. In the event of future recruitment, this is liable to limit the terms of the range of background and experience that could be suitable for future incumbents.

- Do not assume that those reading the document will have any prior knowledge of the job, so structure wording accordingly.

- Ensure that the statements made about reporting relationships are consistent with the organisation chart attached.

7 Completing the position description job evaluation document

Before you start:

- Review the whole document before answering any questions.

- Completion of the document should not be rushed. You may find it helpful to work through the questionnaire and then to review your responses a couple of days later before passing the document on to your supervisor. You may prefer to complete the document in stages. Arrangements should be made to complete the questionnaire without interruptions.

- You should complete the document yourself. You should then discuss your responses with your supervisor to check that you both agree that you describe the position as well as possible. When agreement is reached the front section of the document should be signed off accordingly.

- Please type or complete the document in ink. (Please print) You should cross through any changes that are made after discussion with your supervisor, rather than using white-out. Both you and your supervisor should initial any changes.

- Describe your position as it actually exists. Do not include duties which you only undertake when acting in a different or higher position.

- When answering questions about knowledge and skills, remember that you are describing the contents and requirements of your current job, rather than your individual knowledge, skills or performance.

- Please answer all the questions. This document is being used for general staff positions across the University. This means that some questions will be more relevant to your position than others.

- You may find that you will answer 'high' on some questions and 'low' on others. This is normal and shows the nature of your position, rather than its classification level. It is the combination of all your answers which provides information about the position and determines the classification level.

- You will need to ensure that:
  - you have answered all questions
  - you and your supervisor have discussed the final response to each question
  - once you have both agreed on the responses, you have signed off accordingly.

- Sections 11, 13, 15, 16, 17:

  Please provide a written response to indicate the depth of supervision received and the problem solving abilities required in the position. Examples to illustrate your response should be shown.

- Section 18 (Training and qualifications – this section is not to be used to show the position holder's qualifications and experience. The section is to be completed with the assistance of the supervisor and head/dean to show the qualifications and experience required in the position.

Appendix 2
Job descriptions and person specifications

Health service job description

Position title: Medical Librarian

Department: Resources Centre

Award: Public Hospital Employees Librarians (State Award)
Conditions as per Public Hospitals (Professional and Associated
Staff) Conditions of employment (state) award

Responsible to: Director of Administrative Services

Industrial coverage: Public Service Association of New South Wales

Hours of work: Monday to Friday, 8.00 am–4.30 pm (38 hour week)

Overall objectives of the position:

To provide an information service for Health Service staff which is appropriate, timely and
effective.

Specific function/details:

1   Coordinate and integrate library and other services across the area to provide a
comprehensive Resources Centre for the Health Service.

2   Manager of the Resources Centre and responsible for audiovisual equipment.

3   Select and acquire a collection of books, periodicals, audiovisual and other material to
meet the information needs and interests of Resources Centre patrons.

4   To organise this material for easy retrieval by Resources Centre users. Books will be
classified and arranged by a recognised classification scheme (National Library of
Medicine Classification).

5   Provide bibliographic access to material held in the Resources Centre's collection.

6   Ensure that the collection and equipment of the Resources Centre are adequately
maintained.

7   Prepare journals for binding.

8 Withdraw or replace obsolete material in the Resources Centre collection.

9 Prepare and maintain documentation on the history of the Health Service.

10 Provide an information service both from the collection, with particular use of reference works and indexes, and from the use of appropriate automated online services.

11 When necessary, extend the information services to gather information from outside sources, local and overseas.

12 Provide reader assistance and instruction on techniques of information retrieval, including use of indexes, the catalogue and reference books.

13 Develop and maintain an interlibrary loan system, which utilizes local, state, national and overseas collections, subject to the provisions of the Copyright Act and the Interlibrary Loan Code.

14 Develop and maintain cooperative relations and networks with other libraries and Resources Centres.

15 Report to the hospital Director of Administrative Services and the Library Advisory Committee on information needs of hospital staff and necessary Resourcess Centre development to meet those needs.

16 Administer the budget for the Resources Centre.

17 Develop, implement and maintain relevant policies and systems subject to the approval of the Director of Administrative Services.

18 Review and evaluate Resources Centre performance and systems, using appropriate quality assurance measures, and report results to the Director of Administrative Services and the Library Advisory Committee.

19 Prepare reports and correspondence as required.

20 Carry out the duties of Secretary of the Library Committee.

21 Attend meetings and other professional development activities.

22 Understand and implement Equal Employment Opportunity policies and practices and Occupational Health and Safety requirements.

23 Carry out other duties as allocated from time to time by the Director of Administrative Services.

City Council: position description

Position: Children's Librarian

Classification: Librarian Band 5

Department: Cultural Services

Branch: Libraries

Position objective:

To work as a team with the libraries personnel to provide a professional library service and environment which relates to the City's diverse community.

To encourage the use of the resources for the recreational, cultural and educational requirements of users and potential users.

To liaise with Children's Librarians across the Municipality with particular responsibility for services to children and teenagers.

Key responsibilities and duties

1   Readers advising and resources

- Provide effective professional and individual readers advising, reference and referral services to all library users, with particular reference to teenagers and children within the libraries.
- Communicate in a friendly and helpful manner about the library's resource of print and non-print material to library users.
- Create a professional yet welcoming ambience for users speaking community languages.
- Keep informed through reading literature for adults and children and maintain an awareness of contemporary trends in library science, publishing, TV and films, etc.
- Provide library user education to the community, informally or through semi-formal group discussions, with particular emphasis on sessions to groups of school children, teachers and care givers.
- Liaise between the library users and the Council and when appropriate refer enquiries to other libraries and information centres.
- Provide individual professional service as a priority.
- Perform relief duties at other Branch libraries.

2   Promotion of library services

- Promote the library's resources, services and facilities within the library and out in the neighbouring community to groups and individuals, particularly to children, teenagers, parents, care givers and teachers.
- Promote the use of the library's catalogue of resources, community information and local history, etc. card files, microfiche or computer databases.
- Promote the practice of professional resource sharing between the library and other organisations.

3   **Library administration**

- Maintain the library's resources, systems, facilities, shelf order and signage with other library personnel, as required, with particular emphasis in the children's and teenage areas.
- Participate in and contribute to the ongoing evaluation and selection of the resources of the Branch, through discussion with clientele, staff and regular staff meetings.
- Perform other duties as required.

4   **Programs for children, teachers and parents.**

- Organisation and presentation of story time to pre-school and school age children with awareness and implementation of the skill of professional storytellers, in consultation with the Children's Services Librarian.
- Maintain familiarity with children's and teenage literature and professional developments through reading, attendance and participation at meetings, etc. as appropriate.
- Organisation and promotion of holiday activities, group visits and special activities for example, Children's Bookweek promotion in consultation with the Children's Services Librarian.
- Organisation and presentation of talks to parents, schools and visits to relevant groups in the community in consultation with the Children's Services Librarian.

Organisational relationships

Reports to: Children's Services Librarian (Professional Direction) Branch Librarian

Supervises: Nil

Internal liaisons: Cultural Services Department staff

External liaisons: Local children's centres
Local maternal health centres
Local kindergartens and schools
Local youth groups and centres
Child care workers
Parent groups

Limits of authority

Authorises opening and closing of Council facilities (for example, Branch Libraries). Authorised to issue receipts for monies received in the course of duties.

Accountability

Responsible for the provision of an efficient and effective professional library service based at the Branch library and local community with particular emphasis on children's services.

Personal specifications

Essential:

- Eligibility for professional membership of Australian Library and Information Association.
- Effective communication skills and ability to interact with staff and public of all ages and interest levels.
- Ability to create a positive relationship with children.
- Flexible attitude to technological change and work within a team environment.
- Positive interest in ability to promote the use of the library resources and facilities.
- Demonstrated interest in contemporary literature, TV, film and audiovisual trends for children.
- An awareness of current affairs and contemporary literature for adults.

Desirable:

- One year's previous public library experience.
- Familiarity with and/or knowledge of a language and/or culture other than English.
- Current driver's licence.

University: position description

Job title: Faculty Librarian

Classification: Librarian Grade I

Relationship: Accountable to Senior Librarian
Supervise clerical and technical staff and student assistants as necessary.

Objective:

To assist with the delivery of professional library services to faculty, staff and students

- by providing general reference service

- by servicing the information needs of the Faculty

- by instructing students in the use of the library and its resources and to encourage use of the library as an independent study centre

- by selecting suitable materials for the Humanities and Social Sciences reference, circulating and periodical collections.

Responsibilities

1 Maintain contact with the client group and both assess and monitor their information needs.

2 Market the library's information services to the client group.

3 Give direct and personal aid to the Senior Librarian.

4 Deliver general reference information to staff and students through rostered duty on the reference desk.

5 Assist in the selection, maintenance and evaluation of the Faculty's reference, circulating and periodical collections.

6 Provide specialised information services to clients including online and Internet searching and the creation of files and/or indexes necessary for the efficient retrieval of information.

7 Participate in user education.

8 Assist in monitoring and evaluating the performance of the work group.

9 Interpret and act upon library policies and procedure.

10 Contribute as required to the administration and management of library functions.

11 Maintain records, prepare reports and attend meetings as required.

12 Other reasonable duties as directed by the Senior Librarian.

University: person specification

Knowledge, skills and abilities required for duties of the Faculty Librarian, University Library.

1 **Contact with client group - assess and monitor information needs**
   - good communication and interpersonal skills
   - ability for teamwork
   - evaluation and assessment skills
   - subject knowledge desirable

2 **Marketing library services**
   - good communication skills
   - ability to promote and market library services
   - thorough understanding of library services
   - enthusiasm for library services

3 **Direct and personal aid to members of Faculty.**
   - good communication and interpersonal skills
   - ability for management when necessary
   - ability to respond to authority
   - problem-solving and decision-making skills
   - dependability and reliability
   - subject knowledge desirable

4 **Reference service**
   - in-depth knowledge of reference tools and sources
   - high level of professional skills in librarianship/information management
   - service-oriented communication skills
   - ability to work with people using tact and diplomacy at all times
   - management skills when left in charge of the library at night or on a weekend
   - ability to work under pressure

5 **Collection development**
   - high level professional skills in librarianship and information management
   - ability to evaluate existing collection and establish its shortfalls
   - critical and analytical
   - knowledge of selection sources
   - decision-making skills for selecting materials
   - communication skills to liaise with the Faculty

6 **Specialised information services**
   - knowledge of faculty and student information needs
   - knowledge of current collection and resources
   - knowledge of what is available externally
   - knowledge of bibliographic and full-text databases and their use in research
   - logical, patient and thorough

7 **User education**
   - training and teaching skills

- knowledge of library tools and technology
- innovative and creative with the ability to make education in library use interesting
- patience and tolerance – students are both young and more mature age

8 Monitor and evaluate the work group
- good communication and interpersonal skills
- evaluation skills
- management skills
- problem-solving and decision-making skills
- knowledge and understanding of work groups' goals and objectives

9 Interpret and act upon library policies and procedures
- thorough knowledge and understanding
- good communication skills

10 Contribute to management of library
- management ability
- problem-solving skills
- decision-making skills
- organisational skills
- good communication skills
- knowledge and understanding of library's goals and objectives
- policy-making skills

11 Attend meetings, maintain records and prepare reports
- good communications skills
- ability to work as a team member
- written communication skills
- research skills
- organising skills

12 Other duties as required
- flexibility
- ability to work as part of a team
- ability to work without supervision
- dependability and reliability

Summary

Essential:
- Ability to do or be trained to do the job.
- Ability to work as part of a team.
- Good communication and interpersonal skills.
- High level of professional skills in librarianship/information management.
- Reliability and dependability.
- Motivation and drive/energy.
- Enthusiasm for the job and a desire to learn.
- Logical, patient and thorough.
- Integrity and dedication.

Important:

- Ability to promote and market library services
- Ability to participate in user education
- Ability to work without supervision
- Ability to work under pressure
- Management skills - problem-solving and decision-making, organising skills
- Evaluation and assessment skills
- Critical and analytical skills
- Flexibility
- Innovation and creativity

Desirable:

- Subject knowledge of the Faculty is desirable, but the ability to acquire this knowledge is more important.

Special Library: position description

Position: Librarian

Location: Canberra office

Librarian is accountable to the Library Partners and Committee for the following result areas.

Result areas:

- Information service
- Library development
- Library maintenance
- Expense control
- Staff performance
- Professional self-development

Specific, measurable objectives and action plans within each result area will be set jointly with the Library Committee in conjunction with the personnel and administration manager. They will be used as a basis for annual performance reviews.

Responsibilities, duties and activities

1 Information service

- Ensure that requests for information and materials from members of the firm are effectively and efficiently carried out.
- Guide users to the materials in which they might find the information they require, ensuring that any user of the library is fully aware of the rules and conditions governing the user of the library facility.
- Research and collate for the user all information available in the library on a particular topic requested or if necessary obtain the information from other libraries or information brokers.
- Liaise with library users on a regular basis to ensure that the service being provided by the library staff is of a standard that is both useful and effective from the user's point of view.
- Recommend and implement policies relating to the use of the library and provision of user requested information that will ensure that the library service remains at a high standard.

2 Library development

- Plan long-term goals to ensure the library, in the future, will meet the changing needs of the firm as can best be ascertained.
- Plan long-term goals to improve physical facilities in the library and ensure the facilities reflect recent library science developments where appropriate.
- Make recommendations for improving resources, arrangements or procedures within the overall running of the library.

3 Library maintenance

- Maintain in good order the holdings of the firm's library (books, journals, loose-leaf services) and the library records.
- Purchase and incorporate new and additional materials which are of direct relevance to the work of the firm.
- Ensure that all materials are classified and catalogued.
- Regularly correspond and communicate with legal publishers to ensure that forthcoming publications reviewed are drawn to the attention of the firm's solicitors.
- Ensure that journals are bound in a manner that will not only enhance their value but will prevent issues from becoming lost and/or damaged.
- Remove out-of-date or useless material from the library to make room for items of greater value. This should be done with the assistance of the firm's solicitors.

4 Expense control

- Prepare annual budgets in conjunction with the Accountant and maintain adequate controls to monitor budget performance.
- Continually assess the cost effectiveness of library purchase and maintenance practices and policies.

5 Staff performance

- Establish and maintain clear objectives and standards of performance with each member reporting to this position. Conduct regular reviews of performance emulation to the standards, including reviews in July and January each year.
- Delegate authority to subordinates to enable them satisfactorily to carry out their tasks to the required standards.
- Guide and teach subordinates in all aspects of library procedure to ensure that the library functions effectively if the librarian is away.
- Develop and maintain a continuous program for self-development for library staff in conjunction with the personnel and administration manager.

6 Professional self-development

- Develop and maintain a continuous program of self-development in conjunction with the personnel and administration manager.
- Maintain a high standard of knowledge and expertise by attendance at relevant professional courses, seminars and activities.

Appendix 3
Advertisements

Example 1

Regional Library
Children's Services Librarian – Grade 1

The City is seeking a qualified, energetic and enthusiastic librarian to work in the busy Branch Library. Duties to the position involve assisting the senior Children's Service Librarian in selection and maintenance of materials, participating in the organisation of library programs and story times and providing reader's advising. Work with adults in the library and community will also be expected.

Applicants should be eligible for professional membership of ALIA. Previous experience in a public library would be an advantage.

The salary is in accordance with the Library Officers Award for Librarian Class 1. An optional nine-day fortnight flexitime system applies.

For further information and a position description contact the recruitment office on (12) 334 5678

Applications in writing close at 5.00 pm. on Friday 4 April and should be forwarded to Recruitment Section, PO Box 1380, The City 1234.

The City is an equal opportunity employer and a smoke-free working environment.

Example 2

University Library
Assistant Librarian
Reference Department

Applications are invited from persons with appropriate academic and library qualifications for a newly established position of Assistant Librarian in the Reference Department of the University Library. Duties include the development, implementation and provision of an electronic document delivery service. The administration, coordination and promotion of computer-based information systems generally will also be expected. Reference enquiry work and user education are other important components of the position.

A background in information retrieval and previous experience in electronic information retrieval is required, preferably in an academic library. Good interpersonal skills are also required, to facilitate interaction with users from a wide range of cultural and ethnic backgrounds and academic disciplines. Candidates must feel comfortable working with information technology and should have the ability to work with a variety of computer software and hardware. The position requires attention to detail and organisational ability, as well as an ability to work well under pressure.

Starting salary will be determined according to qualifications and experience within the award range for Assistant Librarians.

A job description and conditions of appointment are available from the Staffing Section, Registry.

Applications quoting the reference number close with the Registrar on 1 April

Application forms are available from the Staffing Section of the Registry (01) 987 654. These forms should be completed, quoting the appropriate vacancy reference number, and forwarded to Registrar, University, PO Box 456, no later than the stated closing date.

The University has an Equal Employment Opportunity policy.

Example 3

The University Library
Clerk Grade 2
Technical Services Division
Ref. 123

The Library is seeking applications from suitably qualified people for the position of Clerk Grade 2 in the Bibliographic Control Unit of the Library's Technical Services Division, and to assist in other sections of the Library as required. Duties will include bibliographic checking of monographs and serials, the preparation of data for the automated system and providing support for some cataloguing operations. Aptitude for detailed clerical work is essential and library experience is desirable.

Applicants should have the Higher School Certificate.

Telephone enquiries: (00) 12 3456 Ms Brown
Closing date: 1 April
Salary: In accordance with award rates

Send applications quoting ref. number and name, 'phone numbers and addresses of two referees to:
        The Personnel Dept
        The University
        PO Box 321
        The City.

Example 4

Special Library
Information Research Librarian

The Corporate Services Division of the Company is seeking to fill a vacancy in the Library. The primary goal of the Information Research Librarian is to provide an effective reference and information service for customers of the Library.

The ideal applicant should have:

- Either a degree or postgraduate qualification in librarianship or equivalent qualification.
- Proven experience after qualification, preferably in a special library.
- Expertise in the user of local and overseas databases.
- Recent experience in reference and information searching.
- Strong experience in the development of intranet services.
- Excellent communication skills

For more information contact Ms Black, telephone (012) 101 1213 or facsimile (012) 101 1214. Applications close on Friday 25 March and should be forwarded with the names of two referees to Ms Black, The Company, Private Bag 123, The City.

The Company has a policy of Equal Employment Opportunity.

References

Accel-Team.com 2003, 'A guide to selecting the most appropriate people', viewed 17 January 2004, <http://www.accel-team.com/job_interviews/job_selct_ interviews_03.html>.>.

Alessandra, Tony 1998, 'Listening attentively', viewed 14 January 2004, <http://www.mentoruniversity.com/tony/lessons/lesson3.html>.

Anandarajah, D, Aseervatham, A, and Reid, H 1998, *Managing finance*, Prentice Hall Australia, Sydney, NSW.

Armstrong, B 1994, 'Customer focus: obtaining customer input', *Australian Library Journal*, vol. 43, no. 2, pp. 108–117.

Auckland City Libraries 2000, 'Strategic framework', viewed 27 April 2003, <http://www.aucklandcitylibraries.com/ process.asp?pageurl=/explore/aboutaz/ ABmission.html>.

Austen, Gaynor 1996, 'Quality management: education in common sense?', in *Best practice: challenges in library management education*, Fay Nicholson and Maxine Rochester (eds), Auslib Press, Adelaide, SA, pp. 5–15.

Australian Library and Information Association (ALIA) 2003, 'Continuing professional development', viewed 17 January 2004, <http://www.alia.org.au/education/cpd>.

Australian Library and Information Association (ALIA) 1990, *Towards a quality service: goals, objectives and standards for public libraries in Australia*, ALIA, Canberra, ACT.

Bannister, Marion 1995, 'View from the practitioner: collaborative decision-making: a practitioner's viewpoint', in *Australian library supervision and management*, Roy Sanders, Centre for Information Studies, Wagga Wagga, NSW, pp. 115–116.

Barlow, Richard 1989, *Team librarianship: the advent of public library team structures*, Bingley, London.

Bartol, Kathryn *et al.* 2001, *Management: a Pacific Rim focus*, 3rd edn, McGraw Hill, Sydney.

Bartol, Kathryn and Martin, David C 1998, *Management*, 3rd edn, McGraw Hill, Boston MA.120

Batten, JD 1989, *Tough-minded leadership*, AMACOM, New York.

Bedeian, Arthur G 1989, *Management*, 2nd edn, Dryden Press, Chicago, ILL.

Blair, Gerard n.d., 'How to build quality into your team', viewed 18 June 2003, <http://www.ee.ed.ac.uk/~gerard/Management/art3.html>.

Bluck, Robert 1996, *Team management*, Library Association, London.

Bolton, Robert 1979, *People skills*, Prentice-Hall, New Jersey, quoted in Kotzman, Anne 1989, *Listen to me, listen to you*, Penguin, Ringwood, VIC.

Bone, D. 1988, *The business of listening: a practical guide to effective listening*, Crisp Publications, Los Altos, CA.

Bouthillier, France 1993, 'Educating librarians and information resource managers: differing management perspectives?', *Canadian Journal of Information and Library Science*, vol. 18, no. 1, p. 34–43.

Bratton, J, and Gold, J 1999, *Human resource management: theory and practice*, Macmillan, London.

Bridgland, Angela and Hayes, Helen (eds), 1996, *Charting the future: strategic planning in the Australasian library and information industry*, Centre for Information Studies, Wagga Wagga, NSW.

Brophy, P and Coulling, K 1996, *Quality management: an introduction for information and library managers*, Aslib, London.

Brown, Dorothea 1995, 'View from the practitioner: dealing with senior management' in *Australian library supervision and management*, Roy Sanders, Centre for Information Studies, Wagga Wagga, NSW, pp. 221–223.

Bryson, Jo 1999, *Effective library and information centre management*, 2nd edn, Gower, London.

Burgin, Robert and Hansel, Patsy 1991, 'Library management: a dialogue – participative management', *Wilson Library Bulletin*, March, pp. 77–79.

Burrell, Jennfier and McGrath, Brad 1999, *Quality in library service: a competency-based staff training program*, Docmatrix, Canberra, ACT.

Butcher, KS 1993, 'Total quality management: the Oregon State University Library's experience', *Journal of Library Administration*, vol. 18, no. 1/2, pp. 45–56.

Carey, Alex 1967, 'The Hawthorne studies: a radical criticism', *American Sociological Review*, vol. 32, no. 3, pp. 403–416.

Carson, PP, Carson, KD and Phillips, JS 1995, *The library manager's deskbook*, American Library Association, Chicago, ILL.

Childers, Thomas and Van House, Nancy A 1993, *What's good?: describing your public library's effectiveness*, American Library Association, Chicago, ILL.

Clack, ME 1993, 'Organizational development and TQM: the Harvard College Library's experience', *Journal of Library Administration*, vol. 18, no. 1/2, pp. 29–43.

Clarke, John [1979], *The Fred Dagg careers advisory bureau*, Fourth Estate Books, Wellington, NZ.

Cochran, J Wesley 1992, *Time management handbook for librarians*, Greenwood Press, New York.

Conflict Resolution Network 2002, 'Mediation', viewed 1 September 2003, <http://www.crnhq.org/windskill11.html>.

Conroy, B 1978, *Library staff development and continuing education*, Libraries Unlimited, Littleton, CO.

Cook, Colleen and Heath, Fred M 2001, 'Users' perceptions of library service quality: a LibQUAL+ qualitative study', *Library Trends*, vol. 49, no. 4, pp. 548–584.

Cram, Jennifer 1998, 'Fishing with grenades or greening the mind: value, values and municipal libraries for the new millennium', invited keynote address delivered at the Country Public Libraries Association of New South Wales 10th Annual Conference, Ballina 1–3 July 1998, viewed 28 August 2002, <http://www.alia.org.au/~jcram/ FishingGrenades.html>.

Crawford, John 2000, *Evaluation of library and information services*, 2nd edn, Aslib, London.

Crook, Alison 1987, 'Human resources development and organisational change', *Education for Librarianship: Australia*, vol. 4, no. 1, pp. 5–15.

Danton, J Periam 1934, 'Our libraries: the trend towards democracy', *Library Quarterly*, vol. 4, p. 16–27.

De Gennaro, Richard 1978, 'Library administration and new management systems.' *Library Journal*, 15 December, pp. 2477–2482.

Department for Culture, Media and Sport. Libraries, Information and Archives Division. 2001, *Comprehensive, efficient and modern public libraries – standards and assessment*. The Department, London, viewed 2 September 2002, <http://www.dcms.gov.uk/PDF/ libraries_pls_assess.pdf>.

DeVito, Joseph A 2001, *The interpersonal communication book*, 9th edn, Longman, New York.

Dougherty, Richard M and Heinritz, Fred J 1966, *Scientific management of library operations*, Scarecrow Press, Metuchen, NJ.

Durant, Colleen and Morley, Karen 2002, 'Mt Eliza leadership index 2002', Mt Eliza Business School, viewed 15 July 2003, <http://www.mteliza.com.au/downloads/ 2002_Mt_Eliza_Leadership_Index_report.pdf>.

Dwyer, J 1999, *Communication in business: strategies and skills*, Prentice-Hall, Sydney, NSW.

Dwyer, J 2000, *The business communication handbook*, Pearson Education Australia, Sydney, NSW.

Ellis, D and Norton, B 1996, *Implementing BS EN ISO 9000 in libraries*, 2nd edn, Aslib, London.

Eunson, Baden 1987, 'Stress management', in *Behaving: managing yourself and others*, McGraw-Hill, Sydney, NSW, pp. 203-233.

Evans, G Edward 1976, *Management techniques for librarians*, Academic Press, New York.

Evans, Margaret Kinnell 1999, *Improving library and information services through self-assessment : a guide for senior managers and staff developers*, (British Library Research and Innovation Report, 172), Library Association, London.

Fayol, Henri 1949, *General and industrial management*, trans. Constance Storrs, Pitman, London. (First published in 1916 as *Administration industrielle et générale*.)

Fine, Sara 1985, 'Interpersonal relationships in a technological age', in *Public libraries and the challenges of the next two decades*, Alphonse F Trezza (ed), Libraries Unlimited, Littleton, CO, pp. 199–207.

Gardner, Neely 1979, 'Current concepts in management', in *Current concepts in management*, Martha Boaz (ed), Libraries Unlimited, Littleton, CO.

Garfield, Charles 1999, 'Peak performance and organizational transformation: an interview with Charles Garfield', *Educom Review*, vol. 34, no. 5, pp. 34–36.

Garlick, Marina 1992, 'Public library standards and evaluation', in *Access and equity: challenges in public librarianship*, Anne Hazell (ed), Auslib Press, Adelaide, SA, pp. 48–54.

Gilbreth, Frank and Gilbreth, Lillian 1917, *Applied motion study*, Sturgis & Walton, New York.

Griffin, Des 1991, 'Management and leadership in museums,' *Australian Library Journal*, vol. 40, no. 2, pp. 125–151.

Grosvenor, Mark, 1998, 'Evolving a strategic plan for high quality, high-speed information and library service delivery', in *Library management into the 21st century '98: maximising the performance of library services through people, new technology, innovative corporate strategies and continuous improvement initiatives, Sydney, NSW, 10–11 September 1998*, IES Conferences, Chatswood, NSW, pp. 37–52.

Hale, Kaycee (comp) 1991, *Study guide for success*, The author, Los Angeles.

Hall, John 1999, 'Training in teamwork in British university libraries', *Library Management*, vol. 20, no. 3, pp. 149–158.

Handy, Charles B 1976, *Understanding organizations*, Penguin, Harmondsworth.

Hawkins, Leo and Hudson, Michael 1986, *Effective negotiation*, Information Australia, Melbourne, VIC.

Heifetz, RA 1998, 'Values in leadership', in *Leading organisations: perspectives for a new era*, GR Hickman (ed), Sage, Thousand Oaks, CA.

Hennessy, JA, *et al.* 1976, 'Finance and libraries', in *Studies in Library Management*, vol. 3, G. Holroyd (ed), Clive Bingley, London, pp. 36–51.

Hernon, Peter and Altman, Ellen 1998, *Assessing service quality: satisfying the expectations of library customers*, American Library Association. Chicago, ILL.

Herzberg, F, Mosner, B and Snyderman, B 1959, *The motivation to work*, Wiley, New York.

Hick, Mike 1998, 'Team effectiveness', viewed 30 August 2002, <http://www.eagle.ca/~mikehick/teams.html>.

Hicks, Herbert G and Gullett, C Ray 1981, *Management*, 4th edn, ,McGraw-Hill, New York.

Hilgert, RL and Leonard, EC 1995, *Supervision: concepts and practices of management*, 6th edn, South-Western College Publishing, Cincinnati, OH.

Hill, Ken 1991, 'Turning a job into a learning process', *The Sydney Morning Herald*, 23 March, p. 81.

Hill, Percy H, *et al.* 1979, *Making decisions: a multidisciplinary introduction*, Addison-Wesley, Reading, MA.

Hilmer, Frederick G and Donaldson, Lex 1996, *Management redeemed*, Free Press Australia, Sydney.

Hiltrop, JM and Udall, S 1995, *The essence of negotiation*, Prentice Hall, New York.

Hobrick, Brice G 1991, 'Creating your library's future through effective strategic planning' *Journal of Library Administration*, vol. 14, no. 2, pp. 37–57.

Horton, Warren 1991, 'Address to the 1991 New Zealand Library Association Conference', Auckland, NZ [unpublished].

Houle, Cyril D 1967, 'The role of continuing education in professional development', *ALA Bulletin*, vol. 61, no. 3, pp. 259–267.

hr-guide.com. 2000, *On-line position description questionnaire program*, viewed 1 September 2002, <http://www.job-analysis.net/G908.htm>.

hr-guide.com. 2000, *Personnel selection*, viewed 1 September 2002, <http://www.job-analysis.net/G908.htm>.

Ivancevich, J, Olekalns, M and Matteson, M 1997, *Organisational behaviour and management*, 1st Australasian edn, McGraw-Hill, Sydney, NSW.

Johnson, David W 1990, *Reaching out: interpersonal effectiveness and self-actualization*, 4th edn, Prentice-Hall, Englewood Cliffs, NJ.

Johnson, Peggy 1991, *Automation and organizational change in libraries*, GK Hall, Boston, MA.

Jordan, Peter and Lloyd, Caroline 2002, *Staff management in library and information work*, 4th edn, Ashgate, Aldershot, Hants.

Jurow, S and Barnard, SB (eds) 1993, *Integrating total quality management in a library setting*, Hasworth Press, Binghamton, NY.

Kanter, Rosabeth Moss 1985, 'Managing the human side of change', *Management Review*, vol. 74, April, pp. 52–56.

Karasek, Robert Allen 1981, 'Job socialization and job strain: the implications of two related psychosocial mechanisms for job design,' in *Working life*, B Gardell and G Johansson, G (eds), Wiley, Chichester.

Kelly, Lauren 1987. 'Budgeting in non-profit organizations', *Drexel Library Quarterly*, vol. 21, no. 3, pp. 3–18.

Kight, DV and Snyder, CA 2002, 'Library staff development and training for assessment of services', *Library Administration and Management*, vol. 16, no. 1, pp. 24–27.

Knox, Jeanette 1988, ['Staff development at Macquarie University'], *Staff Development in Australian Libraries*, no. 5, pp. 5–6.

Koenig, Michael 1998, *Information driven management concepts and themes: a toolkit for librarians*, (IFLA Publications 86), KG Saur, München.

Koteen, Jack 1997, *Strategic management in public and nonprofit organizations*, 2nd edn, Praeger, Westport, CT.

Kotter, JP 1998, 'Successful change and the force that drives it', in *Leading organisations: perspectives for a new era*, GR Hickman (ed), Sage, Thousand Oaks, CA.

Kotzman, Anne 1989, *Listen to me, listen to you*, Penguin, Ringwood, VIC.

Krueger, Karen 1985, 'The planning process', in *Public libraries and the challenges of the next two decades*, Alphonse F Trezza (ed), Libraries Unlimited, Littleton, CO, pp. 35–41.

Lakos, Amos 1998, '2nd Northumbria International Conference on Performance Measurement and Libraries', viewed 12 January 2004, <http://www.library.ucla.edu/libraries/yrl/reference/aalakos/Present/North97/norsum.html>.

Leigh, A, and Maynard, M 1997, *Leading your team: how to involve and inspire teams*, Nicholas Brealey, London.

Levinson, Daniel J, *et al.* 1978, *The seasons of a man's life*, Alfred A. Knopf, New York.

Library Board of Queensland and the Chief Librarians Association (Qld) 1997, *Guidelines and standards for Queensland public libraries*, Library Board of Queensland, Brisbane, Qld.

Losyk, Bob 2002, 'How to conduct a performance appraisal', *Public Management*, 1 April, pp. 8–11, viewed 13 January 2003, <http://www.zigonperf.com/resources/pmnews/conduct_perf_appr.html>.

Lubans, John 2000, 'I borrowed the shoes but the holes are mine: management fads, trends, and what's next', *Library Administration & Management*, vol. 14, no. 3, pp. 131–134.

Lubans, John and Chapman, Edward A (eds) 1975, *Reader in library systems analysis*, Microcard Editions, Englewood, CO.

Lunn, Veronica 1995, 'View from the practitioner: [staff development]', in *Australian library supervision and management*, Roy Sanders, Centre for Information Studies, Wagga Wagga, NSW, pp. 186–187.

Luther, Linda 2000, 'Introduction of performance management into the University of South Australia Library', in *Change in Australian technology network libraries: a showcase of current professional practice*, J Frylinck (ed), University of South Australia Library, Adelaide SA, pp. 142–156, viewed 30 August 2002, <http://www.library.unisa.edu.au/papers/perman.htm>.

Martin, Rebecca R 1998, 'Managing change', in *Creating the agile library: a management guide for librarians*, Lorraine J Haricombe and TJ Lusher (eds), Greenwood Press, Westport, CT.

Maslow, A 1943, 'A theory of human motivation', *Psychological Review*, vol. 50, pp. 370–396.

Masters, Denise G 1996, 'Total Quality Management in libraries', *ERIC Digests*, ERIC Clearinghouse on Information and Technology, Syracuse, NY, viewed 28 August 2002, <http://www.ed.gov/databases/ERIC_Digests/ed396759.html>.

Mayo, Elton 1960, *The human problems of an industrial civilization*, Viking, New York.

McDonough, John J 1985, 'Power and human relations at work: a personal dilemma', *Journal of Library Administration*, vol. 6, no. 3, pp. 51–71.

McGregor, F 1997, 'Quality assessment: combating complacency', *Australian Library Journal*, vol. 46, no. 1, pp. 82–92.

Miller, KI, Ellis, BH, Zook, Eric G, and Lyles, Judith S 1990, 'An integrated model of communication. Stress, and burnout in the workplace', *Communication Research*, vol. 17, no. 3, pp. 300–326.

Mintzberg, H 1973, *The nature of managerial work*, Harper and Row, New York.

Morgan, C and Murgatroyd, S 1994, *Total quality management in the public sector: an international perspective*, Open University Press, Buckingham.

Nankervis, AR, Compton, RL and Baird, Marion 2002, *Strategic human resource management*, 4th edn, Nelson Thomson Learning, South Melbourne, VIC.

National Institute for Occupational Safety and Health (NIOSH) 1999, *Stress at work*, (DHHS (NIOSH) Publication no 99-101), NIOSH, Cincinnati, OH, viewed 26 October 2003, <http://www.cdc.gov.niosh/stresswk.html>.

Nemiroff, PM, and Rasmore, L 1975, 'Lost at sea: a consensus-seeking task' in *Handbook for group facilitators*, W Pieffer and J Jones (eds), University Associates, San Diego, CA, pp. 28–34.

Newnham. Erina 1988, ['Staff development at the South Australian Institute of Technology Library'], *Staff Development in Australian Libraries*, no. 5, p. 9.

Nicholson, Fay and Rochester, Maxine (eds) 1996, *Best practice: challenges in library management education*, Auslib Press, Adelaide, SA.

O'Brien, Linda S 1990, 'Changing an organisation's culture: enhance your library's ability to change and be innovative', in *Papers Presented at the ALIA First Biennial Conference, Perth, WA, 30 September–5 October 1990*, vol. 1, Promaco for ALIA, Perth, WA, pp. 627–640.

O'Sullivan, Tim, *et al.* (eds) 1994, *Key concepts in communication and cultural studies*, 2nd edn, Routledge, London.

Palmour, Vernon E, Bellassai, Marcia C and DeWath, Nancy V 1980, *A planning process for public libraries*, American Library Association, Chicago, ILL.

Penniman, W David 1990, 'On their terms: preparing libraries for a competitive environment' in *The bottom line reader: a financial handbook for librarians*, Betty-Carol Sellen and Betty J Turock (eds), Neal-Schuman, New York, pp. 4–8.

Pestell, Robert and Lihs, Karen 1992, 'What does it cost? A unit cost analysis of the Public Libraries Division, State Library of Queensland' in *ALIA 92: Libraries: The Heart of the Matter: proceedings of the Australian Library and Information Association Second Biennial Conference*, D.W. Thorpe for ALIA, [Port Melbourne], pp. 277–290.

Peters, T 1988, *Thriving on chaos: handbook for a management revolution*, MacMillan, London.

Phipps, Shelley 2001, 'Beyond measuring service quality: learning from the voices of the customers, the staff, the processes and the organisation', *Library Trends*, vol. 49, no. 4, pp. 635–661.

Pitkeathly, Pam 1994, 'Building a high performing library team and creating an exciting working environment' in *Library management into the 21st century '94. Proceedings of the 1994 Australian Library Management Congress, 28–29 March 1994, Darling Harbour, Sydney, NSW*, IES Conferences, Chatswood, NSW.

Poustie, Kay 1992, 'Public library personnel', in *Access and equity: challenges in public librarianship*, Anne Hazell (ed), Auslib Press, Adelaide, SA, pp. 125–129.

Pymm, Bob 2000, *Learn library management*, 2nd edn, Docmatrix, Canberra, ACT.

'Quality rewarded' 1996, *InCite*, vol. 17, no. 12, p. 7.

Queensland Government Workplace Health and Safety 2000, 'Workplace health and safety guidelines for people working in libraries', viewed 14 January 2004, <http://www.whs.qld.gov.au/guide/gde54.pdf>.

Ranieri, E 1999, 'Performance management', presentation to library staff, University of South Australia, Adelaide, SA. Quoted in Luther, Linda. 2000, 'Introduction of performance management into the University of South Australia Library', in *Change in Australian technology network libraries: a showcase of current professional practice*, J Frylinck (ed), University of South Australia Library, Adelaide, SA, pp. 142–156.

Reece, Barry L and Brandt, Rhonda 1993, *Effective human relations in organizations*, 5th edn, Houghton Mifflin, Boston, MA.

Reynolds, Brian A 1986, 'Proactive management in public libraries – in California and the Nation' in *Advances in Library Administration and Organization*, vol. 6, JAI Press, Greenwich, CT, pp. 1–78.

Rider, Fremont 1966, 'Library cost accounting', *Library Quarterly*, vol. 6, pp. 331–381. Reprinted in John Lubans and Edward A Chapman (eds) 1975, *Reader in library systems analysis*, Microcard Editions, Englewood, CO, pp. 9–26.

Ristuccia, Helen 1994, 'Establishing a strategic plan for high quality information delivery – Liverpool City Library', in *Library management into the 21st century '94: Proceedings of the 1994 Australian Library Management Congress, 28–29 March 1994, Darling Harbour, Sydney, NSW*, IES Conferences, Chatswood, NSW.

Ristuccia, Helen 1998, 'Building a high-performing library team and creating an exciting working environment', in *Library management into the 21st century '98: maximising the performance of library services through people, new technology, innovative corporate strategies and continuous improvement initiatives: Papers presented at the conference, Sydney, NSW, 10–11 September 1998,* IES Conferences, Chatswood, NSW, pp. 159–168.

Robbins, SP, Millet, B, Cacioppe, R, and Waters-Marsh, T 1998, *Organisational behaviour: leading and managing in Australia and New Zealand*, 2nd edn, Prentice-Hall, Sydney, NSW.

Rodriguez, Andrea and Prezant, Fran 2002, 'Better interviews for people with disabilities', *Workforce*, vol. 81, no. 8, pp. 38–42.

Rue, LW and Byars, LL 1999, *Supervision: key link to productivity*, 6th edn, Irwin McGraw Hill, Boston MA.

Samuels, Alan R 1982, 'Organizational climate and library change', in *Strategies for library administration: concepts and approaches*, Charles R McClure and Alan R Samuels (eds), Libraries Unlimited, Littleton, CO, pp. 421–431.

Samuelson, Michael 1990, *Supervision and management*, Wiley, Brisbane, QLD.

Sanders, Roy 1993, 'Library management education needs: preliminary results', *Education for Library and Information Services: Australia*, vol. 10, no. 1, pp. 37–46.

Sanders, Roy 1995, *Australian library supervision and management*, Centre for Information Studies, Wagga Wagga, NSW

Sannwald, William 2000, 'Understanding organizational culture', *Library Administration & Management*, vol. 14, no. 1, pp. 8–14.

Sarros, JC and Butchatsky, O 1996, *Leadership*, Harper Business, Sydney, NSW.

Saw, Grace 1989, 'Staff professional development in libraries', *Australasian College Libraries*, vol. 7, no. 1, pp. 17–25.

Scanlan, B and Keys, JB 1983, *Management and organizational behavior*, 2nd edn, Wiley, New York.

Schein, EH 1990, 'Organizational culture', *American Psychologist*, vol. 45, no. 2, pp. 109–119.

Schein, EH 1980, *Organizational psychology*, 3rd edn, Prentice-Hall, Englewood Cliffs, NJ.

Shaw, Ralph R 1947, 'Scientific management in the library', *Wilson Library Bulletin*, vol. 21, January, pp. 349–352.

Shonk, JH 1997, *Team-based organizations: developing a successful team environment*, Irwin Professional, Chicago, ILL.

Simons, Fran 2000, 'Can we talk?', *Australian Financial Review*, April 10, p. 50.

Sirkin, AF 1993, 'Customer service: another side of TQM', *Journal of Library Administration*, vol. 18, no. 1/2, pp. 71–83.

Skopec, E and Smith, DM 1997, *How to use team building to foster innovation throughout your organization*, Contemporary Books, Lincolnwood, ILL.

Smith, John 1982, 'Living in interesting times: the management of change', in *Peebles '82: Proceedings of the 68th Annual Conference of the Scottish Library Association, 3–6 May 1982*, Special Libraries Association, Glasgow, pp. 57–63.

Smith, John 1995, 'View from the practitioner: team management', in *Australian library supervision and management*, Roy Sanders, Centre for Information Studies, Wagga Wagga, NSW, pp. 128–132.

Spring, Tom 1999, *The ten commandments of e-mail*, viewed 30 August 2002, <http://www.cnn.com/TECH/computing/9903/31/commandments.idg/>.

Staff Development in Australian Libraries, 1988, vol. 5.

State Library of Western Australia 2002, 'Customer Service Charter', viewed 18 May 2003, <http://www.liswa.wa.gov.au/custserv.html>.

Stueart, RD and Moran, Barbara B 1998, *Library and information center management*, 5th edn, Libraries Unlimited, Littleton, CO.

Taylor, FW 1947, *Principles of scientific management*, Harper and Row, New York.

Tennant, R 1998, 'The most important management decision: hiring staff for the new millennium', *Library Journal*, vol. 123, no. 3, p. 10.

Todaro, Julie Beth 2001, 'The effective organization in the Twenty-First Century', *Library Administration & Management*, vol. 15, no. 3, pp. 176–178.

Townsend, Robert 1971, *Up the organization*, Coronet, London.

Trahn, Isabella 1988, ['Staff Development at the University of New South Wales'], *Staff Development in Australian Libraries*, no. 5, pp. 6–7.

Turock, Betty K and Pedolsky, Andrea 1992, *Creating a financial plan: a how-to-do-it manual for librarians*, Neal-Schuman, New York.

University of Wisconsin, School of Library and Information Science c2000, 'Communication models', viewed 14 January 2004, <http://www.slis.wisc.edu/academic/syllabi/450/communication/sld001.htm>.

Vallence, Kevin E and Wallace, Laurie 1993, *Quality concepts: an introduction to the concepts, processes and key terms in quality*, Nelson, Melbourne, Vic.

Van House, Nancy A 1990, *Measuring academic library performance: a practical approach*, American Library Association, Chicago, ILL.

Van House, Nancy A. *et al.* 1987, *Output measures for public libraries: a manual of standardized procedures*, American Library Association, Chicago, ILL.

Vincent, Peter 2002, 'Trial and error', *Sydney Morning Herald Weekend Magazine*, March 16–17, p. 1.

Vroom, V 1964, *Work and motivation*, Wiley, New York.

Wainwright, Eric 1988, 'Why some libraries succeed: innovation and change in a service bureaucracy', in *Living together – people, persuasion, power: Proceedings of the 25th Library Association of Australia Conference, Sydney, 1988*. LAA, Sydney, NSW, pp. 293–301.

Walsh, Barbara 1989, *Communicating in writing*, AGPS, Canberra, ACT.

Ward, Patricia Layzell 2002, 'Management and the management of information, knowledge-based and library services 2001', *Library Management*, 23, 3, pp. 135–165, viewed 2 September 2002, <http://www.neal-schuman.com/Ward.pdf>.

Wertheim, Eleanor, *et al.* 1992, *I Win: you win; how to have fewer conflicts, better solutions and more satisfying relationships*, Penguin, Ringwood, VIC.

White, Donald D and Bednar, David A 1986, *Organizational behavior: understanding and managing people at work*, Allyn and Bacon, Boston, MA.

Williamson, Vicki 1995, 'View from the practitioner: [recruitment]', in *Australian library supervision and management*, Roy Sanders, Centre for Information Studies, Wagga Wagga, NSW, pp. 167–168.

Wrege, C and Perroni, A 1974, 'Taylor's pig-tale', *Academy of Management Journal*, vol. 17, March, pp. 6–27.

Young, HC 1976, *Planning, programming, budgeting systems in academic libraries*, Gale Research, Detroit, MI.

Zweizig, Douglas and Roger, Eleanor Jo 1982, *Output measures for public libraries*, American Library Association, Chicago, ILL.

INDEX